Date		
450 A.D.	Flight of North African Christians to America to escape Vandals.	Barbarian incursions into Europe and North Africa.
500 A.D.	Libyan science and mathematics flourishes in west North America.	Byzantine power in North Africa. Islam invades Libya (646 A.D.)
700 A.D. onwards	Islamic inscriptions in western states. Christian Celts in West.	Islam dominates Mediterranean. Arabs cross Pacific to reach west coast of America.
700 A.D. onwards	Byzantine inscriptions. Americans explore Pacific. Hawaii mapped.	Islam and Byzantium in confrontation.
1000 A.D.	First Norse visits to northeast America.	Iceland becomes Christian, but Viking raids continue.
1341 A.D.	Vinland Norsemen revert to paganism. Reversions to barbarism.	1347 A.D. Norse refugees from Labrador reach Iceland and sail on to Norway.
1355–1362	Norwegian expedition seeks lost Vinland Norse settlers.	1362 Norway gives up Vinland and Greenland colonies as lost without trace.
ca. 1350	Vinland cathedral church build in Rhode Island.	
1398	Last Norse-Celtic voyage to North America.	
1492	Columbus reaches Caribbean.	1493 Europe reawakened as to potential of American trade.
1524	Verrazano finds blond people in Rhode Island.	

*The dating is based on coins, inscriptions, and tree-ring analysis.

Saga
America

Other books by Barry Fell

Life, Space and Time

America B.C.

Saga America

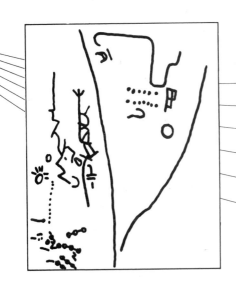

Barry Fell

Times
BOOKS

Published by TIMES BOOKS, a division
of Quadrangle/The New York Times Book Co., Inc.
Three Park Avenue, New York, N. Y. 10016

Published simultaneously in Canada by
Fitzhenry & Whiteside, Ltd., Toronto

Library of Congress Cataloging in Publication Data

Fell, Barry.
　Saga America.

　Bibliography: p. 407
　Includes index.
　1. America—Discovery and exploration—Pre-Columbian.
2. Inscriptions—United States.　3. United States—
Antiquities.　I. Title.
E103.F34　1979　　970.01′1　　79-51440
ISBN　0-8129-0847-3

Manufactured in the United States of America

CONTENTS

FOREWORD

Several years ago, I inquired at Harvard University's Museum of Comparative Zoology for someone to help me classify fossils I had obtained at Jericho, Jordan, in 1961. I was referred to one of the world's leading authorities on echinoderms, Dr. Barry Fell. I arrived at his home for an appointment on a Sunday afternoon, hoping for ten minutes in the schedule of a busy scholar. He saw the fossils and learned that my primary concern was with an ancient inscription cut into each of them, looking rather like the letter "A." It was the beginning of an intense, fascinating dialogue on ancient scripts which lasted through dinner until after midnight.

I left with my head spinning at the amazing work in linguistics which had absorbed Barry's private hours for many years. I realized that I was privy to a framework of research that would yield major new breakthroughs in our understanding of the past—though neither of us could know precisely what these would be.

Three years ago, I received a letter from Dr. Linus Brunner, a noted linguist in St. Gallen, Switzerland, who is probably the world's leading authority on the etymology of the Indo-European and Semitic languages: "The activity of Barry Fell is marvelous. . . . In matters of decipherment he is a great master. I think, like you, he will go down as one of the great decipherers of all time."

Recently Barry shared with me a letter dated September 1, 1978 from the world-famous discoverer of *Australopithecus*, South African paleontologist Dr. Raymond Dart: "What you and your colleagues are doing in New England is basic. The spectacle of its potential repercussions upon mankind . . . is fantastic to envisage."

Barry is truly a remarkable man, talented and knowledgeable in many fields. He has edited several journals, written hundreds of articles, authored and co-authored numerous books. He is a fellow of the American Academy of Arts and Sciences, the Royal Society of Arts, the Epigraphic Society, the Royal Society of New Zealand, the Explorers' Club, and the Scientific Exploration and Archaeological Society.

Growing up in New Zealand, Barry studied Greek, Latin, German, French, and later Danish. He holds Ph.D. and D.Sc. degrees from the University of Edinburgh. He read Gaelic for two years with Mairi nic Asgail. He has acquired a working knowledge of Sanskrit, Egyptian hieroglyphics, Kufic Arabic, and other ancient. writing systems of Africa, Asia, and America.

Decipherment is a special form of linguistics and requires statistical talents and ways of thinking which few linguists possess. Barry has deciphered a half dozen ancient languages and many scripts—far more than any other person in history. Coming as it does upon the trail of his extraordinary data published in *America B.C.*, this book contains fundamental and exciting new findings relevant to the continual rediscovery and re-evaluation of the American past.

Norman Totten

History Department
Bentley College
Waltham, Massachusetts

INTRODUCTION

As America enters her third century of independence, it has become apparent that an overwhelming thirst for historical information has swept the country. In *America B.C.,* issued at the time of the bicentennial in 1976, I outlined our knowledge of the earliest phases of settlement by colonists from Europe and North Africa during the first millennium before Christ. This book carries the story through the time of Christ and on into the first millennium after Christ. It also takes some cognizance of the corresponding arrivals on the West Coast of ancient colonists who crossed the Pacific to find a New World.

The men and women who figure in this sequel were Carthaginians, Greeks, Celts, Romans, Iberians, Libyans, and Norsemen; and on the West Coast, Libyans, Greeks, and Arabs, with traders from China and India. Our history books speak much of the Romans of Rome, the Greeks of Greece, and of each of the others named—always in the context of their homeland. But that is not the stuff of which American history was made. Colonists vanish from their homelands, and none remains behind to write their saga. American history is to be sought engraved on American bedrock, written by the hands of scribes who came here. And to find their antecedents we journey not to Rome, nor to Athens, nor to Tyre and Sidon. No, it is to their ports of departure for the New World that we must turn: to the coasts of Portugal, to the Greco-Roman colonies of North Africa, and to the Norsemen's lairs in the Arctic islands. Those were the places from which men set out to seek the ends of the earth.

In this book I recount, therefore, not only our American researches, but also pilgrimages made to timeworn ruins in the lands I have indicated. To those who still live in these ancient lands of departure, much that we find in America is still intelligible. If you want to know what an ancient American text is saying, take it to an Old World land where similar texts are still to be seen engraved on bedrock, on headstones, and temple lintels. Ask the local people how they read their ancestors' writings; the learned among them still remember.

We in America have spent over a century exploring, recording ancient petroglyphs, classifying them into a dozen different categories, with scores of subdivisions, all supposed to be meaningless markings of religious or magical connotation, and all classified under such names as "Great Basin Curvilinear" and heaven knows what not. The work was well done, the inscriptions accurately recorded by camera and pen; and for that we can be thankful to the archeologists who thus gave permanency to much that is now threatened by modern land use.

But one thing was overlooked. Apparently no one thought to carry copies of the photographs or casts of the petroglyphs back to the Old World, to see what might be made of them. In this book I tell of how this omission is being rectified, of the interesting dwellers in the fringe areas of the Mediterranean to whom I have shown American inscriptions, and their interpretations. I am thus doubly in debt, not only to my good American colleagues—now swelled by many others and not only to thoughtful readers who wrote thousands of letters to me after *America B.C.* was published —but also to new friends across the Atlantic, archeologists and numismatists in Iberia and North Africa, professors in the universities of Portugal and Spain and Libya. Above all, I am grateful to kind and generous hosts in Tripoli and Benghazi, Arab scholars and Islamic historians, Berbers and many others who, in all likelihood, carry the blood of Hanno and Hannibal in their veins, proud descendants of the line of Masinisa, and Bedouins of the desert lands. Arab hospitality crosses all boundaries, and to have been their guest was an unforgettable experience.

Now there is a two-way exchange of information. Archeologists from Iberia and from the North African universities are visiting America to see and read *our* inscriptions. For them, too, it is a moving experience to perceive the long-lost handiwork of forgotten or half-remembered ancestors. We of the New World now can peer further back in time—and into our own remote history—than ever before. And what we see along those remote corridors of time are

Approximate areas of settlement and points of entry via the river systems of early visitors and colonists from Europe, North Africa and eastern Asia. Some of the Amerindian tribes with whom the visitors are believed to have come in contact are also indicated. The southeastern tribes are believed to have descended in part from the Mediterranean colonists shown here as settling that region. The Iroquois are believed to have reached North America after most of these settlements had been made, possibly from South America around 1200 A.D., passing up the Mississippi to drive an enclave into the Algonquian area.

Julian Fernandez and Fell with a cast of the bilingual Latin-Ogam altar fragment from San Miguel da Mota, Portugal, referred to in Chapter 9. Originally identified by Professor Scarlat Lambrino as a dedication to the Celtic god Endobolius on the basis of its Latin text; the Ogam letters were later found to match the American Celtic script and give the consonants of the god's name. *Photo Peter J. Garfall.*

On his 1976 expedition to Portugal, James Whittall located this Celtic stone goddess recently discovered, with others, by a farmer. Whittall's continuing studies of the architecture and distribution of stone chambers in the Iberian peninsula and in eastern North America are throwing new light on the former movement of the Iberian peoples into the New World. *Photo Malcolm Pearson.*

For the North African inscriptions of North America, the greater part of the vocabulary is still in use in North African Arab and Berber communities to this day, where the American inscriptions can usually be identified at sight. Here two young Tunisians, Buazizi Mohamed Lamine and Buazizi Abdesselem Taub, with Fell, find a common bond through modern French. *Photo Peter J. Garfall.*

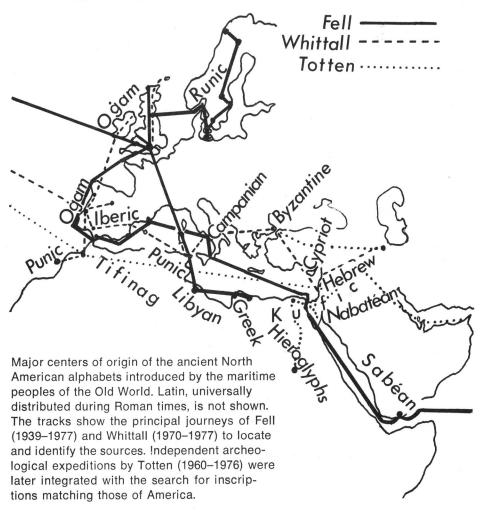

Fell ——————
Whittall - - - - - - -
Totten ············

Major centers of origin of the ancient North American alphabets introduced by the maritime peoples of the Old World. Latin, universally distributed during Roman times, is not shown. The tracks show the principal journeys of Fell (1939–1977) and Whittall (1970–1977) to locate and identify the sources. Independent archeological expeditions by Totten (1960–1976) were later integrated with the search for inscriptions matching those of America.

Professors Janet and Gareth Dunleavy, of the University of Wisconsin, with a half-scale replica of what is believed to be a Colorado form of Ogam writing found by Dr. Don Rickey, historian of the Bureau of Land Management. The inscription was found, with others, within an artificial stone structure resembling a dolmen. *Photo Peter J. Garfall.*

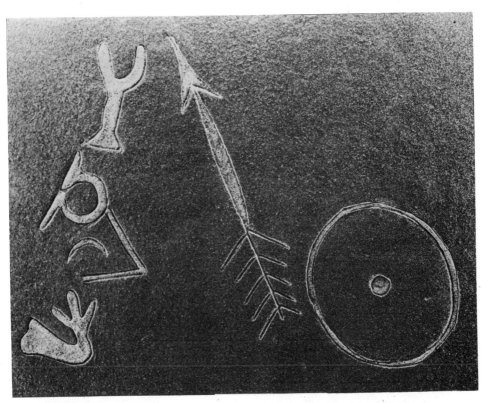

An ancient horoscope for the 25th day of the lunar month of November, the sun in Sagittarius (lower right, and the central arrow, the sign of Sagittarius). To the upper left is Scorpio, below it Libra, and below that Virgo. The moon is in Libra, shown by the crescent, and the angular marking is the astrological symbol "in sextile," meaning that the moon is 60° from the sun. This petroglyph was discovered by Captain J. H. Simpson in 1859, in the pass named for him. He recognized it as writing, which he reported as "hieroglyphics." The Paiute Indians mistakenly attributed this inscription to the Modoc tribe, who are said to have occupied the site 500 years ago. However, the Modoc have no knowledge of the zodiac today. The real authors must be the ancient astronomers of Nevada. Epigraphic Museum replica. *Photo Peter J. Garfall.*

Opposite page: Ancient Kufic script was employed for the Arabic language before the modern Arabic alphabet came into general use in the time of Richard Lionheart's crusade in the twelfth century. This example, possibly dating from about 700 A.D., occurs in Nevada, where it was mistaken for Amerindian markings of about 1000 B.C. It is actually a religious text and reads *Nabi 'Ilah Mohamed*—Mohamed is the Prophet of God—and was probably cut into the rock as part of the permanent school lessons of the Arabic-speaking Libyan settlers of the desert Southwest. See also Chapter 13. *Photo Julian Fell.*

One of the ancient ports of departure for ocean voyages was Leptis Magna, in the Gulf of Syrtis on the Mediterranean coast of Libya. Here the Carthaginians originally had a factory and trading station named Lepqis. In Roman times it assumed considerable importance and was given many splendid public buildings by various emperors and wealthy Carthaginian families who found refuge there after the destruction of Carthage itself. Part of the dockside ruins are shown here. *Department of Antiquities, Tripoli.*

start

2

.3

o

end

In order to learn how to read ancient American inscriptions in the Libyan script, the best school is Libya itself. Markings that archeologists have called "Great Basin Curvilinear," or similar names, and which have been supposed to be meaningless Indian magic signs, are recognized by Libyans.

This letter from a Berber was written a century ago and illustrates many of the writing principles found in ancient Libyan inscriptions. For example, the writing is continuous, not broken into separate lines; instead, it winds like a folded ribbon, the top line reading from right to left, the next from left to right, the third reading right to left. This ancient arrangement is called *boustrophedon:* it was employed by the earliest of the ancient Greek scribes, and the name means "going like a plowman." Almost all vowels are omitted, as in all the most ancient writing, and the context indicates what vowel sounds to supply. By referring to the alphabets on page 227, the consonants can be identified. The following shows how the words are reconstituted by inserting the vowels:

(1) W(a) N(a)k Abd-S(u)l(i)m(a)n w(i) h(u)l h(a)n(a) l(a)h(i) z(e)q d(a)y(i).
(2) T(a)br(a) kit(a)b (e)lh(me)d (a)s(a)d (a)m z(e)r in(i) m(e)d(i)n(a).
(3) W(a)r(ia) n(a)y(a) r(i)h(a)l(a)h(u) (*misspelt*) (a)k(a)m m(e)d(i)n(a) n(i) t(e)n(a)t n(i) m(ai)t(e)n.

The translation runs: *"This is I, Abd-Suliman, who greets you and who prays for your well-being from here. This letter is written to inform you that I am coming on a visit to my home town. Furthermore I intend to stay at a house in town in order to enjoy the company of my brothers."* The opening formula *Wa Nak* also begins Berber autographs both in North Africa and in North America.

glimpses of adventurous sea rovers from a past that is a common heritage of both the Old and New Worlds.

Almost as soon as *America B.C.* was published, I began to receive letters—and later on, personal visits—from men and women of Amerindian descent, some of them of dual heritage, some of them full-blooded American Indians. They spoke of how their grandparents had taught the ancient tribal traditions to them as children, of how their ancestors crossed the great ocean that lies to the east of America, to reach this continent; of how they had been bewildered and confused by the conflict between tribal tradition and what they were obliged to learn in school—namely of an alleged ancestry stretching back across the Bering Strait to Asia. These visitors brought strength and encouragement, wisdom, and, in some cases actual artifacts of the Old World, such as Roman pottery. Their treasured mementos of a past are now becoming intelligible in the light of new investigations. To those Indian Americans, the scions of the sea rovers whose trails we are now following, I send greetings and this expression of gratitude.

And to all those who may chance to read this book go the greetings and good wishes of the investigators whose work is described on these pages.

Saga
America

PROLOGUE

Attic Nights

We were only ninety minutes out from London when already the lagoons and embayments of the sinuous coast of Tunisia were slipping by beneath us. From a height of eight miles, North Africa seemed to have no more topography than a printed map on the page of a book. The Atlas Mountains lay concealed beneath a sea of cloud.

It was not my first visit to the continent, whose coasts I had sailed in earlier years, but I had never before viewed these lands from the air. Now we were coming not only as invited guests of Arab scholars who had visited America to see the ancient inscriptions, but also as pilgrims to pay homage to the land that gave birth to so many of the founding fathers of America's oldest civilization. Above all, I was eager to walk among the ruins of Cyrene, and to see the relics of that seafaring nation from whom had sprung the greatest navigators the world has ever known.

With a thrill of excitement I saw that we were already passing over the ruins of Carthage, historic mother city of the African Phoenicians, whose coins American farmers are now plowing up from the soil of Kansas and Connecticut, Arkansas and Alabama. This, then, was the spot on earth from which those telltale disks of metal had come, crossing the Atlantic by routes known to Plutarch, to serve as currency in distant colonies or to be presented as mementos to hospitable Amerindian chiefs for acts of kindness two thousand years ago.

But although we had found Carthaginian inscriptions and other relics in America, that famous city was not our present destination. We were headed for Libya, the vast and little-known country that lies to the west of Egypt. For I knew that it was in Libya that we

3

would find the answers to many of the archeological enigmas of the New World.

Already the sun was setting and the evening glow had turned the Mediterranean to a sea of gold. Ahead of us, to the southeast, lay our landfall, all Libya under the blanket of night as the earth's shadow swept westward in the wake of the sinking sun. And now the Libyan pilot began the long glide down to Tripoli where, I knew, we would soon be greeted by the scholars at whose invitation we had come. We had new information to impart to university audiences, and for our part looked forward to visiting their excavations and learning of their own discoveries.

I hoped also to learn more of the ships and the ports of the ancient Libyan mariners and planned to visit the places from which their ships once sailed. The Libyan desert is twice the area of Texas. The very hostility of such a hinterland must have triggered the impulse that sent these ancient wanderers to seek a livelihood upon the sea. And when their American descendants occupied the desert states of the Far West, they, too, maintained a fleet, and spent much time upon the waters of the Pacific.

Among the samples we had on board were photographic enlargements of the engraved portraits and associated inscriptions newly identified as being those of famed Libyan kings of ancient times, yet they had been found in the New World. The originals remain in America, but the reproductions, soon to be shown nationwide on television, would be America's token of goodwill; a dossier of ancient Libyan records now sent home from the New World, dealing with events and personages involved in the wars between Rome and Carthage. The names of the two monarchs depicted in the inscriptions were well known in Libya, where they are regarded as national patriots who had defied the power of Rome two centuries before Christ; but their portraits had never before been seen. It was indeed a privilege to be the bearer of such tidings.

Such were my thoughts as we came down into a dense black cloud that overhung Tripolitania. We were enveloped in an electrical storm, whose flashes and thunder seemed like a royal salute for the homecoming of the relics of the Libyan kings. At all events, as we were afterward told, a thunderstorm is a happy augury in a land where water is precious. Soon, we were hastening through the deluge to the arms of welcoming friends.

The Arab scholars who greeted us had worked with us at Harvard the previous summer. Our official host was Dr. Mohamed Jarary, who directs the Libyan Study Center of the University in Tripoli. With him was Professor Ali Khushaim, council member of UNESCO in Paris, distinguished Islamic historian and professor of education. My party included my wife Renée and research photographer Peter Garfall. All five of us were acquainted from previous meetings, so it seemed more like a homecoming than a visit. And so it continued thus in the weeks that followed. When the time came to bring back to America new insights gained from our work in Libya, the country we now left behind had become one of happy memory, of a warmhearted and artistic people, a land of scholars and poets and of practical men and women, a land steeped in history yet now leaping boldly into the twenty-first century.

Tripoli was called Oea by the ancients. With two other ancient cities, Sabratha and Leptis Magna (both now deserted but beautiful ruins newly excavated from the desert sands), the region acquired the Greek name Tripolis, meaning the Three Towns. I was enchanted to find that the Mandaq ash-Shatt ("Beach Hotel"), where we stayed, is built as near as matters on the site of the ancient hostelry where the second-century novelist Apuleius had stayed when on a visit to an old school friend (whose widowed mother, curiously, he was later to marry, precipitating a famous lawsuit over disputed property). From the *mandaq* by day, one can gaze across the Bay of Tripoli, and the desert air is so clear that the long line of ships that constantly streams from the port can be followed to the horizon, where one sees the hull of each ship disappear beneath the earth's curvature while the masts are still visible. No wonder that it was in Libya that the curvature of the earth was first demonstrated! In our misty northern latitudes, the ships fade into distant haze long before they reach the horizon.

Aulus Gellius lived during the reigns of Hadrian and the Antonines, that happy era in the otherwise rather disenchanting age of Imperial Rome. In the short span of a lifetime of only four decades, he somehow contrived to be born, grow up, digest a vast

Arab hospitality made evenings in Tripoli memorable events for us. On this occasion, Dr. Mohamed Sharif, Minister of Education and Harvard graduate (left) gave a dinner for the American party, and distinguished Libyan scholars, representing the Universities of Tripoli and Benghazi. Fell, to Dr. Sharif's left, here presents to Dr. Ahmed Funaish, Vice President of the University of Tripoli, a plaque of greetings from the Epigraphic Society designed by Colonel Robert Vincent, Cherokee member of the Amerindian Advisory Committee of the Society. In addition to the faculty of the Libyan Studies Center, other scholars present included Dr. Ali Hawat, Faculty of Education, Tripoli; Dr. Omar Shebani, past president of the University of Benghazi; Dr. Mustapha Attir, also past president, University of Benghazi; and Dr. Abdul Rachman Ghinnewa, of the Ministry of Education. *Photo Peter J. Garfall.*

The magnificent mosaics of the Roman period in Libya dominate much of the exhibition area of the Archeological Museum in Tripoli. The Fells with, from left, Mr. Abdullah Wahab, Controller of Antiquities; and right, Dr. Abdul Hamid; center, Hussein Abu Sitta, technical staff, who with his colleagues Abdullah Naal and Salim Abu Zaid Bilqasim, gave generously of their own time to aiding our work. Their enthusiasm and kindness was repeated everywhere we traveled in Libya. *Photo Peter J. Garfall.*

Opposite page, below: The nights in Tripoli during the rainy season can be cool, as is evident from this group beside the palms. From left, Dr. Mohamed Jarary, Director of the Libyan Studies Center, University of Tripoli; Barry and Renée Fell; Professor Ali Khushaim, Council Member UNESCO (Paris) and Faculty of Education, University of Tripoli; and to the right Professor Omar Shebani, past president, University of Benghazi. *Photo Peter J. Garfall.*

Professor Ali F. Khushaim, one of the first Arab scholars to visit the Epigraphic Museum, has since written extensively for the Arabic press on the American finds of ancient Libyan inscriptions. Here he holds one of a series of articles published in Tripoli. Now a well-known lecturer in universities in North America as well as in the Arab world, he has become a valued consultant and advisor. *Photo Peter J. Garfall.*

Dr. Mohamed Jarary (left), director of the Libyan Studies Center of the University of Tripoli, with Fell (right) at a university presentation in Libya at which the Mekwsen proclamation was made known to archeologists and historians, and subsequently televised to the nation. *Photo Peter J. Garfall.*

amount of Latin and Greek literature, and then write a précis of hundreds of extracts from ancient writers whose works were wholly lost in the Dark Ages, and whose memory survives today only through the quotations made by Aulus Gellius. By some chance, the manuscripts of this otherwise unimportant writer escaped the holocaust when the Vandals leveled Rome.

He had called his work *Noctes Atticae*—Attic Nights—evoking an earlier era when the educated leaders of Athens would gather in the evening to recite extracts from their writings, or quote from those of other authors whom they respected. It was the age of the symposium, when wine was mixed with spring water, and poets might declaim without risk of insobriety, for the rule of the Greeks was three parts water to every one of wine.

I had all but forgotten the *Attic Nights* until we came to live a short span in Tripoli. There, as we found, the poets and historians and journalists and other writers made a practice of gathering by evening in the Mandaq ash-Shatt, but fifty yards from the Writers Center, there to talk, quote, declaim in the Attic manner. *Ariston men hudor*—"Water is best"—Pindar's maxim is followed to the letter, for Libya is a Moslem land where the word of the Prophet is the letter of the law. (But Arabs have a skill in the making of coffee so potent that verse flows unrestrained when the occasion demands.)

Here in the comfortable lounge of this Arab hotel in an Arab capital of enchanting vistas by day, one finds that the night, too, has its charms: the more so when three or more literary men are gathered, and the conversation flows to the alternating rhythm of spoken English and Arabic. Here it was that Ali or Mohamed would come by of an evening to see how our day had gone, or to plan the morrow, or to introduce us to men of their acquaintance. The Arabs are famed for their sense of obligation to a guest, and their fame is justly deserved. Here it was that I had the privilege of meeting the writers and poets of modern Libya and many visitors from other lands.

Now in my library in Massachusetts, a glance at the Arabic shelves serves to remind me of those Attic Nights in Tripoli. The literary mementos given me to take home to America by distinguished Arab writers trigger the memory. Professor Ali F. Khushaim—the Ali of this book—is represented by his philosophical study *Zarruq the Sufi*. It tells of the days of the decline of the Marinid dynasty in Fez, in the fifteenth century of our era, when Zarruq called upon the people to seek a deeper meaning in life than the luxury of the day provided, a Moslem mystic who trod analogous paths to those taken by some of the medieval saints of Europe. Books by another Ali, too; the poet Ali Abd Sidqi, the warmth of whose ebullient personality crosses the barriers of space and language, as our host Mohamed Jarary translates. Yet a third Ali is the distinguished Ali Mustafa Misrati, with thirty published titles to his credit, ranging the whole gamut of Libyan culture and tradition, his quiet personality and deep-thinking eyes ranging through time as Ali Khushaim interpreted for us. Their books have an honored place on my shelves, and I treasure the generous dedications that these exponents of Arab thought have written on the flyleaves.

In such company, the eminent writers of the past in North Africa live again and are named and quoted. Callimachus of Cyrene, the greatest of the Greek poets of the Alexandrian age, is remembered here, of course, for his Libyan origin. Mention of his name among the company brought to my mind his friend Heracleitus of Caria (in modern Turkey) of whom Callimachus wrote one of the most touching poems in the Greek language when news came to Alexandria of the death of Heracleitus. Not one poem of Heracleitus has survived the two thousand years that separate us from his age; all that we know of him is that his phrases were accounted so beautiful by his contemporaries that they spoke of them as the *nightingales of Heracleitus*. When Callimachus learned that he would never again see his friend, he wrote of his sorrow in words that William Johnson Cory, an English schoolmaster at Eton College, rendered in such noble English a century ago as to ensure his own immortality as well as that of his Greek masters:

> They told me Heracleitus, they told me you were dead:
> They brought me bitter news to hear, and bitter tears to shed.
> I wept as I remembered how often you and I
> Had tired the sun with talking and sent him down the sky.

And now that thou art lying, my dear old Carian guest,
A handful of grey ashes, long, long ago at rest,
Still are thy pleasant voices, thy nightingales, awake,
For Death, he taketh all away, but these he cannot take.

To my Arab friends I spoke the lines, for they happen to be among the few passages of the classics that I like to carry in my head—and found them in turn fascinated by the familiar sense of the poem rendered in an unfamiliar tongue. I was happy to find that this and like literary treasures from North Africa's Hellenic past live on in the minds of modern Libyans, whose homeland gave birth to such mastery of the uttered word.

We in the West learn at school that the Arabs preserved Greek learning when the ancient world collapsed into barbarism, but we do not really appreciate how profound has been the influence of ancient Greece upon the Arab world, nor the depth of feeling that one can find among educated Arabs for the Greeks of ancient time. The nights and days that my Arab friends gave to me and my work were an education in the universality of literature and science, mediated by the enduring influence of Athens. The only acknowledged standard is perfection; seek a match for the master scribes of Ireland, and you are most likely to find it in some masterpiece of Arabic calligraphy.

In the closing passages of my previous book, *America B.C.,* I stressed that many different peoples of ancient time contributed to the history and civilization of the Americas; and I said that if I had given undue prominence to the role of the Celts of Iberia, it was because I was able to recognize Celtic trails more easily.

In the three years that have passed since I wrote that book, our trails have led us into regions of America where North African—and, in particular, Arab North African—pioneers have engraved their names and deeds during the passage of many centuries long past. Through the many kindnesses of visiting Arab scholars, my colleagues and I have been made more sensitive to the traces of the vanished civilization of North African colonists—Greek, Punic, Libyan, and Arab—through the eras of paganism, Christianity, and Islam. This book, inevitably, is dominated by these aspects of our long and complex history—yet it is no more than a collection of first impressions. For what can one learn in a few years of faltering research of a pageant of events that lasted two thousand years! As before, I gladly admit that many errors must be imbedded in an exploratory work such as this. I doubt, however, if the main outlines of my story are seriously at fault, and I would say the same for my earlier work. In any case, time, as always, will be the final arbiter.

Mr. Jefferson Regrets

When the crack of Doom shattered the peaceful dawn twilight of western Connecticut on December 14, 1807, it is unlikely that many of the inhabitants lost any beauty sleep. To begin with, it was already 6:30 A.M. (by the most reliable timepieces, as afterwards established by scientific inquiry), and none but the most abandoned of sluggards would still be abed at that hour in so industrious and God-fearing a community. Besides, it was a Monday, the first of the week. All the more reason for a prompt start to the six days of labor decreed by Holy Writ.

No angelic choir appeared in the sky, nor trumpet sounded, nor even the slightest hint of a crack in the heavenly vault above or in the earth beneath. Within minutes, after some speculative chatter among neighbors, all returned to normal, and good folk went off to work. Not so, however, in the little township of Weston, in Fairfield County. Here, indeed, as was soon established, a highly irregular event had occurred. Not only was the thunderous roar well attested, but there were those who heard the whistle and rushing noise of something like a cannonball flying through the air, and additional plain evidence in the shape of a sinister dark stone that had struck the ground. There were those who claimed to have seen the entire occurrence, in the course of which, after celestial phenomena such as muffled reports and puffs of smoke high above, a missile had descended out of the sky to land on American soil.

Rumors spread. In New Haven, the press spoke of the event as a public occurrence worthy of note. Yale University was induced to dispatch two reluctant and skeptical professors to investigate the situation. In due course, after interrogating witnesses and obtaining the material evidence itself in the shape of the alleged celestial stone, the professors returned to Yale to announce to an astonished faculty that in actual fact *a stone had fallen out of the sky.*

Now, there were those among the university community and the more learned members of the public at large who already had learned through the foreign correspondence of the American Academy of Arts and Sciences that a French government commission set up in 1803 to investigate a similar alleged event at L'Aigle, France, had reported to the Academy in Paris just precisely the same conclusion: that stones do fall from the sky. Since no person could be found who might be supposed to have hung the stones in the sky in the first place, the French savants concluded that the stones must always have been there, and in fact must have fallen from outer space. At Yale the first recorded American event of this extraordinary nature was hailed as a scientific advance of the first order, and curious mineralogists began the examination of the chemical constitution of the rare specimen thus obligingly delivered by a bounteous Providence.

And so, in the course of time, word came to Washington of the Weston meteorite. The Washington of those days was still largely an unrealized dream in the mind of its architect, not yet the gracious and splendid capital city of a great nation, though already showing the first classical facades and spacious avenues, under the watchful eye of President Jefferson. The president himself was the acknowledged master of all matters scientific among the administrators and legislators who were his daily companions. For these men, however, much they might dispute his wisdom in other affairs, Jefferson was the ultimate referee in all questions of natural philosophy.

What, they asked, was Mr. Jefferson's comment on the extraordinary report from the little New England community, backed so surprisingly by the two learned professors of Yale University? For once the great Virginian's star deserted him. Apparently—and inexplicably—he had not heard of the conclusions reached by the French Academy four years earlier. Consequently—and the history of American astronomy reports the comment—Jefferson's reply was to the effect "that he could more easily believe that two Yankee professors lie than accept the notion that stones can fall from heaven."

I like to think of this incident in American history whenever I am shown one of the more inflammatory denunciations of my book, *America B.C.* In some quarters it is commended, and in as many others it is called misguided folly. For every black there is a white, and I guess the only way to look at the matter is to pair off the negative comments with the positive ones and call the score even. To be sure, I still find myself in opposition to a sizable segment of academia, but was it not Jefferson himself who said, "A little rebellion now and then is a good thing"?

I also like to think of the sequel to the Weston controversy. Like all true investigators, Thomas Jefferson soon amended his oversight, and we hear no more of lying Yankee professors. Meteorites were granted recognition and henceforth might land on American soil without hindrance, and with full approval from Washington.

In contrast to his conservative attitude toward meteorites, Jefferson would nowadays be classified as a decided radical with respect to his views on archeology and the ancient history of the Americas. During his term as president of the American Philosophical Society, he disclosed that earlier in his life, before he assumed the burdens of public office, he had personally excavated an ancient Indian mound in Virginia. More than that, he cultivated the acquaintance of leading Indians and had formed the opinion that their ancestors had come to America from overseas. He believed that a study of the Indian languages of America would disclose the places of origin. These views neither shocked his contemporaries, nor those of several later generations. Only after about 1860 did the dogma develop that all Amerindians descend from Asiatics who crossed Bering Strait, and that no visitors from Europe or Africa came to these shores before Columbus. As late as the 1940's, not even the Norse were considered; or at best were regarded as very dubious claimants to have visited Vinland of the sagas. Any who dispute the ivy-league infallibility on these matters are castigated in a manner reminiscent of old-time politics. Historians and archeologists are peculiarly prone to mistake diatribe for logic. Thus an opponent not only is mistaken, but in addition is deluded and has neanderthal proclivities into the bargain. This makes for lively—though not always informative—public discussion.

Those of us who prefer dogma to logic are, it seems to me, repeat-

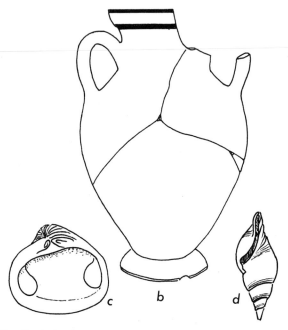

During the Dark Ages in Europe, the memory of the ancient Etruscans was lost, and early archeologists ran the gauntlet of skepticism and suspicion of heresy when they excavated remains of ancient peoples. When in 1498 Dominican friar Giovanni Nanni published the first Etruscan inscriptions (a) which he found on subterranean tombs near Viterbo, Italy, he was suspected of forgery until Swedish excavations in the twentieth century confirmed his findings. Cardinal Perretti (afterwards Pope Sixtus V) collected fossil shells, which he placed in the Vatican Museum; but in 1574 his finds were declared to be merely stones that had come under the "influence of heavenly bodies." Antique vases (b) discovered beneath the ground at Monte Testacea were similarly dismissed as "natural impressions resulting from fermentation of earth by lapidifying juices." In 1580 in Paris a French naturalist named Palissy re-asserted the Greco-Roman view that fossils are the remains of once-living organisms. Archeology in Italy finally emerged as a respectable philosophy when a Neapolitan farmer in 1710 accidentally discovered the ruins of Herculaneum and Pompeii some 60 feet beneath the ground when he sank a well shaft—and found not water, but statues.

The discovery of the buried city of Herculaneum through accident in 1710 led to the modern era of excavation of ancient buried cities. The view shows part of Pueblo Bonito in Chaco Canyon, New Mexico, a relic of the civilization discussed in Chapters 10 and 11, and associated with inscriptions that imply a North African relationship. *Photo Professor Norman Totten.*

ing the performances of some of our medieval predecessors. Let me illustrate this comment briefly by citing a few incidents in the history of the subject.

One of my favorite characters in history is Pope Sixtus the Fifth. Quite apart from his endearing arithmetical name, he was a man after my own heart, for in his spare time he did something that I also have done most of my life: he collected fossils. But unlike the common or garden fossils that most of us addicts assemble, his were very special, in fact unique, for—unlike all other fossil collections—Sixtus V's specimens had the honor of being placed in no less than the Vatican Museum.

Unfortunately, the aura of sanctity that one might suppose would now devolve upon the Pontifical Department of Paleontology did not in fact eventuate. This bad luck was engendered chiefly—my inquiries have led me to discover—from the tiresome fact that he was so incautious as to place his specimens on public display in the revered Museum *before* he had been elected to the supreme office. They were there, indeed, in 1574—six years before Sixtus became the fifth of that name—and when he could claim no infallibility since Felix Perretti was a cardinal at that time.

And that was the undoing of his reputation as a paleontologist. For a disagreeable figure known to us as Mercati, author of a treatise on sports of nature, carefully illustrated the cardinal's fossil sea shells, and then declared that they were not the fossilized remains of sea animals but merely simulations of them, produced in the soil by the mysterious emanations of the heavenly bodies, designed to deceive men. Colleagues of Mercati supported him to a man. In like manner, Professor Olivi of Cremona dismissed as worthless an entire museum of fossils at Cremona, and an eminent botanist of the day, Professor Andrea Mattioli, took time from editing Dioscorides' manuscript on ancient Greek vegetation in order to examine some alleged vases lately discovered in the ground at Monte Testaceo. These objects are what we probably would classify as Etruscan ware today, but Dr. Mattioli would have none of that. He announced his discovery that they were not really vases at all, but "bodies produced by fermentation" of a singular substance that he called "lapidifying juice," the final result of this subterranean chemistry being the said vases. The details of his alchemy he left unexplained.

In those days, strange though it seems, the Italian literati had all but forgotten that there ever were a people called Etruscans. In 1498, six years after Columbus made his first voyage to the New World, a Dominican friar named Giovanni Nanni discovered and published ancient inscriptions, including some that he claimed were the work of the forgotten Etruscans. He had evidently discovered underground tombs of Etruscans at Viterbo, twenty miles north of Rome, where he lived. Fra Giovanni's work was discredited by later writers. For centuries he was called by such choice epithets as "an impudent trifler," a "nefarious impostor" (by Philippe Cluver, the German archeologist), and an English student of the Etruscans called him "a wholesale forger" and several other bad names. Finally, when the Swedish Academy undertook excavations at Viterbo in the twentieth century, old Fra Giovanni was justified. Professor Olaf Danielsson now defends him, for remains of tombs have been discovered that carry Etruscan inscriptions—or rather the fragments of them—and these it appears likely were the basis of the friar's book. His interpretations are no longer acceptable, but the relics he discovered were real.

By the time Cardinal Felix Perretti laid aside his biretta to assume the papal crown, his life had only five years to run. He was fired with the ambition to endow the Vatican with architectural masterpieces. He compelled the engineers and architects of his day to rediscover the Byzantine mastery of the dome, and so endowed Saint Peter's Basilica with the great cupola it now bears. This and many other similar activities apparently left him no time to resume his paleontological studies. In those days, the study of fossils was not separated from the study of ancient relics of mankind, so archeology and paleontology remained under a cloud of suspicion. In France, in a more enlightened atmosphere, a French naturalist named Palissy reinstated the view (held by the ancient Greeks and Romans) that fossils are the remains of creatures that once lived on the earth and in the sea. Some 150 years later, in 1730, his countrymen held a sesquicentennial congress to honor Palissy as the founder of modern paleontology. But meanwhile a dramatic event had occurred, and the entire world was now ready to accept the reality of buried cities and other exciting evidence of the life and times of our remote forebears.

The year was 1710, and the Italian summer was proving unusually dry. Near Portici, on the Bay of Naples, one farmer decided to sink a deeper well in search of water needed for his crops. He went down 60 feet, still without finding any water, when to his ultimate disgust he struck rock. It was highly unusual rock—marble carved in the form of temple columns and steps. Apparently he had encountered a subterranean city. This irritating obstacle was also a marvel of no ordinary nature, and he told his neighbors.

Word of the strange discovery came to the ears of a Swiss engineer named D'Elboeuf, who happened to be staying in the district. He was something of a classical scholar, and he remembered the old tale in the letter that Pliny the Younger sent to Tacitus in answer to Tacitus' request for information on the eruption of Mount Vesuvius in 79 A.D. In the letter Pliny stated that two cities had been totally buried by the great eruption, Pompeii and Herculaneum. In the eighteenth century, no one actually believed so manifestly improbable a story. It was argued that Pliny was well known to have served as governor of Judaea under the emperor Trajan, and doubtless his Hebrew acquaintances had spoken of the legendary destruction of Sodom and Gomorrah. Apparently, scholars said, Pliny had made up a Romanized version of the Bible story for the amusement of Tacitus.

D'Elboeuf thought it possible that the scholars were wrong. Could it be that Vesuvius had indeed once erupted and buried the cities as Pliny claimed? He decided to find out. The owner of the desiccated farm proved very willing to sell his property, and D'Elboeuf hired diggers to test his theory.

"How deep do you want us to go?" they asked.

"No deeper. Dig horizontally instead," D'Elboeuf replied. "Tell me if you break through a wall."

All was done as D'Elboeuf instructed. Before long he found himself crouching in the partly emptied interior of a Roman mansion, with the remains of the furnishings still within. The work of excavation went on, in fits and starts, the "mine" now passing relentlessly through wall after wall, into one house and out the other side, only to enter the next house. Statues came forth from the wonderful mine, and the whole of Europe was astonished to learn that the long-lost city of Herculaneum had been discovered. Later Pompeii was located. Archeology became the ruling passion of the gentry of all countries where Romans had once governed, and spread even further, as related in the chapter that follows.

It was the end of an era, and the beginning of a much more exciting one. For the first time, people learned what ancient cities and houses were like. History came to life, and caught the popular imagination. It has never since lost that fascination, which was sparked by a dry well and an imaginative engineer who had a hunch that the scholars might be wrong.

2

Ancient America — Ancient Treasure

Over the span of fifteen centuries, from 400 B.C. to 1100 A.D., the Western world was dominated by six maritime powers. In orderly succession, their fleets swept the Mediterranean and adjacent seas, planting colonies or merely trading, and leaving behind a record of inscriptions, artifacts, and cultural influences as enduring mementos of their visits. In order of their appearance upon the world's stage, the six nations were (1) the Carthaginians of Tunisia; (2) the Greeks and Libyans of North Africa, often in concert with either Carthage or Egypt; (3) the Romans; (4) the Byzantine Greeks who succeeded Rome; (5) the Islamic powers of North Africa and Asia; and (6) the Norse sea-rovers.

Over that same span of time, six waves of visitors to the Americas left inscriptions and artifacts, and in some cases colonists as well. The mementos they left behind tell us that they were none other than the same six nations whose fleets in turn dominated the Mediterranean and European seas. Thus America shares a history with the Old World, and ancient Americans must have been well acquainted with much of that history as it took place.

These were not the only maritime peoples who visited our shores and sailed our great inland rivers and lakes. Others had come before: Celts, Iberians, and Basques from Spain, earlier Libyans, men of Egypt and Crete; and some, as recounted in my previous book, had settled here as permanent colonists. Others also came later. The record of the earliest visitors is confused by the passage of time and obscured by a lack of any degree of precision in dating their arrivals and departures. Our oldest history is therefore clouded in uncertainty.

But after the fourth century B.C. our visitors began to bring with them—and to leave behind—the infallible date-markers that the modern historian demands: those enduring metal disks called coins. The substance of this book about ancient Americans revolves largely upon the discovery and interpretation of that long-lost coinage now being brought to light by the electronic metal detector.

Two oceans mark the eastern and western boundaries of the Americas. Most of our maritime visitors crossed the Atlantic and then reached the interior of the continents by sailing the inland waterways—particularly the Mississippi and its navigable branches, and the St. Lawrence, with its associated lakes. Ancient ships were purposely constructed with a shallow draft and a flat keel, in order to take advantage of the rivers as natural trading routes. Indeed, the rivers were the only routes open in any virgin land, where forests covered vast areas, and no roads existed. All settlements were necessarily to be found along the natural waterways, and it was the settlements that traders most desired to reach; the easiest way to obtain the natural products of any country is by exchanging imported wares for those desired as exports.

America's second seaboard lies along the Pacific Ocean. Here, too, came ancient traders and settlers, though in fewer numbers and at longer intervals; the Pacific is twice the size of the Atlantic, a much more formidable barrier for ancient navigators to cross. Even so, the peoples of China and of India found their way to our western shores, and they, too, left enduring markers by which we may recognize their calling cards. The ancient Libyans, those descendants of Greek, Arab, and Carthaginian fishermen who dwelt along the Mediterranean shores of North Africa, transcended all others in the spans of their voyages. One of them, Eratosthenes of Cyrene, calculated the earth's circumference, and then showed that if the ocean is continuous, one could sail around the earth in either direction and return to the starting point.

Libyans set out to test his theory. They found that America divides the ocean, and instead of returning to Libya from opposite directions, they found themselves landing on the opposite sides of America. They liked what they saw, and stayed. Some of them established schools of learning here where mathematics, astronomy, navigation, and geography were taught. These early Americans, for such they became, have left behind a fragmentary record of their skills in the sciences. Ancient America, two thousand years ago, became a haven of refuge where learned men from Mediterranean lands imparted their knowledge to the young and engaged in friendly relations with the Amerindian peoples who saw no grounds for hostility. A golden age dawned in the mountainous West where these philosophers made their home, and for centuries a breed of mariners set out from our shores to explore the Pacific and to trade with the peoples of Asia. Then, about a thousand years ago, that civilization began to crumble. By the time the Spanish conquistadores arrived, little remained of its former brilliance.

This book recounts some part of these events. It lays claim to no measure of infallibility and undoubtedly makes unintentional errors; but it nonetheless comes nearer to the truth than was previously possible without the new sources of information yielded by the inscriptions and the buried coins.

In 1974, when I first began to report the inscriptions, with an explanation of how the individual signs were to be identified as letters of alphabets already known from Europe and North Africa, and how the letters spelled words recognizable in known ancient languages of those regions, I found myself in the role of a solitary traveler talking aloud to himself in a wilderness. At first no one took any notice. Later, a number of scholars who had come to suspect that ancient voyagers reached America became interested in my work and encouraged it. Later still, these scholars, and I myself, came under a concerted attack by traditional archeologists on the ground that the ideas we expressed were fanciful and unscientific. Particularly frequent was the criticism that no one else could read the alleged inscriptions, and thus the whole pack of cards rested on the wild imaginings of Fell alone. This criticism was also made when a popular explanation of my work appeared in a nontechnical form as a book.

That criticism is no longer valid. One by one, competent scholars who hold responsible positions in universities and museums are now coming forward with confirmations of the decipherments. At first the confirmations were made by linguists in Europe, North Africa, and the Middle East, and were published in technical papers that they wrote. Later confirmation was reported from American scholars. By that time, I had already received many visits from scholars from abroad, anxious to learn further details of the progress of the research in America. The next step was invitations to address university audiences here and overseas and to carry out research on related inscriptions in Mediterranean contexts.

Now, in 1979, the whole question of ancient American contacts with overseas civilizations has become a lively topic of debate in the universities and archeological societies, both here in America and abroad.

In 1976 in my book *America B.C.* I illustrated many of the mysterious stone chambers that occur in New England and showed that engraved Celtic inscriptions that are associated with them lead to the conclusion that these are ancient temples oriented with respect to the motions of the sun and the moon, such as to imply that they were astronomical observatories, associated with sun worship. This interpretation, which was in accordance with the independent opinions of investigators such as James Whittall and Byron Dix, was roundly condemned at first. But professional astronomers who came to investigate the claims confirmed the astronomical alignments, and soon a technical journal called *Archaeoastronomy* was established to record the new facts. Some critics had also asserted, though without proof, that the stone chambers are in reality only "root cellars" built in modern times by New England farmers, as late as the Victorian period. But a team led by James Whittall discovered charcoal while excavating a chamber at Putney, Vermont, and, in 1978, Whittall announced that the radio carbon age calculated from analyses made by the Geochron Laboratory in Cambridge implied a construction date at least fourteen centuries ago, a full thousand years before Columbus. Further, at other sites in New Jersey that had once been declared modern because of the presence of brass artifacts, radio carbon dating now showed that the sites were occupied around 1250 A.D.

In *America B.C.* I had also reported Carthaginian inscriptions engraved on bedrock in the vicinity of the stone chambers, or actually on the stone lintels and walls of the chambers themselves. Soon afterwards a new source of information appeared, for within six months ancient Carthaginian and Celtic coins were being discovered in the farmlands of the very river valleys where the inscriptions had been recognized.

The finders were farmers and sharp-eyed farmers' sons, and treasure hunters using electronic metal detectors. Thus, after 350 years of settlement since colonial times, only now was the long-hidden evidence of a much older colonial age brought to light. But these new finds, though they represent the oldest coins of America (and also our most artistic antiques, for they were struck from dies engraved by Greek artists), are by no means the first examples of ancient coins to be found in the Americas. We have, in fact, a long history of recovering ancient coins from American soil—coins that, for some unaccountable reason, we have persistently contrived to ignore. Take, for example, the events that occurred some two centuries ago on a stretch of highway only a few minutes' drive from my home in Massachusetts.

The year was 1787, and the Reverend Thaddeus Mason Harris was making his way along the Cambridge-Malden road (now known as Route 16), probably turning over in his mind the prospects of the young Republic, whose very Constitution was that year being hammered out by the Congress summoned for that purpose. As he rounded a bend, he saw before him a cluster of people gathered about some unusual object. As he afterward recorded in a letter to John Quincy Adams, he learned that some workmen had been engaged in widening a section of the road when a pickaxe had struck a horizontal flat slab of stone buried beneath the surface. When the slab was cleared and prized up, it was found to serve as the protective cover of a concealed cache of ancient coins, of which "two quarts" now lay exposed to view, hundreds of small square pieces of base metal (a copper-silver alloy) each bearing unknown signs stamped on both faces. The finders concluded that they were worthless, and passersby, including Harris himself, were invited to take away handfuls. Hundreds of coins were thus dispersed.

Of all the people who carried off samples of these curiosities, Harris alone took steps to place the matter on record. After fruitless attempts to identify the inscriptions (actually Kufic, an ancient form of Arabic) and research in Harvard Library to no result, he had illustrations drawn and these, together with the account he sent to John Quincy Adams, were published by the American Academy of Arts and Science, in Boston. And there the matter rested for nearly two hundred years, until James Whittall, of the Early Sites Research Society, chanced upon the old report written by Harris and took steps to notify me and the American Numismatic Society. Let me now go on to other finds in other states.

Since the early days of the Colonies, American farmers had become accustomed to finding Indian arrowheads in the soil they plowed, and there was scarce a farmer's son to be found who did not own a collection of these telling reminders of an age now passing into history.

But when, in 1797, the first of a new brand of plows began to materialize from the inventive minds of Charles Newbold and his successors, and a furrow could now be cut by an iron plow whose coulter and share reached twice as deep as before, the virgin earth brought to light a wholly unforeseen harvest—buried *Roman coins!* Yet others were discovered deep down in the subsoil when well-shafts were sunk.

Many such finds were doubtless made and never reported in hamlets where no one was on hand with a knowledge of Latin to identify the small green-patinated disks. But in communities that could boast a local judge or country doctor, these occasional fortuitous discoveries provoked speculation and discussion. Those were days when Latin and Roman history were required subjects for any college degree; many professional men could therefore cast their minds back to their school days, and recall having learned that the greatest sea battles in all time had been those fought between the Romans, Sicilians, and Carthaginians. The Grand Armada that Philip of Spain had sent against England in 1588 paled into insignificance when compared with the fleets of Octavian and Antony. So, remembering these things, the learned men of the Republic logically concluded that apparently Roman ships had crossed the Atlantic to visit the Americas and to leave behind these unexpected mementos. But later on, when the Columbus mystique began to evolve in American schoolbooks, and children were taught to believe that the world was considered flat until 1492, the troublesome coins were dismissed from consideration. New finds, as often as not, were ignored. America, it was now argued, could never have been known to the Romans; hence these Roman coins must be some kind of modern intrusion—certainly not related to ancient America.

When the improved iron plows developed in Europe in the course of the eighteenth century, they, too, cut a deeper sod than before, and they, too, turned up ancient Roman coins. In England and France and the Rhineland, all of them onetime provinces of the Roman Empire, the antique coins came to light in very large numbers—as indeed they still do to this very day. (A visitor from England recently mentioned to me that when he passed his boyhood days in Silchester, Hampshire, he sometimes followed the plowman, and considered it very poor pickings if a day's search did not yield three or four coins.) The plows of Europe also yielded stone arrowheads and similar relics of a barbarian past; only whereas these objects lay near the surface in American soil, in the Old World they are found mostly at depths greater than those that yield Roman coins. The English antiquarians interpreted the facts as meaning that the stone artifacts were relics of the ancient Britons, and hence older than the Roman coins that lay above them. All seemed to be logical and in accordance with expectation.

But now a problem arose. As the new plows were introduced into Scandinavia, the deep furrows yielded the same harvest of coins as had those of England, France, and the Rhineland, all once part of the Roman Empire. But Denmark and Sweden and the Baltic Islands had never formed anything other than a barbarian wilderness in Roman times. An attempt during the reign of the emperor Augustus to bring Germany under Roman rule had ended in disaster. In 9 A.D., as an army of three legions under Varus marched across Germany toward the Danish peninsula, a force of German warriors ambushed the Romans at some lonely place, now forgotten, in the Teutoburg Forest. By day's end, 12,000 legionaries lay dead. The shattered remnants retreated behind the Rhine, never again to venture into Teuton territory. How could it be that Roman coins dating from all periods of the empire lie in the soil of northern Europe, so commonly that over 4,000 have been taken from the island of Gotland alone? Scandinavian scholars concluded that despite the fact that the northern lands remained barbarian in Roman times, nonetheless traders from Rome were regular visitors in such numbers as to account for all the coins that the plows reveal.

And this is where the American and the Scandinavian scholars part company. In Copenhagen the King of Denmark was so intrigued by the surprising discovery of the coins that he appointed a Royal Commission for the Preservation and Collection of National Antiquities, and in the year 1816 a famous authority on ancient coins, Christian Jørgensen Thomsen, was appointed secretary to the commission and instructed to prepare public exhibits illustrating the finds. In America no such steps were taken. Local newspapers might report occasional coins plowed up on some farm in the district, but historians ignored them for a hundred years until Frederick J. Pohl in 1961 drew attention to the unexplained questions they raised. Pohl's book, *Atlantic Crossings Before Columbus,* listed some notable finds of Roman coins in American soil. Since then, other historians, notably Professor Cyclone Covey at Wake Forest University, Professor Douglas C. Braithwaite at M.I.T., and Dr. Joseph Mahan in Georgia, have published additional finds. Recently, with the invention of the electronic metal detector, a new precision has aided the discovery of such objects in the field. The conclusions to be drawn from them have become an important part of the historical information we now possess on ancient America.

Let me now return to the events in Denmark, following the appointment of the Royal Commission. These have wide implications. They played a notable role in a revolution that occurred in archeology a few decades after Thomsen was placed in charge of the Copenhagen collections.

Frederik VI had ascended the Danish throne at a difficult time for the neutral countries of the north, during the upheaval of Britain's long struggle with Napoleon. The British Navy demanded the same rights of search and seizure as had disturbed Anglo-American relations in 1812, but the Danes, unlike the Americans, could not match material resources to their will. They suffered disastrous attacks on their fleet—and eventually on Copenhagen itself—at the hands of the British. Frederik found respite from these troubled days by taking a close personal interest in the archeological researches he had initiated in his country. This interest was maintained after his death in 1839 by his successor, Christian VIII, who personally collected ancient coins and appointed another archeologist, the classical scholar Brøndsted, to be curator of his private collections; after Christian VIII died, the royal collection was united in the national collection, and Denmark thereafter assumed a commanding role in all researches and publications dealing with ancient coins and their implication in archeology. For this reason, and others, my wife Rene and I learned Danish in 1950–52, and then spent a year in Denmark in 1953 assimilating the classical riches of that country, little dreaming that twenty-five years later we would encounter in the New World a similar set of unresolved problems for whose solution the Danish scholars had provided the key.

In 1816 Thomsen found himself confronted by a heterogeneous assemblage of miscellaneous objects of metal and stone, recovered from Danish soil and from ancient burial mounds, totally without any order. In the background stood an eager and impatient king demanding solutions to these mysteries regarding the unknown history of his country in the ages that came before the Vikings.

After pondering the matter for three years, Thomsen hit upon a purely practical expedient. He separated the collection into three lots: one group comprised artifacts made of stone, another those made of bronze or copper, and a third group comprising objects made of iron. To each of these groups he then added other objects such as pottery or wooden implements recovered from bogs, fragments of textiles and leather garments, if such objects were known to have been found in direct association with any of the stone or metal artifacts.

Then, by consulting the oldest surviving writings from ancient times, such as the Iliad and the Odyssey (thought to date to about 800 B.C.—no decipherments of older documents had yet been achieved in 1816), he found that very little reference at all was made to iron, but a great many references to copper and bronze. He inferred from this that the use of iron—or, more significantly, the art of smelting iron ore, must have been a later discovery, after bronze alloys had been developed. Presumably, the few references to iron in the oldest documents related not to the ores of iron (such as red oxide), but to iron meteorites such as those

A   B   C

Islamic coins have been found in hoards of hundreds in both America and Scandinavia. Some of the Islamic coins found in America may have been brought by Norsemen, as thousands of such coins of the ninth to eleventh centuries are found in the soil of Scandinavia. A, coin of Samarkand struck in 903 A.D. and found at Gulland, Denmark. The central inscription reads: "There is no god but God alone, and no partner for him." The marginal inscription reads, "In the name of God was coined this drachma [dirhem] in Samarqand." B, C, Medieval Islamic coin of North Africa from a buried hoard found in 1787, during road-building excavations between Cambridge and Malden, Massachusetts. *(Redrawn Fell, after original engravings located by Whittall.)*

Roman coins of the era 337–383 A.D., all found in 1977 by metal-detection apparatus within an area of beach of about one square yard, at Beverly, Massachusetts. It is typical of beach finds that coins of similar dates occur in association in very limited pockets. Similar associations occur with Spanish coins of the sixteenth and seventeenth centuries, and these are known to come from offshore wrecked ships. Mounting evidence now shows that Roman wrecks also lie offshore on the east American coast. *Photo Malcolm Pearson, coins in the Whittall collection.*

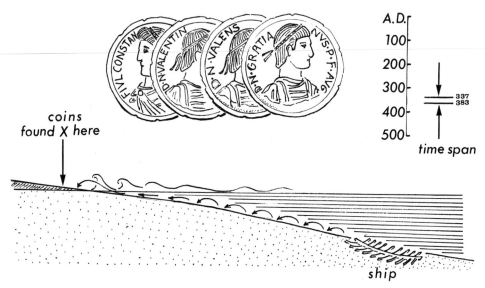

coins
found X here

A.D.
100
200
300
400
500

337
383

time span

ship

Coins of the Beverly Roman wreck include examples only of late-fourth-century issues and prove to belong to the reigns of four consecutive emperors: Constantius II (337–361 A.D.), Valentinianus I (364–375 A.D.), his younger brother Valens (364–378 A.D.), and Valens' nephew Gratianus (367–383 A.D.). The 58 emperors of Rome issued numerous coins, of which about 3,000 kinds are commonly found in Europe. If coin finds are due to random losses, then the chances of any one emperor's coin turning up are on the average roughly one chance in 60. But for a single find-site to yield a run of coins of closely consecutive rulers, spanning only four decades, the chances can be estimated as less than one in 100,000. Thus the coins are not being found as a consequence of accidental losses (as archeologists have always assumed), but are strongly correlated with some factor linked to the short time span from 337 to 383 A.D. The only reasonable explanation is that the money chest of a merchant ship carrying current coin in use around the year 375 A.D. is the real source of the Beverly coin supply. For the past 1600 years onshore currents have drifted the coins toward the beach, where they are thrown up by waves in heavy weather.

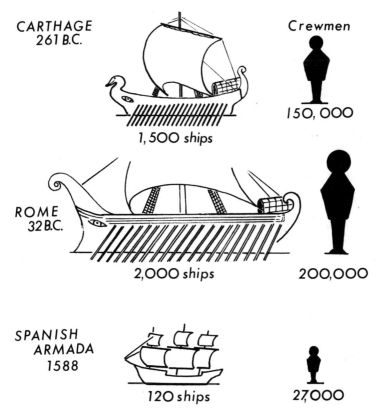

CARTHAGE 261 B.C.

Crewmen

1,500 ships

150,000

ROME 32 B.C.

2,000 ships

200,000

SPANISH ARMADA 1588

120 ships

27,000

Relative naval strengths of Atlantic powers, based on records of battle fleets and support vessels participating in naval wars. Naval strengths are a reflection of overall maritime resources, including the uncounted mercantile vessels and crews. As ancient historians record, both Carthage and Rome had adequate reserves for mounting transatlantic navigation.

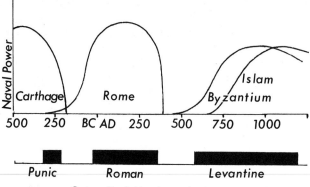

Coin finds in America

The frequency of finds and their range in time for ancient coins in American soil is a direct reflection of the rise and fall of naval power in the Mediterranean. This shows that ancient coins must have been brought to America during the respective epochs of shipping activity on the part of the Carthaginians, Romans, Byzantines, and Arabs. Archeologists hitherto have contended that no shipping came to America in ancient times, and that all ancient coins found in America are coins that have been accidentally lost in modern times by collectors of such coins. If this were true, all coins of all periods and of nonmaritime nations as well as naval powers would be equally represented in the American finds. Treasure hunters have learned by experience that consecutive runs of dated coins indicate the presence of a sunken wreck. There is no reason to suppose that Roman coins on American beaches behave differently from those on Mediterranean beaches—or that rules applicable to sunken Spanish coin cannot be applied to sunken Roman coin.

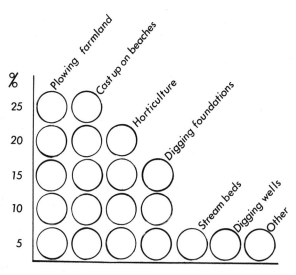

How ancient coins are discovered in America. As in Europe, most discoveries are made by farmers and country schoolboys. With the development of metal detectors, important finds are now being made on beaches after storms. In the nineteenth century coins were also found in Indian mounds, but unfortunately no detailed records were kept.

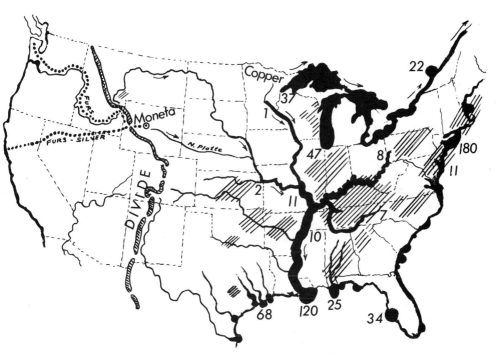

The geographical distribution of finds of ancient coins in North America shows a strong correlation with navigable coastal and riverine waterways. Relative traffic density in modern times is shown by the bold face numbers, which represent millions of tons of traffic per annum. Petroglyphs depicting ancient coins extend the range to the ancient equivalent of the Oregon Trail, extending across the prairies to Moneta in Wyoming. The latter town appears to mark the site of the annual fur market in Roman times, lying near the North Pass in the Great Divide, and thus as convenient for ancient trappers as the nineteenth-century Wyoming markets were for trappers and buyers of the Astor company. The route also gave access to Nevada and Californian silver. In the north, the Michigan copper mines linked both with the upper Mississippi traders and with ships on the Great Lakes.

New techniques were brought into use to speed the decipherment of difficult inscriptions from Spain, Portugal, and North Africa, as well as North America. Here Dr. Sentiel Rommel at the University of Maine has programmed a computer to plot the relative frequencies of sounds in sample languages, for comparison with corresponding plots of sign frequencies in undeciphered inscriptions. *Photo Dr. Julian Fell.*

Malcolm Pearson, archeologist-photographer since the 1930's, prepares to take off on a flight over a site area designated by James Whittall, who will also accompany him. Pilot Charles Burnham is fellow member of the Early Sites Research Society and Epigraphic Society. *Photo James Whittall.*

Above: Aerial geography and the analysis of space-satellite photos is the special skill of **Professor Noel Ring of Norwich University,** Vermont, lecturing on the persistence of ancient field boundaries into modern times. *Photo Peter J. Garfall.*

Left: A metal detector employed by Jesse Ray Kelley of Waldron, Arkansas, proved effective in locating buried ancient coins and other metallic objects. His discoveries include a specimen of the same Carthaginian coin as that from Connecticut shown on page 56. *Photo Professor Norman Totten.*

Although numerous American inscriptions had been found in the peculiar Ogam script of the Celts of Iberia, it was not until the spring of 1977 that the first example of a Celtic inscription in alphabetic script was discovered. This boundary marker, written in the Celtiberian dialect of Gadelic (ancient Gaelic) and using an alphabet similar to Irish, but related also to Phoenician, was found by Barbara Jean Woodward in the woods at Ardmore, Oklahoma. Gloria Farley, president of the Eastern Oklahoma Historical Society, immediately secured a latex impression for the Epigraphic Society, permitting this plaster replica to be made and studied. The three lines of text read, from above down, and left to right,

AOS NOUG
FIRID
AILG

which may be translated as "Tribal land as far as this Boundary Stone." Similar words still occur in modern Irish Gaelic to this day. The inscription is believed to date to about the time of Christ. *Replica Gloria Farley, photo Peter J. Garfall.*

Celtic scholars from Britain, Canada, and the United States
now began to visit the New England sites believed to be the work of
Iberian Celts of two thousand and more years ago, Ogam inscriptions
were reported from various parts of North America, and a Romano-
Celtic coin, excavated in Champaign, Illinois, yielded a date of ca.
third century A.D. Here Professors Gareth and Janet Dunleavy, of the
University of Wisconsin, Milwaukee, inspect the Ardmore cast. *Photo
Peter J. Garfall.*

Archeologists at the University of Benghazi confer in 1977 on new finds
from America. From left, Fell, Dr. Fauzi Gadallah (Professor of Ancient
History), and Dr. M. El-Ghannai (Chairman, History Department), both
of the University of Benghazi; Dr. Mohamed Jarary (University of
Tripoli), and Dr. E. D. El-Mehdiwi (Education Administrator, University
of Benghazi). *Photo Peter J. Garfall.*

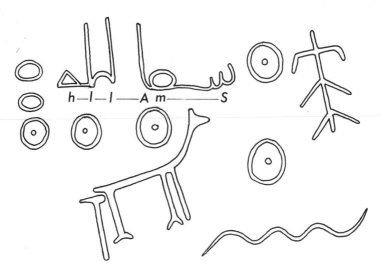

Two inscriptions of differing age occurring together on a rock face at an intersection of caravan routes near Figuig Oasis, south of Oran, North Africa. The oldest is the graffito *Sam Allah* (Exalted is God), dating from some time after 650 A.D. The seeming prehistoric symbols—the sun, water, a camel, and matchstick figure—from their symmetric distribution around the Arabic text were added later by illiterate, and probably pagan, Bedouins. Feeble desert varnish is present over the incised markings. *(Record by Flamand (1901), transl. Fell.)* Inscriptions are often found in which later additions are superimposed over older material. Thus, if dealing with readable texts, the decipherment neglects irrelevant parts of the petroglyph of different age, just as studies on historic New England colonial tombstones ignore modern defacements added by vandals. This procedure, often not understood by archeologists, leads to complaints that the decipherer "chooses to read parts of an inscription and ignores other portions."

Reluctance to recognize Old World affinities still characterizes the attitudes of many archeologists. As recently as 1977, a prominent English spokesman denied that any connection exists between the pyramids of Egypt and those of America; the latter being considered mere "temple platforms," devoid of a royal tomb. As the diagram shows, the royal tomb of the Mexican pyramid at Palenque has, in fact, the same basic relationship to the overlying pyramid as occurs in the Egyptian pyramids.

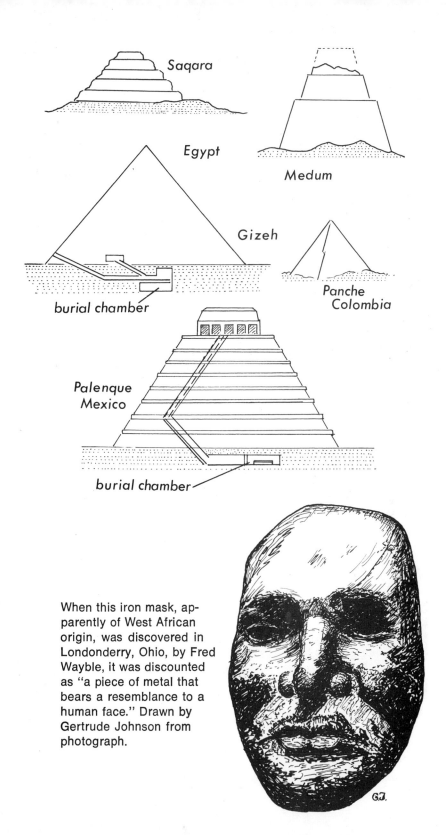

Saqara

Egypt

Medum

Gizeh

burial chamber

Panche
Colombia

Palenque
Mexico

burial chamber

When this iron mask, apparently of West African origin, was discovered in Londonderry, Ohio, by Fred Wayble, it was discounted as "a piece of metal that bears a resemblance to a human face." Drawn by Gertrude Johnson from photograph.

GJ.

Above, Professor Ivan Van Sertima, authority on African language and literature who is engaged on researches into ancient American contacts with black Africa. *Photo Smithsonian Institution. Below,* Dr. Edgard E. Torres Mosquera of Colombia, whose excavations of the ruined Panche pyramid are disclosing new evidence of ancient American connections with Egypt.

known to the Eskimo in Greenland. Last, on grounds of common sense, he reasoned that stone would be utilized by primitive man long before he learned the art of working metals. In 1819 the collection was opened to the public in a display in the University Library in Copenhagen, and the explanatory labels offered the suggestion that there had apparently been a Stone Age, followed by a Bronze Age, which in turn was followed by the Iron Age. Coins associated with some of the finds implied that in Denmark the Iron Age had begun about 400 B.C., when the earliest Greek coins began to be used by traders in Europe; evidently, therefore, the Bronze Age represented an older epoch in man's history, and the Stone Age a still older era.

Thomsen offered these proposals merely as reasonable inferences, with suggestions on how future inquiries might be directed to check the validity or otherwise of the proposals. Swedish scholars became highly interested in these ideas and set about further investigation in Sweden. Danish researchers now had an added incentive to intensify their own inquiries at home. By 1836 the collections had outgrown the available exhibition space at the university and were removed to a new museum established in three halls in the Christianborg Slot (Palace). Thomsen now assigned one gallery to the Stone Age, one to the Bronze Age, and one to the Iron Age. He also wrote the first guidebook in which antiquities were thus classified in what now came to be known as the "Three-Age System." The first foreign nations to study—and then accept —Thomsen's proposals were the Swedes, and then the Norwegians and Germans—all of whom had suffered from the same lack of direct evidence in the shape of Roman occupation ruins and inscriptions.

Thus, out of the original paucity of evidence from Scandinavia, the least promising area as it had seemed for recovering ancient history, had come forth a usable and essentially logical classification that now transformed the archeology of the northern countries into the most advanced anywhere in the world. By 1849 an English translation of a book explaining the system had appeared, written mainly by Thomsen's assistant and successor, Worsaae. At this point the British were in no mood to accept such ideas, and most of the archeologists of the day clung to the older biblical dogma of a universal deluge (to which all fossils were to be assigned as the remains of sinners and animals drowned by the Flood). The notion of an evolutionary progression from one level of culture to another higher level seemed unfamiliar and improbable. And when, thirteen years later in 1859, Charles Darwin added fuel to the fire by proposing a general theory of evolution, archeology was beset by raging bishops and other furious clerics who denounced the stupidity of Scandinavians and the impiety of biologists. Yet, within the space of a decade, most thinking people had come to realize the essential good sense of the Three-Age System, and had quietly adopted it.

While Britain and France painfully adapted to the flow of ideas from Scandinavia, the Danes had been ranging far ahead. Thomsen and Brøndsted were both expert numismatists, leading world authorities on ancient Greek and Roman coins. They had observed the associations occasionally to be seen between particular ancient coins and particular types of artifacts, and had been able to subdivide the Iron Age into three parts. The first, from about 400 B.C. to the time of Christ, was dated on the basis of coins of the Greek states and of the Roman Republic. As the artifacts showed Celtic influences, they called it the Celtic Iron Age. Next came what they called the Roman Iron Age, from 1 A.D. to about 400 A.D., coinciding approximately with the span of the Roman Empire, and signaled by artifacts of a kind showing evident Roman influence, or actual importation from Italy, and coupled with Roman coins of the emperors. Last came a more vaguely defined era, called by the Danes the Nordic Iron Age, spanning the period from 400 A.D. to the onset of Viking times in 800 A.D. It was signaled by the occasional presence of coins of that range in dates, derived from the Frankish, Byzantine, and Anglo-Saxon mints. In England, where these refinements took root more easily than the original proposals, similar divisions were recognized; the name Anglian Iron Age being substituted for Nordic Iron Age. At the same time that divisions of the Stone Age and the Bronze Age were recognized, such well-known and universally used terms as Paleolithic and Neolithic were introduced; the former and older period characterized by chipped stone implements, the latter and younger by polished stone implements. The divisions of the Bronze Age were found to vary from one region to another, with alternating fashions of burying or cremating the dead to serve as markers.

These lively developments in European archeology were less enthusiastically accepted in America, for the obvious reason that most American Indian tribes presented anomalous cultural features. Arrowheads, for example were chipped from stone, hence "Paleolithic," yet contemporary with such objects are copper bracelets and knives and polished stone amulets and tobacco pipes—a veritable hodgepodge of "ages" on the European system. These anomalies, coupled with a steadily growing mine of misinformation on the supposed uniqueness of Columbus' voyage, led to a deep schism of American archeological thinking from its European equivalent, and ultimately to the impasse in which American archeology now finds itself in the grip of a dogma that prejudges all new evidence of Old World connections as forgeries, misinterpretations, and surreptitious importations of ancient objects in modern times. As in *America B.C.,* one purpose of this book is to restore the long-neglected evidence, to add new evidence, and to make inferences accordingly.

One main point must now be made: the whole essential basis of modern archeology is the original Three-Age System developed by the Danish scholars and, with the refinements they added later, almost the entire classification of the periods from 400 B.C. onward has been carried out on the basis of dates yielded by ancient coins. The men who initiated and carried through these reforms were expert numismatists, specialists in the coinage of the Greeks and the Romans. And nearly all the more modern extensions of this dating method to other parts of the world has been performed on the basis of ancient coinage. America stands alone in having ignored these important developments. The time is long overdue to rectify the oversight. Here, as elsewhere, study of our ancient coins provides a means for dating the American cultures over the past two thousand years, and for determining the transoceanic connections of American colonists, many of whom stand in the line of descent of major Amerindian tribes.

In parts of North Africa, north of the Sahara Desert, very ancient writing systems that range back over 2,000 years are still to be found in use by isolated tribes. They were formerly more widespread than today, with the result that ancient rock inscriptions in these archaic alphabets can nowadays be found in areas where only Arabic is spoken and written today. Some of the ancient inscriptions closely match those of North America. Also, some of the earliest Arabic inscriptions, written in an alphabet called Kufic, closely match some of the North American inscriptions, both as to alphabet and as to language. Thus the importance of North African studies to American history is obvious. Further, as I pointed out in *America B.C.,* the old language of the religious chants of tribes such as the Pima in Arizona is so rich in Arabic vocabulary that the chants can be translated in the same way as correspondingly ancient language in North Africa.

New methods are appropriate to our times, whenever advances in technology place them within our grasp. Computer-drawn frequency diagrams for the various sounds or letters in ancient inscriptions sometimes are a valuable aid in identifying the parent language. At my request, Dr. Sentiel Rommel of the University of Maine kindly devised a program that simplifies this operation (page 36).

Aerial photography is not a new tool in archeological research, but some aspects of its application have not previously been used here. For example, Professor Noel Ring is now making use of aerial surveys, not only in planes that she flies, but also from photographs taken in infrared light from high-flying U-2 planes and from earth satellites flown by NASA. It is her belief that studies of such photographs disclose ancient field patterns, and the manner in which ancient fields have been incorporated into modern fields that share the same boundary lines (page 37).

Yet one more new aspect of archeology in America is its extension to examining and surveying potential sites now covered by the sea. Based in Washington, D.C., the Scientific Exploration and Archeological Society was established primarily for this purpose by marine archeologist John Gifford and two international attorneys, Talbot Lindstrom and Steve Procter, in 1971. Known by its acronym SEAS, the group has extended its survey activities to the Red Sea and Saudi Arabia, thus gaining experience in Old World evidence of trading routes by examining sunken ships and ports and other types of submerged sites, and is now actively engaged in seeking out New World parallels. SEAS members regard their work as essentially a survey, to seek out and define important underwater areas for more detailed investigation by major academic institutions. As our work in inscriptions and the discovery of ship-related artifacts (such as coins washed ashore on beaches) goes ahead, it is naturally to SEAS that we turn for further advice and planning, and when feasible these underwater archeologists respond with enthusiasm by initiating a scuba-diving operation.

But whatever the advantages of new methods and new tools for research, nothing can replace the time-honored methods of our predecessors in the field. Exploration, no matter how it is expedited by modern transportation, still demands, in the final reckoning, actual visits to the ancient occupation sites, and personal search of the rock-faces and caves for inscriptions left behind by earlier visitors. In the western states of America, and in British Columbia, a devoted company of explorers has placed on record, by camera and pen, the details of thousands of ancient inscriptions carved or painted on bedrock. These records have been careful and objective, and such names as Robert Heizer and John Corner have become a part of our resources on account of the meticulous detail with which they published their findings. Although, with various companions, I covered some 20,000 miles while researching this book, my major resource has still been the work of my predecessors. To them, whenever possible, we turned for advice and guidance; also to regional archeologists well acquainted with particular areas, including some of the most remote parts of the desert plateau. The help we sought was generously given, and some of the pictures in this book stem from that aid.

The Carthaginians in America

In the year 1558, when Elizabeth I had just been crowned queen of England, an obscure French churchman, the Abbé Amiot, became the literary sensation of Europe. He had discovered ancient Greek manuscripts by a historian named Plutarch in monastery libraries in Italy, and he published a French translation of what he found. His great find comprised a series of biographies of many of the most famous men of ancient Greece and Rome, together with literary and scientific essays on a variety of subjects.

In London, Sir Thomas North brought out an English translation of Amiot's French version, and this in turn became the source of many of the plots of William Shakespeare's historical plays. Not until 1624 did the original Greek appear in print. Among the lesser known of Plutarch's wide-ranging writings is one that is apparently the script of rough lecture notes that he used as a teaching philosopher in the academies of Greece. In it Plutarch discusses an ancient Carthaginian manuscript he says he found in the ruins of that city, one dealing with voyages across the Atlantic. Few—if, indeed any—English or French literary men of Amiot's time had sailed the Atlantic; at all events, not one of them noticed anything unusual about the Carthaginian passage.

And so it was not until America celebrated the 400th anniversary of the voyage of Columbus, in 1892, that a historian in New York noticed Plutarch's account of the parchment from Carthage, and realized that it presented a truthful and verifiable description of routine voyages made to and from America. In May 1942, when the U-boat blockade of Britain was mounting in intensity, a chance decision of military and naval authorities placed me on board a ship whose commander was under orders to sail from Britain to

New York by the so-called Iceland route, then adopted as a make-shift means of skirting the blockade. The ship was the *Port Nicholson,* and she made the crossing safely, set me ashore in Nova Scotia, and then sailed on to her doom. The following day, she and two other ships came to rest on the seabed off Cape Cod, their hulls blown open by torpedoes. Years later, when I read Plutarch, and Verplanck Colvin's 1893 discussion before the Albany Institute, New York, it was at once as clear to me as it had been to Colvin himself that Plutarch's account of the sailing directions of the Carthaginians is indeed the truth. My own voyage of 1942 had covered the same track, and the sequence of landfalls and sightings had been just as he described.

Colvin's deductions were published by the Institute in 1898 and, sad to say, aroused little interest. A quarter of a century later, Samuel Eliot Morison, the biographer of Columbus, dismissed as poppycock all reputed voyages to America before Columbus. Since then another fifty years have gone by, and with their passage has come a shift of opinion. Already a number of American historians accept the reality of Norse voyages in the eleventh century, and some admit to even earlier voyaging. But one thing has always crippled speculations on the subject: the lack of tangible proof that such voyages occurred. And it is just that area of uncertainty that demanded detailed research.

As in the case of the work done in preparation for writing my previous book, far-ranging travel was required. My colleagues and I visited the ancient sites of Carthaginian settlements in North Africa and Spain, and also the ruined cities of peoples who were allies of the Carthaginians, or whose mariners sailed on Carthaginian ships. We visited archeologists and historians who work on these Old World sites and discussed our American finds with them. Then, encouraged by their enthusiasm and obvious confidence in the validity of our researches here, we returned to America to implement their suggestions. We consulted widely with American investigators interested in the problem, sought and obtained their assistance where special skills were demanded. Then, finally, some of the colleagues overseas whom we had visited now came to America to see for themselves the evidence we had reported, and to lend us their skills. But before I deal with our American work, let me first review what had been done in Europe and North Africa by earlier investigators, before the American aspects became apparent.

. Who were the Carthaginians, and why do we associate them with long sea voyages? The Phoenicians, as most people know, were an ancient trading people of Semitic origin (at least in part). They spoke a language akin to that of the ancient Hebrews, and frequently wrote it in much the same alphabetic letters as the ancient Hebrews used. Their best-known homeland is the war-torn country we presently call Lebanon, and their most famous ancient cities were Tyre and Sidon. However, around 800 B.C. they established strong trading posts along the North African coast, west of Egypt and as far afield as Morocco and southern Spain. One of these settlements grew into a powerful city-state, apparently named Kharkhedona, and located in a bay at the northern tip of Tunisia. The Greeks and Romans—and we today—call this city Carthage.

Thus the Phoenicians were now separated into an eastern or Lebanese branch, and a western or Carthaginian stock. Both groups were famous for the purple cloth they manufactured by a secret dyeing process utilizing the pigment of a sea snail called *Murex*; the Greeks named the traders who brought such wares "The Purple-People,"—*Phoinikoi*—from which we get our word Phoenician. The Romans called them *Punici,* which means the same. However, as most of the historical events that linked the Romans and Phoenicians in alliances (and later in enmity) concerned only the western Phoenicians, we usually restrict the use of the word "Punic" to serve as a synonym for Carthaginian. Thus we speak of the Carthaginians as using the *Punic* language.

As time went by, the Punic dialect and alphabet came to differ from that of the Lebanese Phoenicians. Punic often has very long tails on the letters, and is apt to be carelessly written so that different letters often look the same. It is an easy language to recognize when written, but a hard one to read because the writing often is so bad.

From early times, the Carthaginians were famed mariners. They had to be, for their principal wares were rather cheap imitations of Greek and Egyptian goods, and their principal buyers were savage or semicivilized peoples in distant lands that produced the raw materials the Carthaginians needed to supply their factories.

Tin is one of the raw materials essential in the manufacture of hardened bronze, and hence for the making of swords and other weapons, armor, and domestic tools; for bronze is an alloy of tin and copper. Somehow the Carthaginians learned that a supply of tin existed in an unknown land to the north of Spain. They themselves obtained it by bartering with the Celts of northwestern France. As no other source of tin was available to the Greeks and Romans, the Carthaginians established a complete monopoly, which they jealously protected by blockading the Straits of Gibraltar so that no foreign vessel could leave or enter the Atlantic without their knowledge and permission.

The Illyrian historian Strabo, who lived in Yugoslavia in the same century as Christ, recounts an ancient story of how Romans tried to discover the source of the tin. A Roman captain masqueraded as an ally of the Carthaginians and took his ship into the port of Gades (Cadiz) in southern Spain. When his spies reported that a Carthaginian trader was about to sail for the Tin Isles, the Roman vessel sneaked along astern. The Punic captain soon discovered that he was being followed, and he ran his ship ashore on the coast of Portugal, he and his crew making their way overland back to Gades. When he told his story, he was rewarded by the merchant princes of the town and given a new ship to replace his loss.

At length the Carthaginians themselves tired of being dependent upon the Celtic middlemen of France, and determined to find out for themselves exactly where the mines were located. A navigator named Himilco sailed from Gades, following the usual northern track skirting the coast of Portugal, and then northeast across the Bay of Biscay to Brittany. Here he asked which ships were bringing tin to the Breton market, and learned that the vessels were manned by Celts related to the Bretons by race and language, and who came from an island that lay to the north of Brittany. Following these directions, Himilco now seems to have encountered the Channel Islands, and then the coast of Britain—either Cornwall or Devon. As commercial interests invariably governed Carthaginian policy, it is not surprising that the record of Himilco's voyage is woefully incomplete. We cannot tell if he established trading relations with the ancient Britons or not, for Punic sources are silent on the matter, and direct archeological evidence in the shape of Punic inscriptions in Britain are not forthcoming for his particular voyage. It stands to reason that Carthage would not advertise such matters to the world at large, for the merchant princes who constituted her government certainly would not permit the release of such information.

It is commonly stated—and with much less justification—that there is no archeological evidence to show that Carthaginians ever reached Britain. One Spanish archeologist, Professor Antonio Arribas, has even been led to conclude that the absence of evidence of Carthaginian visits to Britain means that the tin mines of Cornwall had already been exhausted by the fourth century B.C. The latter conclusion is demonstrably wrong, for the British tin mines of Cornwall are well known to have served as the only source of tin for Christian Europe all through medieval times, until the discovery of tin ores in Bohemia. Substantial quantities of tin were still being taken from the Cornish mines until the end of the eighteenth century.

Furthermore, recent excavations in Cornwall have disclosed that near Chun Castle, Morvah, an ancient Iron Age tin-mining industry was still in operation in the Dark Ages, because some hut floors datable to the sixth century A.D. yield hearths with slag and other evidence that tin and iron were smelted there at that time. Equally decisive are other new finds made at a Romano-British site near Chysauter village, Madron, in Cornwall. Tin was mined and smelted here from about 100 B.C. to sometime in the third century A.D. The operations appear to have been in the hands of the Britons themselves. There is no evidence of Roman control of the industry which, however, would most certainly be encouraged by the Romans. We must therefore conclude that tin was apparently mined continuously in Cornwall from Bronze Age times onward, right through the Roman occupation and on through the Dark Ages and medieval times until the modern era. Consequently, the alleged absence of evidence of Carthaginian visitors is in no wise to be interpreted as implying the exhaustion of the Cornish mines during the era of Carthaginian dominance. All the evidence points to the contrary.

Besides, there is other information. Within the last twenty years, new excavations have been carried out in Cornwall and have disclosed the presence of what look very much like some of the most conspicuous of the trade goods distributed by Carthaginians. These are glass beads, whose manufacture was essentially a Phoenician industrial secret until their subjection by Rome. What appear to be Phoenician beads have been excavated from a hill fort known as Castle Dore, near St. Sampson, Cornwall. The inferred date span of the site ranges from sometime before 200 B.C. (when the walls of the fort were reconstructed) down to the first century A.D., when the site was temporarily abandoned. It was certainly still in use in 50 B.C., when an inner rampart was built. Radford and his colleagues who made the excavations recovered imported glass beads and bracelets, and concluded that the community using this refuge drew its wealth from two sources: agriculture and mining tin and iron. Thus, as investigations continue in Cornwall, the previously inferred "absence of Carthaginian evidence" has been progressively weakened. Even on the facts already cited, we would now be justified in concluding that Carthaginians really did visit Britain, as historical tradition has always claimed. But there is more to come.

About 600 B.C. a colony of Greeks from Asia Minor had established a trading post on the south coast of Gaul. They named their town Marsalia—the modern Marseilles—and by trading with the Gauls, established a lively commerce between the Greek mainland and France. From the Gauls they learned of the existence of tin mines in some land to the far north, approachable by the sea route around Spain were it not for the embargo imposed by the Carthaginians. Between 310 B.C. and 306 B.C., the navies of Carthage and of the Sicilian Greeks became involved in a conflict that stretched both antagonists to the limit. It came to the ears of one Pytheas, a Greek mariner of Marsalia, that the Carthaginians had been forced to withdraw most of the blockading ships of the Straits of Gibraltar, in order to put together a great invasion force of 1,500 vessels that was about to descend upon Sicily.

The Greeks of Marsalia saw that their chance had come to discover the secret of the location of the mysterious Tin Isles, the

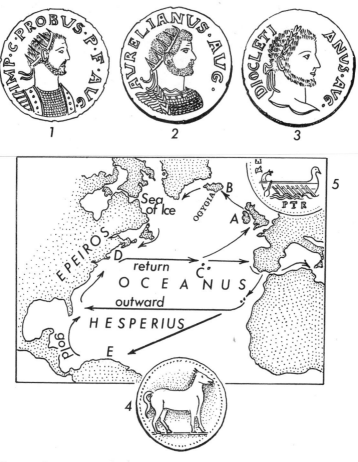

The northern outward route followed by Carthaginian ships, as recorded by Plutarch went by way of Iceland (Ogygia), and the return route followed the anti-trade winds around latitude 40° N, back to Spain and Carthage. It is likely, however, that many ships followed the outward route used by Columbus, in tropical latitudes, thereby gaining the benefit of the westward-blowing trade winds. Diodorus of Sicily implies that this route was followed when he speaks of an island resembling Cuba that, he says, the Carthaginians discovered.

Later mariners used similar routes. For example, the Roman emperor Constans, using a ship similar to that depicted on his London medal (shown at 5), sailed in pursuit of Celtic pirates who had raided Wales. They led him to an Arctic island—presumably Iceland—for Roman coins of the third century (shown at 1, 2, 3) occur in Iceland. An unknown person buried a crock of Roman coins on the coast of Venezuela, E, containing hundreds of examples from the reigns of all the emperors of the first three centuries after Christ. Carthaginian coins were found in a crock buried in the Azores, C, and presumably these were relics of visits by Carthaginian traders; these latter specimens are now lost, but probably resembled the example shown at 4.

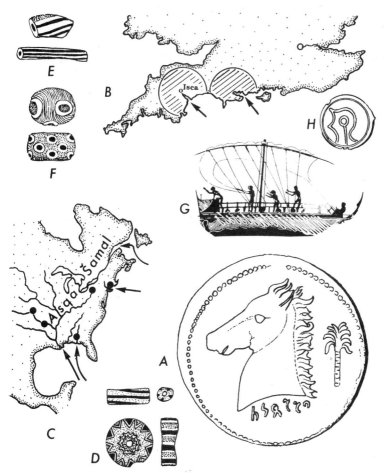

In Britain the principal evidence for Carthaginian visits, apart from
records by ancient historians, lies in the differential distribution of
Carthaginian coins, A, which cluster around two main ports of entry, on
the Esk River in Devon, and Poole Harbor in Dorset; and in the presence
at sites where tin was mined of glass beads E, F, of Phoenician type.
Later Greeks visited Britain, G, and the ancient British tribes minted tin
coins, H, in crude imitation of Greek coins. In North America ancient
Carthaginian coins are found on coastal sites and along navigable
inland rivers, C. Beads of Phoenician type have been found in ancient
Indian mounds, D. Whereas Plutarch used for America the name "Continent (Epeiros) that rims the western Ocean," the Carthaginian name
appears to have been *Asqa Samal* (Great North Land), for this phrase
occurs on a later Libyan inscription recording the flight overseas of
North African Christians persecuted by the Vandals (see Chapter 8).

Left: Carthaginian coins found in America all have one characteristic in common. All belong to the earliest issues of Carthage, those of the fourth and early third centuries B.C. All are the work of highly skilled Greek artists; all bear an obverse face that is a copy of the coinage of the Greek city of Syracuse, in Italy, depicting the nymph Arethusa surrounded by dolphins; all of the American examples that are well enough preserved to be legible prove to have the Greek legend misspelt. In the example illustrated above (found by Frederick J. Gastonguay at Waterbury, Connecticut) the legend reads SYRAKOSCAN, instead of the correct spelling SYRAKOSION. It would seem that these coins were either the work of Iberian Greeks, or intended initially for circulation among Iberian Greeks, whose dialect had diverged from that of Greece. However, it is possible that the misspellings may have an actual function—such as deliberate secret mint marks to indicate the source or date of the minting. *Photo F. J. Gastonguay, courtesy Professor Norman Totten and Vincent Terullo.*

Symbols of Carthage, 1. According to legend, a horse's head in the ground was the oracle's prediction of how the founders of Carthage would recognize the site destined for the city. This emblem, together with a palm tree, was used as the coat of arms of Carthage, as on the American example of an early coin, the reverse face of the same coin from Waterbury, Connecticut, shown on the reverse face. The Punic letters beneath spell the word O-M-M-Q-N-T (*ommachanat,* reading from right to left), literally "in camp," and believed to signify that the coin was a military issue intended for use as pay for mercenary Greek and Iberian soldiers in the Carthaginian army. The Punic lettering shows some Iberian influence, as if the die had been engraved by an Iberian Greek. *Photo F. J. Gastonguay, courtesy Professor Norman Totten and Vincent Terullo.*

Opposite above: Symbols of Carthage, 2. Two views of a white limestone horse's head discovered in North Salem, New York, in the immediate vicinity of stone chambers like those reported in *America B.C.* The head is now in the ownership of K. C. Hughes. *Photo James Whittall.*

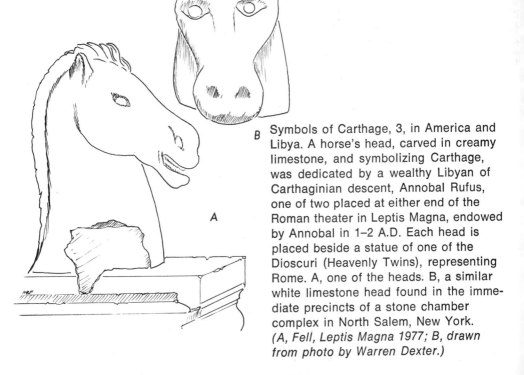

Symbols of Carthage, 3, in America and Libya. A horse's head, carved in creamy limestone, and symbolizing Carthage, was dedicated by a wealthy Libyan of Carthaginian descent, Annobal Rufus, one of two placed at either end of the Roman theater in Leptis Magna, endowed by Annobal in 1–2 A.D. Each head is placed beside a statue of one of the Dioscuri (Heavenly Twins), representing Rome. A, one of the heads. B, a similar white limestone head found in the immediate precincts of a stone chamber complex in North Salem, New York. (A, Fell, Leptis Magna 1977; B, drawn from photo by Warren Dexter.)

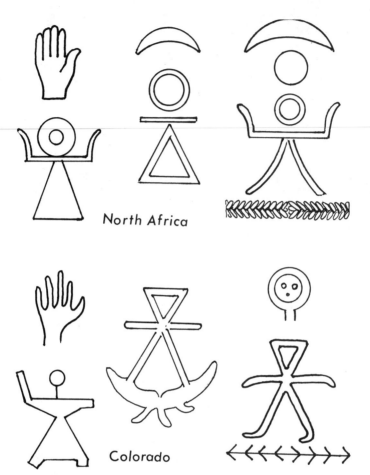

Symbols of Carthage, 4. *Above,* typical symbols of the goddess Tanith (spouse of Baal) and related signs, seen on Carthaginian tombstones in North Africa. *Below,* corresponding petroglyphs from Colorado discovered, but not then recognized, by Professor Julian H. Steward in 1936–1940. *Information in part by courtesy of Aileen Alexander.*

More American examples of early Carthaginian coins. *Above,* obverse
and reverse faces of specimen found in Alabama *(photos courtesy Dr.
Joseph Mahan).* The name in Greek is here again misspelled
SYRAKOSCAN. *Below,* a later minting of uncertain finding place, but in
the possession of a Pennsylvania owner. Here the goddess Arethusa
has been transformed into a Hellenistic version of the Carthaginian
goddess Tanith, and the palm tree lacks roots. The name on the obverse
is misspelled SYRAKOSIAN, believed to be the normal Iberian Greek
form of the genitive case, meaning "Of the Syracusans." In both cases,
the reverse die shows that the coin is Carthaginian, not Syracusan,
though the upper example was initially misreported as a Greek coin of
Syracuse. *Lower photos courtesy of Gloria Farley.*

Kassiteridae of which their Gallic informants spoke. Sneaking by the Pillars of Hercules now ineffectively patrolled, Pytheas found himself off the Portuguese coast with no pursuing Punic ships in view. He set his prow to the north and inevitably made the discovery of the Cornish mines. But he was more than a mariner-explorer; his ship was equipped with instruments to measure the elevation above the horizon of conspicuous stars at night, and of the noonday sun. He was already aware of the fact that the stars revolve daily about a pole located (in his day) in a dark spot of the sky between four stars of the constellation called the Bear. He was also aware that when a ship sails northward from Sicily to Marseilles, the north celestial pole is seen to rise some 9 moon-diameters, or 4.5 degrees, higher in the sky.

Pytheas now observed that as he sailed from Gades northward to Cornwall, the celestial pole rose a further 26 moon diameters, or 13 degrees. He and his fellow sailors had never seen the Bear hang so high in the midnight sky before, and they marveled at the sight. He then sailed even farther north—probably as far as the Baltic—and once again saw the Bear rise even higher. When the expedition returned, all on board noticed that the sequence of changes reversed; the north celestial pole sank back toward the northern horizon. It was as if the Greek ship had sailed over a curved surface; and since Pytheas had some conception of the distances he had covered, he was able to provide the Greek astronomers with the first hints as to the shape of the earth.

As we now realize, Pytheas exerted a long-enduring influence on Greek science as a result of his observations. Never before had any Western navigator been able to sail so far north; Carthaginian commercial interests would not permit it. So only now, for the first time, could astronomers take account of such important new evidence as to the curvature of the earth's surface.

For us in America, the voyage of Pytheas can be seen as a major landmark that led eventually to the discovery of the Pacific coast of both continents, from Alaska in the north to Chile in the south. For, fifty years after Pytheas, a great Libyan scientist was aided by the polar observations in devising an ingenious method of calculating the size of the earth; and, as a result, an expedition was sent out to investigate the matter. As suggested in a later chapter (page 265) that expedition probably discovered and settled California.

But the purpose of this chapter is to examine the sailing activities of the Carthaginians, so I return now to Cornwall and its tin mines. In this context, Pytheas was able to confirm and to locate the mines of which his Celtic informants had spoken in Marsalia. The conclusion of the Carthaginian war with Sicily restored the blockade at the Straits of Gibraltar; once again the trade with Britain became the exclusive prerogative of the western Phoenicians.

But trading practices had advanced a notch since Himilco's original voyage. The merchants of Carthage found themselves handicapped by having no national coinage—until now all trade had been carried out by direct barter and exchanges of goods. This might suffice for dealings with barbarians and semicivilized peoples, but availed not at all in recruiting an army of mercenary soldiers in Sicily, most of which had now become a colony of the Carthaginians. The Greek and Libyan warriors who formed a major part of the Carthaginian army and navy demanded pay in the form of negotiable securities—to wit, coins of good repute, struck with designs recognizable at sight by Sicilian tradesmen, and containing precious metal exactly equal to the face value of the coin. Faced with this demand, the Carthaginian administration authorized the issue of coinage. The finest Sicilian Greek artists were engaged to prepare dies from which the coinage was to be struck and were instructed to make one face of each coin match the coins of the principal city of Sicily—Syracuse—depicting therefore the Syracusan emblem, the nymph Arethusa, surrounded by dolphins. The reverse face of the new coins was to carry a design based on the coat of arms of the city of Carthage, depicting the head of a horse and a palm tree. Legend said that the site of the future city was recognized by the founders of Carthage by a prediction that a horse's head would be found marking the spot. Forever afterward, wherever Carthaginians settled, they dedicated a sculpted marble or limestone head of a horse; even in far-distant New England, when Carthaginians came, they brought with them this ancient emblem (see pages 56 and 57).

By about 325 B.C., the new coinage was in existence and already circulating wherever Carthage had business dealings. One of the factors that must have influenced the Carthaginians to issue the coinage would be the inescapable fact that the Celts of France had already become acquainted with the coinage, in silver and gold, issued by Philip III of Macedon, father of Alexander the Great. For reasons not entirely clear, the Celts were not merely interested in the new Greek coinage, they were positively intoxicated by it. The demand was insatiable. Immense numbers were struck, first by the Greeks, then, when the demand exceeded the supply, the Celts themselves made plausible imitations. These Gaulish copies contained the full monetary value in precious metal, but the design left much to be desired. Some very strange and crude copies of Philip's portrait and the charioteer on the reverse came into circulation (page 146).

Knowing of the Celtic infatuation for Philip's Macedonian coinage and the widespread dispersal of such coins across Europe and into Britain, together with the numerous Celtic imitations, it seemed obvious to me that the Carthaginian coinage, itself a close copy of the renowned coins of Syracuse, ought to have been equally popular with the Celts—particularly with the Celts who engaged in commerce with the Carthaginians. Would not this provide a test for discovering if Carthaginian traders had really visited Britain in order to purchase tin?

By 1977 it had become important for us in America to know the answer to this question, because we were now discovering in American soil those very Carthaginian coins that had been brought into use in Europe and the Mediterranean lands around 325 B.C. Even that very day late in 1977, when our party took off from Boston Airport for London and Tripoli, Professor Norman Totten, who saw us off brought news of yet one more discovery of a Carthaginian coin in Syracusan style—this latest in Connecticut. Inquiries among British numismatists disclosed that coins of the Mediterranean states are rather rare in British soil prior to the Roman occupation, but there is one exception to this rule: coins of Carthage. In fact, such coins are classified as comparatively common in southern England, where they have been found by farmers and country schoolboys. Not infrequently they find their way into private collections.

Two additional facts emerged, both of interest to us in America. First, the coins that occur in British soil are not the prime coinage in precious metal, but subsidiary coins of the same design; struck in copper, bronze, or debased silver. Evidently these base-metal coins were struck for use in dealing with barbarian peoples. Greek and Latin authors reported that the Carthaginians themselves found the native tribesmen of Spain very willing to exchange silver and gold for iron tools. They deemed the soft precious metals of little worth, since they were useless for making tools. They set a high price upon iron, whose metallurgy they did not understand and whose tensile qualities they esteemed. Doubtless the Cornish tin was readily exchanged for attractive and artistically struck base-metal coins that could be used as ornaments, and which, in any case, could not be imitated in Britain, and hence were immune from forgery. Indeed, Carthaginian coins produced from the dies carved by Greek engravers would constitute a hard currency among the barbarians and would acquire a locally inflated value.

The other interesting observation of British numismatists concerns the geographical distribution of these Carthaginian coins. There are two primary areas (page 55, map B); one of them centered about the mouth of the River Esk, in Devon, the other around the harbor of Poole, in Dorset. These two places on the south coast appear to have served as major export-import centers. Presumably not only Cornish tin, but other products (such as furs and skins) from areas farther east, were all channeled into markets located at the two harbors, with a resultant higher concentration of Carthaginian coinage in the country surrounding the two ports.

With these valuable hints from British colleagues, I returned to America to analyze the corresponding information for our newly discovered American series of Carthaginian coins. Professor Norman Totten had already concluded that the American specimens are to be assigned to approximately the period 325 B.C. on the grounds of the extremely high artistic merit of the coins. We know that expert Greek artists were initially employed on the production of dies for the Carthaginian mints, whose establishment is believed to date from this epoch. After examining series of Carthaginian coins in the collection of the National Museum in Tripoli and other examples, I agree with Norman Totten's finding. Thus our

American examples are apparently coeval with the oldest examples found in Britain.

Second, I found that without exception the American examples, like those found in Britain, are all of base metal. Third, our American examples all come from sites in the near vicinity of navigable rivers, or the coast itself in the neighborhood of natural harbors.

The conclusion to be drawn from these facts must surely be that Carthaginian coins in America owe their presence here to the same factors that cause them to be present in southern Britain: Carthaginian coins were brought here by Carthaginian traders. These traders were dealing with so-called barbarians (in the Greek sense of the word, meaning semicivilized peoples who did not form part of the Greco-Roman cultural area); barbarians who set value upon artistically produced coins struck on base metal, and who had wares to offer that the Carthaginians found attractive. North America has no known tin of commercial significance—certainly none that could have any value to the Carthaginian metallurgists. Thus it was not tin that attracted the Carthaginians here. Before examining the question further, I now return to Plutarch's statements about what he learned about Carthaginian sailing routes from that parchment that he says he recovered from the ruins of the old city.

Plutarch lived during the first and second centuries A.D. He was born either at the end of the reign of Claudius, or else at the beginning of Nero's reign—i.e., between about 45 and 55 A.D., for he tells us that he was a young lad when Nero visited Athens, and he died in 120 A.D., during the reign of Hadrian. Thus, when he talks about finding the parchment in the ruins of the "old city" of Carthage, he is referring to the city that was destroyed by order of the Roman general Scipio Aemilianus in 146 B.C., two centuries before Plutarch's own day. Hence the sailing routes referred to are not necessarily those of the people who had resettled Carthage soon after the time of Christ, but those of the ancient Carthaginians, before their suicidal confrontation with Rome. See now what Plutarch has to say—I summarize his long narrative in a few words.

Sail westward from Britain (Plutarch writes) and you will pass three island groups on a northwest bearing, where the sun sets in midsummer. These are equidistant from one another, and also from an island called Ogygia, which lies in the arms of the ocean

Soon after the 1976 publication of *America B.C.,* in which inscriptions in ancient Mediterranean languages were reported from the eastern parts of North America, it was discovered that many supposed Indian petroglyphs of the western states are also ancient inscriptions. *Above,* a prayer for rain in the Punic language of Carthage, at Massacre Lake, Nevada, originally reported by professional archeologists in 1958, though not then recognized as writing. The letters read from right to left Q M-T-R I-B (May the clouds spew forth rain). *Below,* a Punic dedication in the same script and language from Constantine, Algeria "Mutum-Baal, son of Aram, dedicated this tablet." *Epigraphic Museum, photo Dr. Julian Fell.*

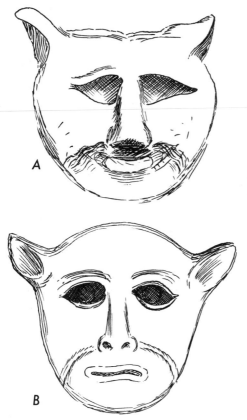

Carthaginian rural satyr masks with Pan's ears: A, carved on rockface near Wichita, Kansas; B, from Sardinia (in Carthaginian occupation until the Punic Wars). Carthaginian coins of the fourth to third century B.C. have been found along the Arkansas River, both upstream and downstream from Wichita. *(A, from color slides sent by the owner-finder, Darrell D. Kellogg.)*

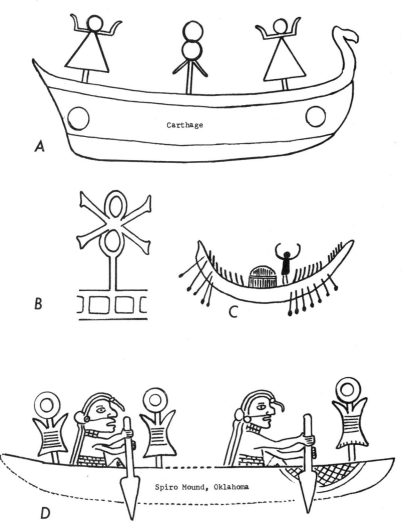

Carthaginian ship motif, A, showing symbols of the goddess Tanith, apparently signifying the special relationship of the goddess to ships and sailors and implying her mystical presence on board. B, similar symbol from Egypt indicating the corresponding role of the goddess Neith for Egyptian mariners, and C, her presence on board as a giant figure among the oarsmen. D, an American example from Spiro Mound, Oklahoma, engraved on shell, and showing symbols of Tanith between the paddlers of a canoe. *(D, courtesy of Peabody Museum, Harvard University.)*

Opposite: A gold zodiac, of which the lower portion is shown here, was discovered in the Cuenca area, Ecuador, and is now in the Crespi collection. It is lettered in the Paphian script of Cyprus, carelessly executed; the language is close to Minoan-Hittite. The portion shown reads from the lower right corner, horizontally in sequence as follows: Wi-tu (The animals), Sign of Aries Le-la (Ram); Sign of Taurus, Gu-da (ox); Sign of Gemini, Po-re-si-za (Divine friends); Sign of Leo, errone-ously, should be Cancer, Me-nu-si (Crab); Sign of Cancer, erroneously, should be Leo, Pe-su (Cat); Sign of Virgo, Ma-ra-te Yo-we Sha-lo (Virgin Daughter of Jove). *Continued in next illustration.*

Continuation of plate shown in previous illustration. Beginning at lower right, reading to left, in sequence upwards: Sign of Libra, U-ke ka-sa-ra-lo (Scales or Claws); Sign of Scorpio, Ku-ne pe za-mi-ra (Venomous tailed-beast); Sign of Sagittarius, O-ku (Archer); garbled sign, should be Capricorn, ma-?-sha, intended for ma-sa (Goat); Sign of Aquarius, si-po (Libation-bowl); damaged sign of Pisces, Ki-tu (Whale). This zodiac, absurdly attributed to alien spacemen by a recent author and ignored by archeologists, is derived from Cyprus, probably copied in Central America from a Cypriot original, sometime before ca. 300 B.C. For further details on American zodiacs see Fell, *Occa-sional Publications of the Epigraphic Society. Replica by Veronica Wilcox, Epigraphic Museum, photo Peter J. Garfall.*

five days' sailing from Britain. (This is a reasonably accurate summary of the relations that the Orkneys, Shetlands, and Faeroes have to one another and to Iceland, which is Ogygia, since it lies at the distance stated. An ancient ship would sail from 100 to 125 miles a day.) Then, Plutarch goes on, if you continue to sail westward for another 5,000 stades (500 miles), you will reach the northern coast of a continent (*Epeiros* is the word used) that rims the great Ocean. (South Greenland fits the distance and direction stated.) Then, he says, if you sail along this coast in a southward direction, you will pass a frozen sea and come to a land where Greeks have settled and intermarried with the native barbarians.

The frozen sea was something Plutarch could not credit. He gave it as the literal translation of the document he had seen, but then expressed his own opinion that this must be some old and confused notion, and that presumably a muddy sea was intended. Actually, as George Lechler has pointed out in his analyses of Norse sailing routes, the southern part of Davis Strait, between Labrador and Greenland, becomes an impassable mass of floating ice during the summer season, when northern navigations could be performed.

As for the land where the Greeks had settled and intermarried with the native barbarians, Nova Scotia and New England lie in the position Plutarch gives, for he says they lie in the same latitudes as the Caspian Sea. Turning now to the authoritative two-volume *Dictionary of the Micmac Language* of Nova Scotia and Maine, prepared by the great lexicographer of the Micmacs, Dr. Silas Rand, we find that the one and most striking fact he was able to elicit as to the relationship of the vocabulary, after a lifetime's work among the Micmacs, was the prevalence of Greek roots (of which he lists over fifty illustrative cases). Rand believed that this implies a former connection between these Indians and Europeans who spoke either Greek, or a language like Greek. At all events, he was of the opinion that the Indian dialects of Nova Scotia and Maine must have been derived from some Indo-European source.

The appendix at the end of this book gives a representative selection of such Greek-related words. These imply a derivation from the Greek spoken in North Africa in Ptolemaic times, around 300 to 100 B.C., words that were part of the everyday language of Libya and Egypt. They are primarily technical words, such as might well be borrowed by an Algonquian population into which Greek-speaking mariners had intermarried. I should stress that present-day cultural leaders of the Micmac people have visited me, have discussed these views, and have adopted the late Dr. Rand's dictionary as the basis for the revised dictionary (using modernized spelling) now in preparation by the Micmac Cultural Center in Nova Scotia. I stress this, because in a recent statement issued by the Department of Anthropology of the Smithsonian Institution, it is claimed that neither Micmac nor any other American Indian language has any relationship to Greek or any other identifiable Old World language. This statement is at total variance with the facts, is in direct conflict with the views of Silas Rand, the only lexicographer of the Micmac language, and consequently is also at variance with the basic materials on which the present revision of the written Micmac language is being carried out by Micmac scholars of Micmac descent at the Micmac Cultural Center. Similar erroneous claims have denied that Celtic roots occur here.

Thus, in contradistinction to the opinion of the Smithsonian Institution's recent (1978) statement, Micmac scholars have long been well aware of the Greek content of the Micmac language. Plutarch's statements, derived from Carthaginian sources, is in good agreement with known fact. I reiterate my own view: namely, that the Greek of Micmac is more appropriately to be called Ptolemaic Greek, and that it came to Nova Scotia and Maine from North Africa, where numerous Greek-speaking communities existed in Classical times. Presumably the vectors of this North African Greek to northeastern North America would be Libyan sailors recruited from such cities as Cyrene and Ptolemais during the fourth and third centuries B.C., when Carthaginian interests were predominant in the land to the west of Egypt.

After discussing the religion of these settlers, Plutarch refers to their special devotion to Hercules and Saturn (whose festival is celebrated at thirty-year intervals when the planet Saturn passes through the constellation of the Bull), and concludes by saying that all of the men of Greek descent still view Europe as their original home. He says that they jokingly refer to themselves as inhabiting the true continent, since it forms the entire rim of the Atlantic

Ocean, whereas they refer to Europe as a "mere island," since Europe is surrounded by the ocean on three sides. Finally, he says that it is the lifelong aim of every colonist of Greek descent to revisit their homeland at the end of their working life, and that to do so they sail eastward to Carthage. Do not every year hundreds of thousands of modern Americans feel that same urge, and sail eastward—in sky-ships?

As I pointed out in *America B.C.,* there is a second route to America: one that makes use of the favorable trade winds that blow from east to west in latitudes south of 30° N. It was the route followed by Columbus which leads from the Canary Islands to the Caribbean. The disadvantage is the vast ocean gap to be covered, as opposed to the route described by Plutarch. His northern route also has east-to-west winds (produced by the polar high), and has a comforting chain of island halfway-houses. It is the route followed by the Norsemen. But its disadvantage lies in the severer weather. However, in 1977 Dr. Timothy Severin demonstrated that even a frail Irish Celtic skin-boat can sail that route, as Irish historians have always claimed. I see only sweet common sense in Plutarch and the Irish sages, and have little patience with the armchair critics of Washington. Many people feel the same way.

Although no Carthaginian antiquities or coins seem to have been reported as yet from Cuba, it would appear that this island was known to the Carthaginians, as evidenced by the following passage from the historical writings of the Sicilian annalist Diodorus Siculus, who flourished in the first century before Christ. He writes:

> The Phoenicians were at a very early period driven by the violence of the wind far beyond the Pillars of Hercules [i.e., Straits of Gibraltar], out into the Atlantic Ocean. To the west of Africa, at many days' sailing distance from that continent, they discovered an enormous island that was fertile and finely watered by navigable rivers. This discovery was soon known to the Carthaginians of Africa, and to the Tyrrhenians [Etruscans] of Italy. The Carthaginians then undertook a voyage to this new region, after one of the hostile invasions by Moors and Tyrians, in the course of which they passed through the Straits of Gibraltar, advancing beyond Cadiz [which lies outside the Pillars of Hercules], till they reached this region and there made a settlement. But the offi-

cial policies of Carthage caused the settlement to be withdrawn, and a strict prohibition was enforced, preventing any citizen from attempting any future encroachment.

Two interesting features can be found in the passage quoted. One of them, a reference to a "hostile invasion (of Carthaginian territory) by Moors," is discussed later in this book in Chapter 11, Arabs Before Islam: the Moors were Arabs, and when the Sicilian annalist records them as invaders of North Africa at least two centuries before Christ, he runs counter to our modern schoolbooks, in which the Arabs are said to have entered Africa at the time of the Moslem expansion, in the seventh century after Christ. The other matter of note is the reported restrictions on the movement of Carthaginian citizens beyond the Straits of Gibraltar; I think we may detect here the Carthaginian government's increasing dread and jealousy of Roman power, now burgeoning in Italy; fear that Rome might outflank Carthage if the secret of the Atlantic islands should become known. Whether or not this interpretation be correct, the stage was already set for a naval conflict of such ferocity as was unknown before, and probably unmatched in any period of history. This we must now examine, for its consequences were felt even across the Atlantic.

America and the Punic Wars

The greatest war in Classical times was the life-and-death struggle between the two powers of the western Mediterranean: Rome and Carthage. It was fought out in three agonizing episodes that left Rome exhausted and Carthage in total ruin, her surviving population scattered across North Africa as refugees in the powerful Libyan Empire that arose from the ashes of the cities of the western Phoenicians.

Certain unexplained features of the great struggle require re-examination in the light of the new discoveries in America. In all probability, America played a significant role in this great historical event. I believe the role was a passive one, but nonetheless critical for the initial phases of the struggle, during the third century B.C.—and significant for Americans, too, for it was their first involvement in world affairs.

Every Roman history textbook sets out at tedious length the causes of the struggle between Rome and Carthage. There is no need to dwell upon them here, since our interest is in America. The causes can be summarized in a few words: greed, competition and jealousy. During the fourth century B.C., Rome had expanded her political and military control to embrace the greater part of Italy, as one by one the independent Etruscan, Celtic, Campanian, and Greek city-states of the peninsula fell into her orbit. In the interim, Carthage had invaded the islands of Sicily, Sardinia, and Corsica. By the beginning of the third century B.C., Carthage had adjusted the weights of her coinage to match those used in Egypt and Cyprus. Now one great common-market trading community extended from Egypt across North Africa to Spain. Most of it was under the control of the wealthy financiers who also comprised the Council of One Hundred that governed Carthage, and which selected the two *suffetes* (or "judges" in the Hebrew sense) who put their wishes into effect.

By midcentury, two powerful nations were in confrontation. Rome guarded the access to the pine forests of Italy and Gaul which yielded the timbers required for building ships and in particular for maintaining a powerful navy—something still quite unfamiliar to Romans. Carthage exercised a total control of tin, the essential component of bronze, still the major metal of weapons of war and industrial and household tools, as well as the sole metal employed in Roman currency. The Roman Senate comprised patrician families to whom wealth was rapidly becoming a means of power, and from whose ranks the two consuls were chosen to put their wishes into effect. Conflict between Carthage and Rome was inevitable. A pretext for Roman interference in Sicily was afforded by an appeal from Sicilian Greeks in 264 B.C.

The First Punic War lasted from 264 to 241 B.C. and was marked by the greatest sea battles in classical history. By totaling the more significant losses mentioned by the ancient historians, I find that Carthage suffered at least the following staggering losses:

Date B.C.	Battle	Roman Fleet	Carthaginian Fleet	Carthaginian Losses
260	Battle of Mylae	150 ships	150 ships	50 ships
256	Battle of Ecnomus	230 ships	230 ships	84 ships
255	B. of Hermaean Cape	200 ships	200 ships	100 ships
242	B. of Aegates Isl.	200 ships	100 ships	100 ships

Total Carthaginian Losses   334 ships

Each Carthaginian ship of the line was a quinquireme: a ship so large that it required five rowers to each oar on account of the length of oar needed to reach the sea. There were fifty or more of these large oars—making a crew of at least 250 rowers—together with officers and 120 marines, for a complement of 400 men. Thus the losses of men in these great battles were staggering. After the Battle of the Hermaean Cape, Carthage simply could not replace her naval losses any more; the final Battle of the Aegates Islands was really a mopping-up operation by the Romans. Rome, too, suffered severe losses, but contrived to replenish her navy and to rebuild her ships sufficiently to outmatch the Carthaginians. Rome had access to the pine forests of Italy, but Carthage lacked naval timber. Recoveries of sunken ancient wrecks show that pine was the favored wood. Spain had pine forests in the interior, but no Carthaginian had yet penetrated there. In any case, the transportation through mountainous terrain was impossible. Then where did Carthage obtain such large quantities of lumber as to permit the repeated rebuilding of her navies in the face of such losses? The ancient historians are silent. It is also significant that Carthage was unable to rebuild her fleet after the Battle of Cape Hermaea, and only the shattered remnants went out to meet the Romans—and destruction—in the final Battle of the Aegates Islands. Apparently something had gone awry with the supplies of timber needed by the Carthaginian shipyards.

Consider another unexplained and mysterious event in Carthaginian history—not mentioned at all by the ancient historians, but discovered by the painstaking researches of modern numismatists. While the initial issues of Carthaginian coinage were silver pieces, on the model of those issued by such powerful Greek cities as Syracuse, the nature of the coinage underwent a sudden and dramatic change around 300 B.C., when very large quantities of gold coins began to be minted. More accurately, the coinage was gold to which a small amount of silver had been added: the light-yellow metal called *electrum* by the ancients. At the same time, the emblem Arethusa disappears from the coins, to be replaced by a Tanith, the native Carthaginian goddess, spouse of Bel, who was depicted as a Classical portrait of a woman bedecked with pendant earrings and necklace.

What was the origin of the gold, and why did it appear so suddenly and in such large quantities in the currency of a city which, for most of her history, had not found it desirable or necessary to issue any coins at all? It has been suggested that the Carthaginian mariners may have discovered a source of gold on the west coast of Africa, or in the Gulf of Guinea, where Hanno sailed. If so, it would be the famous *Guinea-gold* that supplied the British mint during the eighteenth century, and which led to the name "guinea" being applied to the standard gold piece that financed George III's armies during the Revolutionary War.

If West Africa were the source of the sudden gold hoards of the Carthaginians, would it not have continued thus for as long as the Carthaginians had a merchant navy—or a single ship, for that matter—available to coast Northwest Africa as often as required? Carthage still had merchant ships—and ten naval ships as late as the Third (and final) Punic War with Rome, in 149–146 B.C., the last years of her existence. Yet the gold coinage ceased to be struck in any significant quantities after 241 B.C., when the First Punic War came to its disastrous end.

From the ancient historians we learn that when the Second Punic War began in 218 B.C., Carthage no longer regarded her navy as of any great significance as a weapon of war, and the entire series of campaigns for the whole eighteen years of the Second War was conducted as a land operation. The invasion of Italy by Hannibal was performed not by landing troops from transports (as had been the case when Pytheas found the Gibraltar fleet diverted to Sicily), but instead by crossing the Alps from Gaul.

Putting together the facts elicited by numismatists and those derived from ancient historians, we find that

(1) There was a sudden unexplained increase in holdings of Carthaginian gold between 300 B.C. and 241 B.C.
(2) Carthage was unable to replace any of her naval quinquiremes after 255 B.C. and ceased to be a major naval power after 241 B.C.

Is it possible that these unexplained facts are in some way related to America? Until 1976 we had no tangible evidence that Carthaginians were ever present in America, though a careful reading of Plutarch implies that they did make regular voyages to northeastern North America. We are in possession of more historical facts than before 1976, and the time is ripe to take another look at the unexplained questions.

A few months after the first Carthaginian coins had been recognized in North American sites, but before I had had time to inquire into

The Phoenician metalworkers of Cyprus were influenced by both Babylonian and Egyptian art and religion, and produced engraved and cast dishes, bowls, and statuettes that reflect a blending of both civilizations. Their wares were distributed by Carthaginian traders, the silver and gold finding buyers in the Mediterranean, their bronze penetrating far afield to find markets among the barbarians. The bronze examples from the northern Andes probably exchanged hands in return for the gold of Columbia (El Dorado). Shown above are representative engraved motifs from a Phoenician silver dish from Cyprus.

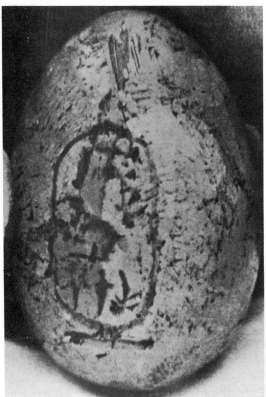

Alabaster egg carrying the cartouche (official name seal) of the Egyptian pharaoh Tutankhamen, discovered in Idaho around 1900 and long supposed to be an Amerindian artifact. In 1977, when the Tutankhamen exhibition reached Washington, Kathy Kincaid, a great-granddaughter of the finder, recognized the cartouche and submitted the artifact to curator Frank A. Norick of the University of California, Berkeley, for examination, when the identification was confirmed. It is possible that the artifact is one of a series of Egyptian exports to Iberia during the period 615–395 B.C., when, according to the Portuguese numismatic authority Professor Antonio D. Simoes, trade was actively pursued by Egyptian vessels visiting Salacia and Olissipo (modern Lisbon); the artifact could later have been brought to North America on a Carthaginian or Iberian ship. *Photo Professor Paul Cheesman, Dr. Julian Fell.*

Metal urn decorated with Phoenician themes in the upper part which depicts the goddess Astarte, and with Egyptian-inspired ornament below, apparently African rain-dancers. The style, of mixed derivation, recalls the work of Cypriot Phoenicians around 600 B.C., when such objects were manufactured for distribution and sale, mainly to semi-civilized barbarians, by the traders of Carthage. The urn was discovered in an excavation carried out by the Middlebury Archeological Research Center near the junction of the Susquehanna and Chenango Rivers, New York. Phoenician inscriptions had earlier been recognized in the Susquehanna region by Philip Beistline and Dr. William W. Strong. *Drawing G. Johnson after photo Salvatore M. Trento.*

Another presumed Cypriot Phoenician reproduction of Babylonian religious artifacts for sale to barbarian peoples by Carthaginian traders,
found in Ecuador and now in the Crespi collection at Santa Maria
Auxiliodora. *Replica by Veronica Wilcox after photographs by Paul
Cheesman of the original; photo Peter J. Garfall.*

Found by Ecuadorian farmers near Cuenca, this reproduction of a Babylonian deity appears to be the product of a Cypriot Phoenician workshop of the period 800–600 B.C., and presumably was shipped to America by Carthaginian traders in return for Colombian gold. *Replica by Veronica Wilcox after photo by Professor Paul Cheesman of original in the collection of Padre Carlo Crespi in the Church of Santa Maria Auxiliodora in Cuenca. Photo Peter J. Garfall.*

the distribution of similar coins in the tin-mining regions of southern Britain, I received a welcome visit from Professor Paul Cheesman, a reader of *America B.C.* His own interest in the early history of the Americas had led him to travel widely in Central and South America, as well as in Polynesia, and he had made a remarkable collection of photographs of artifacts and inscriptions that had come to his notice. These he generously offered to place at my disposal for study in the hope that decipherments might be effected.

Most remarkable of the artifacts depicted in his photographs and color slides are a large number held in the storage rooms of the Church of Santa Maria Auxiliodora in Cuenca, Ecuador, assembled by Padre Carlo Crespi, a Catholic priest, primarily from material discovered by members of his parish. This region was the former Inca northern capital and is noted for its buried hoards and underground chambers with remarkable contents.

My attention was attracted by a number of items that appeared to be of Cypriot-Phoenician origin, imitations in bronze of ancient art objects of Assyria whose originals were carved in massive stone (pages 80 and 81). As is well known, this type of artifact was a speciality of the Phoenician factories of Cyprus and was intended for sale to the Carthaginians, who, in turn, distributed it to barbarian peoples. Among the latter, these were regarded as treasures of great price—almost as the work of gods—and presumably very handsome profits were to be reaped by the Carthaginian merchants who took the trouble and risk of shipping such artifacts to distant countries.

So elaborate and so varied were the other artifacts present in the Crespi collections (and bronze was by no means the only material), the gold and carved stone represented in the photographs, and inscriptions, could not possibly be forgeries, despite the tendency of a certain class of archeologists to call anything they do not understand a "forgery." A forgery of what? And who could or would make such things, only to bury them in the ground to await some chance discovery by a peasant? These, I concluded, were no forgeries, and other competent archeologists of the museums and universities of Mediterranean lands, to whom I have shown enlarged copies of Paul Cheesman's photographs, agree

Padre Carlo Crespi of Santa Maria Auxiliodora, Cuenca. *Photo Professor Paul Cheesman.*

Professor Paul Cheesman and Fell with replica of Cypriot gold plate in the Crespi collection. *Photo Peter J. Garfall.*

During the last days of Carthage, the quality of the coinage deteriorated. These examples circulated in Tunisia and Libya and are now in the National Archeological Museum in Tripoli. So far as is known, late Carthaginian coinage is lacking from American sites; presumably a reflection of the disastrous losses of shipping during the First Punic War with Rome, and a consequent collapse of the trade with North America. *Photo Peter J. Garfall.*

that their presence on American archeological sites must have some other explanation.

Soon after Paul Cheesman's first visit to me at Harvard, I received through James Whittall, of the Early Sites Research Society, a photograph of a remarkable urn of the same Phoenician aspect—found, however, by a member of Salvatore Trento's MARC team in New York—buried in the ground in a stone-rimmed underground chamber, near the Pennsylvania border. This urn (page 79) shows a combination of Egyptian and Semitic art, again suggesting the workshops of Cyprus as the most likely origin of the piece. Excavations near Seville, at or near the site of the pre-Carthaginian city of Tarshish (Tartessus) have disclosed other examples of mixed Egyptian, Phoenician, and Greek influences in a variety of art objects apparently distributed from Tartessus.

When first confronted with these extraordinary artifacts, my first thoughts (after recovering from the initial astonishment) had been that these might be trade objects—or personal treasure—brought to America by emigrants from Tartessus, at an epoch when belief in such gods as the winged Babylonian deities and the winged bulls was still current. But later, when I had seen the nature of the artifacts present in North African and Levantine museums, my opinion gradually changed in favor of a much later distribution —at an epoch when the gods depicted were regarded rather as antiques from a distant past. In short, I began to consider the possibility of their being merely trade items, shipped to the Americas by Carthaginian wholesalers based either in Spain or in Carthage itself, and intended for no other market than that of the Amerindians.

Undoubtedly, such artifacts would arouse the surprise and admiration of Amerindian buyers. And if, in addition, they were offered for barter at landing points in Panama or the Caribbean coast of Colombia or Venezuela, would they not attract substantial gold? For gold was not highly regarded there—save as a metal easy to work into complicated jewelry or cast or hammered into figurines.

The dates of Carthaginian contact with North America, yielded by the coinage we are now recovering from North American sites, match the sudden influx of gold in Carthage. I now propose that an American source for the Carthaginian gold coinage should seriously be considered, and that the gold was bartered for the bronze art manufactures of the Cypriot Phoenicians.

This brings me to the second of the unresolved questions set out on page 76; the source of the pine lumber which built the great fleets of Carthage, and whose supply suddenly dried up at the end of the First Punic War in 241 B.C. I now propose the following explanation:

An export trade of Cypro-Phoenician mass-produced bronze art replicas was carried out by Carthaginian ships visiting America. Substantial gold was acquired in return, but insufficient to provide adequate ballast. To meet this need, the Carthaginian ships picked up shipments of large pine logs from the Algonquian tribes of northeastern North America, to whom they traded adequate stocks of iron-cutting tools, axes, and other desirable items, including occasional bronze art replicas (as in the case of the New York urn), and also low-value Carthaginian coins of attractive appearance, glass beads, and the like. Such trade, profitable alike to the Amerindian and the Carthaginian, would result in a steady input of gold and lumber on the home markets in Carthage, would yield the timbers needed to build ships, and provide them with straight masts and oars, and in addition would yield the Carthaginian state the gold ingots required to produce the coinage that apparently financed the military and naval operations of the Sicilian War, and later of the First Punic War. Much of the gold coin would be dispersed as military pay to the mercenaries hired among the Greeks of Sicily and the Libyans of North Africa; a fact which would account for the occasional hoards of Carthaginian gold coins found in those countries to this very day.

Following the disastrous series of naval defeats in the First Punic War, American lumber would no longer attract a lively market in Carthage. For the Suffetes—or the Council of One Hundred—apparently decided never again to attempt a naval confrontation with Rome, and the Carthaginian navy now languished in favor of a land-based army. In preparation for the Second Punic War, the military leaders of Carthage—men of the Barcine family—chose instead to go to Spain, to establish a new colony there to replace the loss of Sicily, which the Romans had seized. In Spain the Carthaginians discovered adequate sources of precious and base metals in the mines of Andalusia. Hence the whole impetus that had led to the growth of trade with the Americans would now cease to have any appreciable effect; the circumstances in which Carthage now found herself made such long and arduous voyages across the Atlantic no longer worth the expense and trouble. Such lumber as was needed could be obtained from the cedars of the Atlas Mountains, or the oak forests of maritime Spain and Portugal; the vast needle-forests of North America were once more left undisturbed.

Those mariners or trade agents who had chosen to live among the Algonquian peoples and to take American wives would presumably decide whether to return or to stay among the peoples of the New World. Those that remained and their descendants would doubtless be included among the migrant "Greeks" of whom Plutarch spoke.

Events now occurred that were to place America and North Africa in a wholly unforeseen relationship, destined to endure for many centuries.

In Search of Plutarch's Greeks

The discoveries of the American examples of Carthaginian coinage and trade goods in 1976 and 1977 had provided such astonishing confirmation of Plutarch's writings of the second century A.D. as to convince me that he was speaking the truth when he said his account was based on ancient parchment records that he personally had recovered from the ruins of Carthage. What, then, are we to make of his additional statements that Greeks had settled among the barbarian peoples of the Western Epeiros (the continent that rims the Western Ocean, as he called it)? Plutarch states that these Greeks had intermarried with the barbarians, had adopted their language, but had blended their own Greek language with it. He further states that the Greek settlements known to him were about a bay in the same latitudes as the Caspian Sea. This last statement indicates New England, New Brunswick, and Nova Scotia.

Plutarch was writing at the beginning of the second century A.D. At that time, the world had long been known to be a globe, and lines of latitude and longitude had been invented back in the third century B.C. by the North African mathematician-geographer-astronomer Eratosthenes. Because of the depth of ignorance into which Europe fell in the Dark Ages, at times we are apt to forget how advanced were the ideas of the ancients, and how much they knew about the earth and about astronomy and navigation.

Since the Greeks of Europe seem to have said little if anything about the subject of Plutarch's comments, and since the Greeks of North Africa took the path of science that led to the discovery that the earth is a globe, and then set about mapping that globe, it is only logical to conclude that the Greeks of the American

Epeiros, mentioned by Plutarch, would have to be North African Greeks—if indeed they existed at all. Therefore it was with special pleasure and gratitude that I received, at the end of the 1977 summer season, an invitation from the University of Tripoli to extend our research by examining the related sites along the North African coast, most of which lie in the Gulf of Syrtis and around the Cyrenian peninsula to the east of Egypt. This 2,000-mile seaboard lies almost entirely within the ancient—and modern—confines of the land that the Greeks called Libya.

Under the patient guidance of Dr. Mohamed Jarary, director of the Libyan Study Center of the University of Tripoli, we were able to study the sites and archeological collections and inscriptions, the ports ancient and modern, and general lay of the land, from Oea (ancient Tripoli) and Leptis Magna (a now-deserted city, and one of extraordinary beauty), across the Gulf to ancient Berenike (modern Benghazi), and over the peninsula of the five Greek cities called the Pentapolis, to historic Cyrene, the capital of Greek North Africa. Professor Ali Khushaim was our companion and guide in the Tripolitanian region, where the streets, temples, and public and private buildings of ancient times are preserved in astonishing perfection among the dry desert sands. Here I was able to absorb the atmosphere of the homelands of the ancient Greeks of North Africa, and so return refreshed to the American scene to resume the hunt for clues to our vanished past.

The numerous colored mosaic floors that have been recovered from these ancient cities depict scenes in the daily life of people in Classical times. Here, as elsewhere in the Mediterranean, the era of Greek hegemony was followed by a Roman phase, and most of the best-preserved ruins date from the first and second centuries of our era, during the early part of the Roman occupation. But Rome was culturally the child of Greece, and it is hard—and rather pointless—to distinguish between specific Hellenistic and Roman influences, for they are blended. The people are depicted in the mosaics with features resembling those of North Africans today; we customarily call them Arabs, for modern speech is Arabic, but their ancestry is a blend of European, Arab, and Berber. I believe Plutarch's Greeks were just such a people, inheriting the maritime traditions of a varied ancestry, and speaking a dialect of Greek strongly influenced by North African vocabulary. Indeed, from comments made by the historian Polybius, when he visited North Africa in the second century B.C., it is plain that he regarded the North African Greeks as a people now considerably different from the Greeks of Greece. They called themselves Greeks, but, as Polybius says, they were olive-skinned and represented a fusion of Greek and North African. They were, in fact, Libyans.

Never was there a people more passionately devoted to the sea than those whom the Greeks named Libyans. By this the Greeks meant all the communities of the northern fringe of Africa, bordering the Mediterranean Sea from Cyrene in the east, on the Egyptian border, to Mauretania on the Atlantic, encompassing the lands that in modern times we call Libya, Tunisia, Algeria, and Morocco. By Classical times, the North African Greeks had the character of their modern descendants; an olive-skinned race of mixed origin, distinguished therefore from the *Aethiopes,* the dark-skinned Africans whose homeland lay to the south of the Sahara.

A long chain of ruined cities, more or less enveloped in desert sands, marks the maritime of North Africa where these seafarers once lived. Their cities were beautiful, and the ruins of them are still beautiful; their marble, limestone, and porphyry columns gleaming in the bright desert sun in stately series along the deserted streets and marketplaces. North African archeologists have extracted from the houses and temples of these cities a truly wonderful array of mosaics and statues that depict the life and aspirations of the citizens of a noble civilization. When Libyan kings ruled as pharaohs over Egypt, their ships sailed to the Atlantic ports of Spain and crossed that ocean to leave enduring records in the Americas. When the first crossing of the Pacific was achieved, a Libyan queen was spouse to Egypt's pharaoh.

Courage, tempered by a thirst for adventure, moderated by the need to supplement the meager produce of a desert heartland with protein yielded by the fisheries of the Mediterranean, first led them to go to sea. But intellect stimulated by the scientific discoveries of the Alexandrian and Cyrenian philosophers encouraged them to sail farther afield. Thus, in the end, they crossed the oceans and set foot upon the New World; to found American colonies which, like those of the ancient Greeks and Phoenicians, were independent, though doubtless retaining an affectionate regard for the motherland.

Who were these ancient Libyans? What were their antecedents, and how did they come to occupy the coasts of North Africa? Ancient chronicles have not been overly informative on how this vast stretch of territory acquired its populations; but enough has been translated or deciphered to permit a brief sketch of events during the thousand years before Christ, when the chief elements of the constituent races entered the region. To this has recently been added an outline of a succession of still-earlier native cultures of hunters and artists who have left a record of their life in the form of rock engravings and carvings.

About 20,000 B.C., during the period that archeologists call Magdalenian, a hunting culture arose in North Africa, similar to that of Spain and France. The people left a record of their life in the form of remarkable rock engravings of elephants, rhinoceros, hippopotamus, giraffes, and crocodiles. The North African archeologists call this the phase of the *Hunters*.

Following this phase came more settled people, owners of herds of cattle. These they depicted in polychrome paintings in the highest style of prehistoric art. This is called the *Pastoral* phase.

Then arose the civilization of people whom Herodotus called the *Garamantes*: chariot-driving warriors who also rode horses, so that the name *Horse* phase is applied to the period. The art style deteriorated, and much abstract delineation is evident.

The Horse phase may be contemporary with the first historical records of the Libyans; namely, those found on ancient Egyptian monuments depicting battles with the Sea Peoples. According to the great steles of Rameses III, a major invasion of the Nile Delta was attempted around 1200 B.C. by migrant warriors arriving by ship from the northeast, presumably from Anatolia (modern Turkey and neighboring coasts) and Philistia (Lebanon and neighboring parts of Palestine). These seaborne warriors belonged to a half dozen different tribes, distinguished by their helmets and shields. Among them were the Shardana (or Sherden) who carried round shields, broadswords, and who wore feathered warbonnets (see page 101).

The Egyptian army under Rameses III was armed with bows and arrows and, as the monuments depicting the Battle of the Nile Delta show, the invaders were struck down before they could land. The defeated remnants of the Sea Peoples then retreated westward into Libya, to vanish from history for two centuries. During this period, the Shardana apparently recovered from their defeat, learned the art of fighting with the bow and arrow, and then hired themselves out as merceneries in the armies of the last Ramesside pharaohs of the now-decadent Twenty-first Dynasty of Egypt. By about 950 B.C., a chief of the Shardana named Shishonq revolted against the Egyptian monarchy, installed himself as pharaoh in the city of Bubastis, and thus established the famous Twenty-second Dynasty—the Libyan Dynasty of Egypt and Libya combined as one powerful kingdom. The Shardana had never forgotten their seafaring tradition, and Egypt became a maritime power under the Libyans. Exports of alabaster vases carrying the various seals (cartouches) of Libyan pharaohs are now being discovered in tombs in Spain. The name Shishonq, carried by at least four Libyan pharaohs, is also found in American inscriptions, but it is not yet known whether these are contemporary with the famous kings of that name; in one case, at least, it is clear that an American record of the name Shishonq is of much later vintage, merely cited as an ancestor of a Libyan monarch of the second century B.C.

The Shardana and other tribes of Sea Peoples depicted on the Egyptian monuments are shown as light-skinned warriors resembling the ancient Greeks and Hittites. Thus they probably spoke a language related to the Anatolian branch of Indo-European tongues, heavily interlarded with Semitic vocabulary reflecting the origin of their civilized institutions. The Berber language may be derived from this invading stock.

Around 750 B.C., the Egyptians expelled the Libyan monarchs, who then returned to Libya. Meanwhile, colonies of Phoenician traders were being established at various points along the North African coast, notably at Carthage in modern Tunisia, at Lepqis (later called Leptis Magna) near modern Tripoli, at Oea (Tripoli itself), and at the site of the future Greek city called Cyrene in the eastern part of modern Libya. The Phoenician settlers, who later became independent of the parent cities of Tyre and Sidon in Phoenicia (Lebanon), and eventually founded the Carthaginian Empire, introduced a language similar to ancient Hebrew.

Around 650 B.C., Greeks from Sparta established a settlement which superseded the Phoenician village in east Libya and became the famous city of Cyrene. Greek influence spread over the neighboring region, where eventually five cities rose and comprised the kingdom of Cyrene. The lands that lay between Cyrene and Egypt —namely easternmost Libya and the Siwa Oasis region (called Ammonia)—were inhabited by people of mixed Phoenician and Egyptian origin, the most important of whom were the Adrymachids. According to the Greek traveler Herodotus, these people adopted Egyptian manners. Inscriptions in Libyan characters—but containing Egyptian vocabulary—are thought to be Adrymachid in origin. So also, apparently, are Libyan inscriptions that use Egyptian hieroglyphs (see page 98).

The last of the major invasions of North Africa was made by the Romans after the wars with Carthage, in the second century B.C. It used to be thought—and is still mistakenly taught—that Arabs of the armies of Islam first came to Libya in the seventh century A.D. However, as will be explained in Chapter 11, researches on the ancient Libyan inscriptions of both America and North Africa have now proved conclusively that Arabic language came to North Africa long before Islam. In all likelihood, some of the so-called Sea Peoples were really Arabs.

From these diverse stocks arose the North African populations who now speak Arabic. The Berbers are also of diverse racial origin, but the origin of their language is uncertain, though it may have been one of those introduced by the Sea Peoples.

The mixture of racial stocks and parent tongues brought a potent resource of varied talents to North Africa. Under the intellectual leadership of the Cyrenian Greeks, Libya became the major source of learned men at the court of the Ptolemies in Alexandria, during the era that followed Alexander the Great. The neighboring native Libyans retained old customs and continued to practice the art of rock engraving. The so-called *Round-head* phase, in which dances and religious festivals are depicted both in Libya and in North America, is often associated with texts in the Libyan script. After 100 A.D., the Romans introduced the camel into Libya, and thereafter the rock art is dominated by engravings of camels. This phase is totally lacking from American rock art.

The last-mentioned fact is important, for it gives us the first clue as to the date when Plutarch's Greeks—Libyan Greeks—came here. It must have been at some epoch antecedent to the so-called *Camel Period*, yet later than the *Roundhead Period*—between Alexander the Great and the conquest of North Africa by the Romans. We can narrow our search, then, to approximately the interval between the end of the fourth century B.C. and the first century B.C.

With these clues I returned to the American scene to examine new evidence with fresh eyes.

While I had been concentrating on the Libyan, Carthaginian, and suspected Greek aspects of American history, James Whittall, in pursuit of his studies on Iberian stone chambers, had made one more expedition to Spain, Portugal, and Morocco. Professor Norman Totten also visited Morocco. Both he and Jim were successful in locating more inscriptions, Iberian and Libyan, and these I will discuss later (Chapter 8, page 164). However, one inscription that Jim copied from a lead lamina in the National Museum of Archeology in Madrid proved to have unexpected overtones. It had been found in eastern Spain, near Pujol. It appeared to be Iberic; the script contained numerous letters that matched those of the Iberic alphabet. However, by this time, it had been clearly established that the old Iberic language is Semitic, and closely related to classical Arabic—so much so that a good classical Arabic dictionary is all that is needed to decipher most Iberic texts if they are written in known forms of the Iberian alphabets.

But the lamina of Pujol proved to be quite refractory. Although it is well preserved, and almost all of the letters quite easily distinguishable, no sense whatever could be made of the text, whether it was read backward or forward. Apparently it was not written

Skorpious   L----.-I----A---N----E.

① m ——— ẖ — q   b ——— y — ' — G

② O — ph — i ——— s   z(e) ——— t(e)

Plutarch's American Greeks can be recognized from their inscriptions as Libyans of mixed descent from Spartan colonists of Cyrene (see map), Berbers, and early Arabic speakers of Libya long antedating the Moslem invasion of North Africa. Their vocabulary survives among such tribes as the northeastern Algonquians (see appendix), and includes many words of Coptic and Arabic derivation, as well as the more easily recognizable Greek elements detected by Silas Rand a century ago when he compiled the Micmac Dictionary. Above, A, B, typical Greek fret motifs found in Colorado petroglyph areas by Professor Julian H. Steward in the 1930's, and noted by Harold S. Gladwin on Hohokam pottery in Arizona. C, a petroglyph from Nevada previously called "Great Basin Curvilinear" is actually a warning: "Crush scorpions underfoot." D is a bilingual Arabic and Greek semiliterate petroglyph, also from Nevada, warning the passerby: "Look out for snakes."

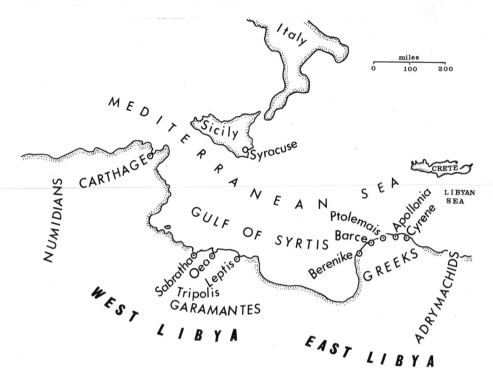

The homeland of the Libyans in ancient times. To the extreme east lived tribes called the Adrymachids who spoke a language midway between Phoenician and Egyptian, and who used Egyptian hieroglyphic writing. To the west lay Cyrene, with five Greek cities founded by Spartans. Farther west lay the Berber tribes, and Carthage dominated the seaward regions. People speaking dialects similar to Arabic also lived along these coasts and used the alphabet called Numidian or Libyan.

Irregularities of spelling and writing persisted among nonacademic Greeks well into Christian times. This fragment of a Byzantine hymn shows writing similar to the Greek of American inscriptions: "The trumpet of doom, the end of the world, in dread the graveyard shall open up."

Similar pottery painted decoration in Arizona and Greek Mediterranean
sites. Long after the so-called geometric style passed out of fashion in
Greece, it persisted at Iberian Greek sites such as Emporion, and in
isolation for much longer in America. a, Arizona, Snaketown, Santa
Cruz red-on-buff. b, Cyclades, brown-black-on-buff. c, Arizona, Snaketown, Sacaton red-on-buff. d, Emporium, Spain, black-on-buff and
orange-red. e, Snaketown, Sacaton red-on-buff. f, Attica, Greece, brown-
black on brown-buff. g, Snaketown, Arizona, Santa Cruz red-on-buff.
h, Greek meander of wide-ranging occurrence in Mediterranean.
i, Snaketown, Arizona, Santa Cruz red-on-buff. j, Attic geometric style,
Greece. k, Swastika from Athenian black-figure vase. l, swastika from
Snaketown, Arizona pottery, Sacaton red-on-buff. m, letters of the
Greek alphabet occurring on Sacaton and Santa Cruz pottery, Arizona.
n, Arizona, Santa Cruz red-on-buff, female dancing figures in geometric
style. o, Protocorinthian, Greece, male dancing figures in geometric
style. (Arizona data from Gladwin, Haury, Sayles and N. Gladwin, 1937.
Mediterranean data compiled by Fell.)

King Mekusen of Libya notifies his American compatriots of the death of his father King Massinissa in 148 B.C., and of his claim to the throne of Egypt. Portion of a proclamation on gold found in Ecuador. *Photo courtesy of Professor Paul Cheesman, intensified by Peter J. Garfall. Crespi Collection.*

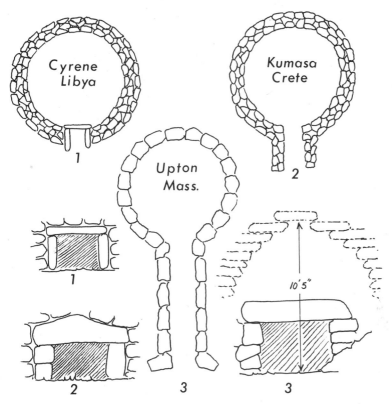

1, Beehive tomb or *tholos,* near Cyrene, eastern Libya. 2, Similar *tholos,* believed to date from Classical times and reflecting Libyan influence, at Kumasa, Crete (after Sir Arthur Evans, 1964). 3, Upton chamber, Massachusetts, completely subterranean. Later forms of the Libyan *tholos* consisted of an earth mound surrounded by a circle of stone, or a stone wall—these latter known to be of Roman date.

Professor Linus Brunner, the distinguished philologist and Classical scholar of St. Gallen, Switzerland. His recently published Polynesian dictionary is the first to offer a logical analysis of much of the vocabulary of the Polynesian languages, demonstrating a common origin with Semitic, and in particular with North African Semitic tongues that contained loan words from Egyptian and Greek. When Fell used cryptographic analysis to analyze a dialect of ancient Greek in Spain that employed an Iberian alphabet, Brunner was prompt to confirm the finding and to deduce the equivalent Attic Greek.

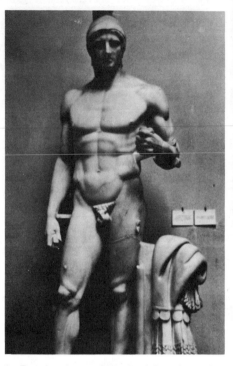

The Spartans of Libya retained the warlike habits of their ancestors in Greece, and thus maintained their independence for nearly a thousand years. The warrior here depicted on a vase excavated in a Cyrenian tomb in 1969 dates from about 550 B.C. His helmet and spear and round shield appear also on American inscriptions, and a bronze circular shield engraved with fighting gladiators has been dredged from Boston harbor.

In Roman times, Classical Greek sculpture continued in Libya, as exemplified by this helmeted warrior, probably dedicated to Mars. *Photo Peter J. Garfall, by permission of the National Archeological Museum, Tripoli.*

Tennessee

In addition to Greeks, ancient Libya also was the home of other warrior peoples. At the close of the prehistoric period of Libya, around 1200 B.C., a series of invasions of North Africa by maritime peoples whom the Egyptians called by the common name Sea Peoples took place. Conspicuous among the invaders who seized and settled the land to the west of Egypt were the Shardana (or Sherden), whose warriors wore a leather kilt and a crown-shaped feather warbonnet. They carried circular shields, and fought with swords and spears. As depicted by Egyptian sculptors, they were evidently of Aryan stock, and may have spoken a language akin to Hittite. They may also be ancestral, in part, to the white Berbers of North Africa. Others of the Sea Peoples who probably settled in Libya included warriors whose helmets carried two horns, similar to those used by the ancient Teutons. By the tenth century B.C. the Libyans were powerful enough to seize Egypt and established the XXII or Libyan Dynasty. During the 200 years of their rule the Libyan pharaohs made Egypt into a leading maritime power. Early voyages to America may have begun at this time, and some remarkable bas-reliefs in Utah (see page 102) suggest a possible link with the Libyan kings. *Epigraphic Museum, photo Peter J. Garfall.*

Large cliff petroglyphs without explanatory inscriptions near Vernal, Utah. They seem to depict a warrior people rather like the ancient Libyans. *Photo Dr. Julian Fell, from replica after photo by Professor Julian Steward.*

During the first millennium B.C., a steady increment of Semitic settlers occurred in Libya: Phoenician traders and apparently Arab fishermen and hunters. These olive-skinned people are depicted in mosaics of the Roman era, sometimes hunting, but most often as sailors and fishermen. Inscriptions after 200 B.C. show that Arabic language, with Berber loan words, was employed in the cities. *Es-Saraya el-Hamra, Tripoli, photo Peter J. Garfall.*

In Greek and Roman times, North African mosaic art reached its peak. The artists used the medium to depict daily life, and from these lasting records we can envisage the background from which arose many of the early colonists of America. All varieties of offshore and onshore fishing provided a major activity of the maritime Libyans, as shown by the abundance of floor mosaics excavated in public and private buildings of the ancient cities of the coast facing Crete. Here Mr. Abdullah Wahab, Controller of Antiquities, exhibits one of the choicest maritime pieces in the collection of the National Archeological Museum, Tripoli. *Photo Peter J. Garfall.*

Fishermen who have let out a seine net approach the shore while companions on the beach prepare to pull in the draw lines. National Archeological Museum, Tripoli. *Photo Peter J. Garfall.*

A hitherto-puzzling problem has been the occurrence in the Mediterranean, Britain, Scandinavia, and North and South America, of identical labyrinth patterns, derived from the religious art of Knossos, in Crete. Here is a graffito engraved on a wall in Pompeii, south of Naples, and dating from before 79 A.D. The cursive Latin reads: "The Labyrinth maze, here dwells the Minotaur." *Epigraphic Museum, photo Peter J. Garfall and Dr. Julian Fell.*

The same pattern as seen at Oraibi, New Mexico. *Epigraphic Museum, photo Peter J. Garfall and Dr. Julian Fell.*

The same pattern from Cuenca, Ecuador. *Photo Professor Paul Cheesman.*

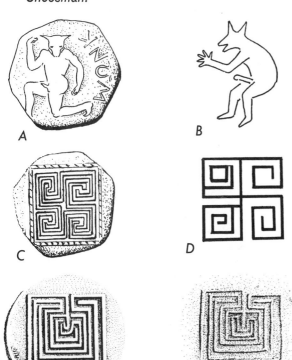

A

B

C

D

E

F

The discovery in America of ancient coins, and many recognizable petroglyphs depicting ancient coins (numoglyphs), provided the key to understanding the widespread distribution of the labyrinth pattern. A, C, E, are coins of Crete which circulated in North Africa and elsewhere, together with American petroglyphs B, D, F evidently copied from them. The Minotaur, B, appears in various Texan petroglyphs, where simplified labyrinths also occur. Two types of labyrinth are shown; D from Colorado, F from New Mexico.

The poor people of Libya lived in simple wigwamlike dwellings in country districts and consequently would readily adapt to the simplicity of life in a colonial setting. But the ports from which they sailed became splendid cities during the Hellenistic and Roman eras, and most of the American colonists would be as familiar with such urban grandeur as were the Pilgrims of modern Colonial times before they sailed from England. These two views show part of the Forum in Leptis Magna, Libya. *Department of Antiquities, Tripoli.*

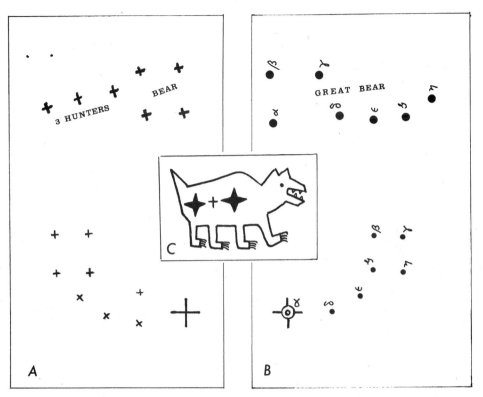

Plutarch tells us that the Greeks who settled in America were deeply interested in astronomy—as indeed they would have had to be in order to find their way across the ocean, using the stars as their guide. These maps show a mirror-image presentation of the north polar stars. A, a map of the stars around the north pole of the heavens, drawn by an Amerindian (Pawnee) astronomer on buffalo hide, and now in the Field Museum, Chicago. In the various Amerindian tongues, the name "Bear" was applied to the four stars forming the bowl of the Dipper, and the three stars of the handle were called the three hunters (or, the hunter and his two dogs). The polestar, to the left, was called The-Star-That-Does-Not-Move. B, in a European map of the same region, the stars are shown as seen when gazing upward, whereas the American map shows them projected onto a plane table. The Dipper is traditionally called Ursa Major, or Great Bear, and the other group to the left, that includes the polestar itself, is traditionally called the Little Bear. The Arabs called the Dipper Al-Dubb—The Bear—and the Little Bear was called Al-Dubb al-Asgar, which means the same. The Phoenicians called Ursa Major "Dub," which also means "Bear." The universality of the association of "Bear" with this polar constellation is evidence of the early contacts between astronomers of the New and Old Worlds. C, an ancient petroglyph of New Mexico symbolically links the Grizzly Bear with the guiding stars.

The shared traditions of celestial mapping and associated mythology that link the Amerindian and European astronomers is well illustrated by this star-map of 1603, drawn by John Bayer (1572–1625) of Bavaria, as part of his atlas of astronomy called *Uranometria.* Compare with the American star maps on page 107.

The Inyo Zodiac, in an area of petroglyphs discovered by J. H. Steward in 1929, east of Little Lake, Inyo County, California, but not hitherto recognized as a zodiac. The sun is shown to the right in the position it occupies at the time of commencement of the New Year in ancient America—the spring equinox. The constellations are shown in the order in which the sun passes through them, beginning on the right of the top row: Aries (March), Taurus (April), Gemini (May, the lower of two signs), Cancer (June, placed over Gemini), Leo (July), and Virgo (August); passing to the lower row, and reading now from left to right: Chelae, The Claws of the Scorpion, later separated as Libra (September), Scorpio (October), Sagittarius, shown as a bow (November), Capricornus (December), Aquarius, shown as a water hieroglyph (January), and Pisces, usually given as a whale in ancient zodiacs, but here apparently damaged (February). *Epigraphic Museum replica, photo Peter J. Garfall.*

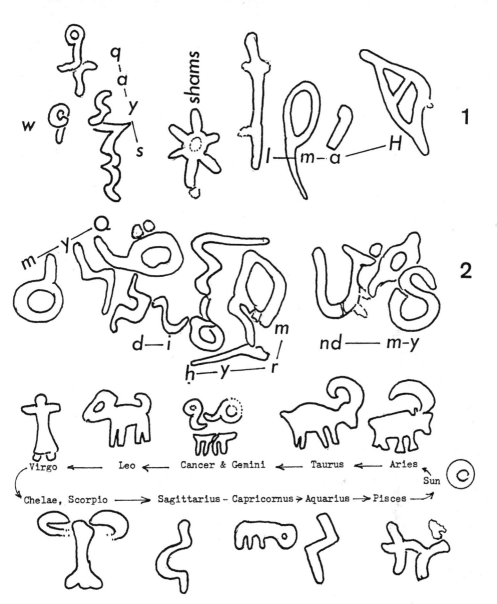

Professors Heizer and Baumhoff discovered two lines of inscription written above the Inyo Zodiac. It proves to be Kufi Arabic, and translates as

(1) When the Ram and the Sun are in conjunction (Spring Equinox)
(2) Then celebrate the Festival of the New Year.

An identical instruction was deciphered from the Libyo-Egyptian tablet found at Davenport, Iowa, a hundred years ago, and subsequently claimed to be "a forgery made by a nine-year-old boy" whose alleged "confession" still exists. As, however, the Inyo inscription is attested as ancient by archeologists of the highest repute, and its subject matter and Arabic inscription unmistakably clear, it is now equally obvious that the Davenport Inscription must also be genuine and ancient. The Davenport tablet is described in *America B.C.*

The Greek letters H-Y-D identify this Oklahoma petroglyph as Taurus, the Bull, a constellation of which the most conspicuous stars are the Hyades, forming the horns, head, and shoulders. The petroglyph was discovered on the cliffs of the Cimarron River by Gloria Farley. *Replica, after photo by Gloria Farley.*

in the Iberic language—but then what was it? I checked the relative frequencies of the letters and noticed that the resultant spectrum was rather similar to other Indo-European languages that occurred in Europe in Classical times. I re-examined the text with this in view, only to discover to my surprise that it is in fact written in Greek! No such text had ever been found before: this strangely-spelled Greek written in Iberic letters.

I published an account of the lamina in the 1976 volume of the Epigraphic Society's series, and suggested that the dialect might be Catalan Greek, since historical records implied that ancient Greek settlements had been made in Catalonia in the sixth century B.C. Archeological finds confirmed this tradition, but until now had not disclosed any document inscribed in the Greek language.

No sooner had the first copies of the Epigraphic Society's volume reached Europe than I received an immediate letter of congratulation from Dr. Linus Brunner, a Classical Greek specialist and sometime professor of classics at St. Gallen, Switzerland. Dr. Brunner followed his initial enthusiastic letter by other letters in the course of which he reconstructed what the Classical

(Athenian) Greek would have been, had the Pujol scribe written his report in that noble tongue. He also suggested a few alternative readings which I was glad to accept. Here is the final version of the decipherment, incorporating the suggestions of Professor Brunner; the original decipherment is given in the appendix at the end of this book.

> He sailed away from the harbor of Ptolemais in Libya. The ship came into collision with another ship from Thebes. The entire aft section and quarterdeck was damaged. Thieves cast a boarding net on the ship and one lawless barefooted ruffian stole the cabin trunk belonging to [Jose?] and which they had failed to keep locked. Cinnamon shipped from the island of Cyprus was in the trunk. He [Jose?] lodged a complaint with a magistrate, denouncing the Egyptians. The magistrate, a lictor, gave authority for the robber to be seized, whereupon the police made the arrest and cast him in prison.

Evidently this is a fragment of a report on a voyage, apparently made to the owners of the ship that was damaged and looted. The writer appears to have been only partly literate (or else writing in a language other than his native tongue). The importance of the fragmentary document lies in the proof it affords that Greek mariners were active in Spain in Classical times, and that their trade extended to Egypt, Cyprus, and Libya. No exact date can be suggested for the document, but it is unlikely to date from Roman times (Latin letters replaced the Iberian script by the time of Augustus, when Spain had been a Roman colony for two centuries). Probably the document dates from about 300 B.C., around the time of Pytheas of Marsalia, when Carthaginians still dominated western Mediterranean shipping.

That was not the end of the matter. While traveling in the remote country districts of Portugal where there are ancient stone chambers that so much resemble those of New England, Jim had encountered a word *forno* used by the country people for these structures. On his return, as no such word appeared in standard dictionaries of Portuguese, I suggested that perhaps Jim might gain some insights by referring his translation problems to Professor John R. Fonseca of the State University of New York. Professor

Fonseca is an enthusiastic member of the Epigraphic Society and is well versed in the history and literature of his Lusitanian ancestors. From Dr. Fonseca's translation and commentary on the difficult dialect Jim had encountered, it became apparent that highly localized patches of "fossil" language exist in the Iberian peninsula. The puzzling word, he explained, literally meant "oven."

While I was in Libya, I learned that beehive tombs, or *tholoi*, exist in the vicinity of Cyrene. They much resemble the New England beehive chambers, and some at least are known to be no older than Roman times. The nearest overseas territory to Cyrene is the island of Crete, some 180 miles away—one-and-a-half days' sail by ancient ship. The work of Sir Arthur Evans in Crete had disclosed close trading and cultural contacts between Knossos, the onetime capital city-state of Crete, and Libya. Evans had also recognized in Crete the same *tholoi* that characterize Libya, and indeed other parts of North Africa as far west as Algeria. From Classical writers he learned that these tombs, for such they are, were regarded as of African origin. They had apparently been adopted by the early Greek colonists of Cyrene, and by them perhaps the fashion had been passed to Crete. The Cretan examples contained multiple burials (see page 99). Later, simple burial mounds of earth replaced these corbel-built structures, the last remnant of the stonework persisting as a stone wall surrounding the earth mound. What now interested me was to learn the word used for these chambers in Crete is *forno*—a dialectal corruption of ancient Greek *phournos,* meaning an oven. But in Libyan Arabic, *furn* is the word we had learned to use when asking for a certain kind of unleavened bread, baked in a stone oven called a *furn*. It was apparent that we were on the trail of one of the ancient Greek words that had passed into both Libyan and Portuguese speech, and which in both regions had acquired the secondary sense of a stone chamber of the ancients, irrespective of the original sense of the word. In the form *fern* I learned it had also passed into the Berber tongue, though I could not discover if the word was ever applied to the ancient beehive tombs.

From the lamina of Pujol, and the curious distribution of the word *forno* in its special sense, my impression was that ancient Greeks in southeastern Spain and also in Portugal not only traded with the Greeks of Cyrene and Ptolemais, but also shared special vocabulary with them and with Crete. Thus apparently we should now widen the sense of the word "Greeks" as used by Plutarch to include not only the North African Greeks, but also those of the Iberian peninsula, of whose very existence we had only shadowy hints until now. Also, it would appear, the Greeks of Crete, or perhaps other non-Greek people of Crete, should also be considered in any effort we were to make in America to trace the colonists of whom Plutarch had written so confidently.

By this time, various correspondents, colleagues, and people who had read *America B.C.* were sending in a stream of valuable information on inscriptions and artifacts found in all parts of North America and Central America. Some of these now began to engage my attention, for there was clear Greek or Cretan influence to be seen. Readers of *America B.C.* will recall that in the closing chapter I cited, without explanation, the remarkable petroglyphs on rock faces and ancient buildings in the Hopi-Hohokam region, New Mexico, that rendered the complexities of the famous labyrinth of Knossos, Crete in the most exact detail. At the time I could offer no explanation beyond the obvious fact that a transmission of a complex pattern had occurred between the Old and New Worlds.

Among the new materials I now received was a photograph (page 104) of another very exact petroglyph recording the labyrinth, obtained by Professor Paul Cheesman in Ecuador. Other examples came from such widely scattered countries as Italy (Pompeii, page 104) and the island called Gotland in the Baltic Sea, southeast of Sweden. One Cornish lady wrote to tell me of the occurrence of the same design on rocks near her home in Tintagel, Cornwall.

It became apparent that in all cases outside the Americas it can be shown that coins of Crete are either known to have circulated during Classical times, or are virtually certain to have done so because coins of other neighboring Greek states have been recovered there. All cases occurred in areas known to have been very active trading centers, yielding thousands of ancient coins in the soil and brought to light by modern plows or by excavation. Many of the ancient coins of Crete carried exact replicas of the labyrinth pattern, combined with varying additional details, and sometimes an engraving of the bull-headed monster, the Minotaur, said by legend to have inhabited the labyrinth (pages 104 and 105). As also became obvious, and is explained in later chapters, a certain category of circular petroglyphs formerly thought to be "Indian shield designs" or "sun-symbols" comprise something quite different: namely, representations of ancient coins. Such petroglyphs, called *numoglyphs,* occur both in Europe and North Africa as well as in North America. Their presence implies that the coins whose designs they imitate were also present. There can be little doubt that the exact reproductions of the labyrinth pattern of Knossos, wherever they occur, were originally copied from actual coins of Knossos that had reached the places where the corresponding numoglyphs are found. Hence in North America, and in Central America, at sites ranging from central Texas to New Mexico, and southward to the northern Andes, the precision with which the Cretan labyrinth is rendered is now to be explained by the presence in the Americas of coins brought from Crete. Cretan coins circulated beyond the borders of the island, and Libya is a near landfall for Cretan sailors. Probably, then, Plutarch's Greeks were involved in the transmission of the coins to the New World.

Now for the first time, it seemed, it was becoming possible to account for the widely scattered labyrinth designs in America. Just as the wide scattering of these complex engravings in the Old World could be associated with ancient traders who distributed Greek coins as part of their commercial activities from the third century B.C. onward, until Roman coinage replaced the Greek, so also the wide scattering of labyrinth carvings in America could be attributed to the transmission of the design, by hand-held coins or copies of them, across the continents, north and south. The labyrinth appears also in various partly degenerate forms, as in Texas for example, and is as often as not associated with petroglyphs depicting bull-headed monsters, just as the ancient coins of Knossos would show the labyrinth on one face, and the Minotaur on the other.

I was now convinced that we were really on the track of Plutarch's Greeks. From the numerous letters and copies of publications on American petroglyphs that correspondents and colleagues now began sending in, it was possible to follow the Greek influence southward into the Gulf of Mexico and westward into New Mexico, Colorado, and Arizona. At the request of Harold Gladwin, our respected mentor in perceiving Mediterranean affinities in American art, Dr. Ralph Philbrick, director of the Santa Barbara Botanic Garden, now placed in my hands the entire series of volumes of *Medallion Papers,* deposited in the library of the Botanic Garden at the time when Gladwin himself was director. These not only recorded his historic analyses of tree rings of the Southwest (on which the whole archeological dating of the Southwest cultures is now based), but also included numerous photographs and drawings of the artifacts uncovered during Gladwin's excavations of the Hohokam culture, covering the period from shortly after the time of Christ up to about 1400 A.D. In these artifacts the influence of Greece was strong, though probably (as inferred above) mediated by North Africa, for Libyan script occurs. On page 97 are shown some of these patterns, together with a partial Greek alphabet, and also comparable Old World examples of the same designs.

With the aid of Ruth Hanner and of Aileen Alexander of Santa Barbara, at that time a student at Harvard and taking tutorials with me, a further collection of petroglyph records was made on the basis of the professional reports of such eminent archeologists as Professors Julian H. Steward, E. B. Renaud, Robert F. Heizer, and Martin A. Baumhoff. These explorers were content to discover and record petroglyphs, without attempting to assign meanings to them, nor recognizing any of them as actual written inscriptions. But Heizer and Baumhoff observed the varying amounts of dark discoloration (called desert varnish) that had formed on the petroglyphs, and had estimated that this atmospheric oxidation of the engraved surfaces would require two to three millennia to develop, though exact rates of oxidation can not as yet be determined. From these resources other Greek affinities could be observed, many of them approximately dated (by desert varnish) to between 1,000 B.C. and 1,000 A.D., and some of them including actual Greek inscriptions. It was evident that these were by no means of the same or even similar ages. For example, some were clearly Christian and Byzantine, and must represent a later visitation or settlement; a fact confirmed by the association with them of Islamic inscriptions written in the Kufic alphabet that dates between 650 A.D. and about 1200 A.D. Others, on the other hand, appeared to be older, resembling in style the Iberian pottery decoration of the fourth or third century B.C., where old Attic designs of several centuries earlier persisted long after their disappearance in Greece itself. The American examples might well be later even than the Iberian ones; but whatever their absolute date, the connection with the Mediterranean models was clear enough. Also from the East—from the mounds of Tennessee, for example— came artifacts of the same genre. All these, I believe, are part of the cultural bequest of Plutarch's Greeks.

While my colleagues and I were speculating on the manner of transmission of these Old World artistic motifs to the Americas, and theorizing that some of our American petroglyphs might be copies of ancient Mediterranean coin designs, unknown to us some alert young Americans were actually discovering the very clues that we sought. Word of the finds came in letters from readers of *America B.C.* These exciting discoveries introduce the next chapter.

Roman Visitors

In scanning the many reports in British numismatic journals of the findings of juries called to serve on judicial inquiries into the ownership of treasure trove, I have time and again been struck by the fact that so many notable discoveries of Roman and Saxon coins have been made by farmers' sons. In so many cases, a lad walking home from school, or two schoolboys exploring caves or crags on a weekend, have spotted something glinting in the soil or an unusual object half-concealed in the dust. The outcome has been a precious fragment of history, an unknown coin of a vaguely remembered Saxon king, or a relic of a Roman emperor. More often than not, the coins are common ones; but their very presence and location adds always a little to our knowledge of the past, and often an admiring jury or the British Museum finds public occasion to congratulate the young explorers on their discoveries.

It is therefore no surprise to learn that American schoolboys have been quietly but efficiently making similar discoveries on our own soil, so far from the orbit of the emperors, yet not so far as to lie beyond the reach of the greatest civilization of ancient times. The first American example of an ancient coin of the Greek city of Thurium was found by Elbert Martin, then a fourteen-year-old, in Oklahoma in 1954. A notable discovery of ancient Roman pottery was made in Alabama by two other fourteen-year-old boys, appropriately representing the old and the new America; one was a fair-haired son of Celtic stock, the other descended from the Muscogees of Alabama. Years later, the Muscogee, by now a commander in the U.S. Navy, wrote to tell me of the discovery and later brought examples of the artifacts for identification. I asked him to put on record in the Epigraphic Society's *Occasional Publi-*

cations an account of the find, and the document he sent is so charmingly evocative of youthful exploration that I select it to introduce America's Roman age through the eyes of one who took part in unveiling it. Here is the substance of the account as Commander Gene Andress gives it. Note how the boys first took stock of tribal tradition before setting out on their successful adventure.

Late in the summer of 1942, when I had just turned fourteen, I went to visit relatives near Gadsden. On a nearby farm lived a lad of my own age named Doug Davis. He began to tell me the local Indian traditions. There were still many Cherokees and Muscogees (Creeks) who lived in the area, as well as numerous village sites and Indian mounds along the nearby Coosa River. We talked about "lost treasure," and met an old Muscogee chief who told us about ancient legends of white men who had sailed up the Coosa a thousand years ago to trade for wood, furs, and metals.

Being even at that age of a skeptical academic bent I checked in the local library and found references to Welsh princes having sailed the Coosa around 500 A.D. Even this vague literary confirmation greatly sparked my interest. Chief Tappawingow further told us of a cave near an ancient trading village known as Tulla, not too far away, where relics could still be found. Typically adventuresome teen-agers, we set out to find this place, some five miles to the south, from his fairly precise directions. . . . I can yet feel the thrill of the search after these 36 years.

After several days of rowing an old boat and tramping the woods along the Coosa we located the place as he had described it, only to find it was now the property of a power company. Ignoring the keep-out signs, we clambered over several fences, to find a kind of sink-hole at the foot of a strangely shaped peak in the crumbling rock face. We began to dig, as others apparently had before us. Soon we found arrowheads, to our great delight. Further down we encountered what appeared to be the opening into a cave which had markings under the entrance overhang. After several days of digging into the cave we began to find broken pieces of pottery. Just before the vacation was over I found the small vase (page 125, Illustration B), which I imagined to be a a "magic potion bottle."

Our parents thought we had been fishing every day, for we told no one about our activities, partly because it was *our* place, and partly out of fear of the power company. We didn't even tell Tappawingow because he drank and talked a lot.

The following summer I visited there again, and Doug showed me a whole box filled with other similar artifacts he had since found and which he kept hidden in the family cyclone cellar. When we tried to revisit the site we found it full of water, and a man on horseback chased us back to our boat, yelling invectives of the redneck caliber. So we had to stay away. But Doug in compensation let me pick about two dozen items from his box, including what I now know to be an oil lamp from three similar ones he had, and I recall that he had about half-a-dozen of the small vases, all exactly similar. Since then I have not seen Doug again, nor revisited the site. Later, when I showed the items to various history professors I was discouraged to be told they were "worthless" or "meaningless," though nonetheless one professor persistently used to ask me to let him have the worthless objects. In the course of time, unfortunately, many of them have been lost or stolen, until I placed the last remaining three in a safety deposit box, where they lay until I was reminded of them by reading *America B.C.,* and then wrote to you.

We Muscogees await our Schliemann, and in the meanwhile I prefer to let the site remain untouched in relative seclusion; but I hope that competent researchers will conduct a proper dig and I will be glad to lead them to the site when the occasion demands.

The artifacts that Gene Andress brought proved to be Roman, similar to some that have been found on board a wrecked vessel dating from Republican times, about 100 B.C., found in the Mediterannean and carrying a cargo of ceramic lamps from a factory in Pompeii in Campania, south of Naples.

As already mentioned, Roman coins are found in America in the same kinds of contexts as they occupy in those parts of Europe that were never part of the Roman Empire. They are evidently the relics of Roman traders who came here—or perhaps, more accurately, relics of traders of countries that used Roman imperial coinage, such as Spain and Britain and the lands of North Africa. Although hundreds of Roman coins have been found here and in Central America, some old finds had been misidentified or not understood. Thus, from letters I received after *America B.C.* was published, some of these old records now appeared as new, for they yielded new information.

One of the most welcome of the new discoveries was brought to my attention in a letter from Gordon A. Price of Wiggins, Colorado. It was a tiny, thin copper disk, only half an inch across (12 mm.), found in Champaign, Illinois, in May 1885, by one of his forebears, than an eight-year-old boy named Alexander. With the coin Mr. Price sent a copy of a notarized statement made by the boy's father, relating that the coin had been found during city excavation, under four feet of undisturbed clay. The coin was described in the statement, and was certainly the same as the specimen I now saw before me; but all efforts Mr. Price had made to have the coin identified had proved fruitless.

This is not surprising, because the coin is an example of a group of little-known Celtic imitations produced in Britain at the end of the Roman occupation. They are called *minimi,* and the first major discovery of such coins was at the old Roman city of Verulamium, in England, in 1934. In 1951 English numismatist Philip V. Hill wrote the first general account and classification of these tiny coins. The Champaign example falls in the most degenerate class, believed to have been struck by the ancient Britons during a period of extreme coin and metal scarcity, after the Roman legions left Britain. It is shown, enlarged, on page 153. What makes this find so interesting is that it occurs along a transcontinental track from New England to the Northwest coast, followed by the Celts when they left New England, eventually to settle in British Columbia, Washington, and Oregon. Ogam stones are found at intervals along the transcontinental route, as well as inscriptions in Gaelic using Iberian alphabetic letters. At the Pacific end of the trail, the inscriptions are painted in red and apparently are not many centuries old. These are discussed later in this book. Here I wish merely to report that the first Celtic coin ever to be found in America—and indeed the first British *minimum* to be found outside of the British Isles—comes from Illinois and dates to approximately the late fourth or early fifth century A.D. The design on the coin, very barbarously executed, is an attempt to depict an unidentifiable Roman emperor, on the obverse, and an effort to copy the figure of Victory commonly found on the reverse of late Roman copper coins. For fuller details on these peculiar British coins, reference may be made to Price's 1951 paper. If Price has dated them correctly, these coins were produced by British Christians before the landings of the Angles and Saxons had plunged Britain into a nightmare of pagan barbarism destined to last for four centuries.

Was the coin brought here in ancient times? The notarized details make it clear that it is certainly not a modern "intrusion." Most likely the man who carried it to America was a British Celt who found America more attractive than his own land, now threatened on all sides by savage Teutons. Was the bearer a Christian, then? Probably. Later chapters in this book show that America in the fifth century A.D. had become a land of haven and refuge for Christians all over the western part of the Old World. From Morocco, Libya, Spain, and Britain people took ship for Asqa-Samal (as the Libyans called America, "The Great North Land").

Were coins useful in America at that date? Even such a miserable coin as the pathetic *minim* of the beleaguered Celts? Yes indeed, as the following pages will show.

In the 1880's a number of very peculiar inscribed stone and ceramic artifacts were discovered in Ohio. They were generally reported by the local doctors or lawyers of the township nearest to the farmer who had plowed up the object. It seems from contemporary newspaper accounts that what usually happened was (1) a farmer plowing his field would notice that his previous furrow had dislodged an unusual "Indian" curio. Pocketing it, he would take it back to the homestead that evening, and in due course place it on the mantelpiece. (2) The object would next come to the attention of either the local doctor, making a house call, or the local lawyer collecting a mortgage payment. The visitor would offer the farmer a dollar or two for the curiosity, and then later present it to a local historical society or perhaps make a public statement. (3) Hebrew being about the only script known to the local country gentry in those days as resembling in any way the Iberian script on the artifact, the latter would be declared a "Hebrew holy stone" or some such similar designation. In certain cases, such a determination was actually correct, as local clergymen acquainted with biblical Hebrew and rabbis in eastern cities would confirm. But usually the inscription, though called Hebrew, was not Hebrew. In due course, a Hebrew scholar, on examining such a misidentified artifact, would denounce it as a forgery. Thus, unfortunately, many important Iberian artifacts were dismissed as worthless pranks, and together with them some genuine Hebrew texts in unfamiliar Libyan Hebrew were also condemned.

Thanks to the historical research of two Ohio investigators, Professor Robert Alrutz, a zoologist of Denison University, and Dana C. Savage, of Dover, Ohio, we are only now beginning to learn the truth of this tangled web of misidentifications and mis-understandings. As both of these gentlemen have put much time and research into tracing the history of the stones, not yet published, it would be improper for me to elaborate at this time; beyond reporting that they asked me to examine the inscriptions, which I have done. One of them, the curious object depicted on page 157, is highly relevant to this chapter, and I am grateful to Professor Alrutz for allowing me to illustrate it.

Though disregarded at the time of its discovery ninety years ago as just one more of the notorious "Ohio Hebrew forgeries," it is in fact absolutely genuine, and cannot possibly be a forgery. It resembles one of the very barbarous bifacial massive coins produced by the Celts of northern Italy in imitation of the large Etruscan bronze coins, called *Aes Grave,* made in the days of the Roman Republic, in the fifth century B.C. The resemblance is superficial, however. The true nature of the baked ceramic object is given by the inscription, in retrograde Iberian Greek letters (quite similar to Phoenician letters). In the Roman alphabet, the words are ODAKIS EBIOM. This is a formula that has been known to numismatists since the 1920's, but was totally unknown in 1880, when the Ohio object was found. ODAKIS is the Iberian form of a Greek word that means *currency.* And EBIOM is merely an alternative spelling of the possessive case name of a Portuguese Celtic city, usually called *Evia,* on the site of the modern town of Alcacer do Sal, known to the Romans as Salacia. The Ohio artifact is, in fact, a crude and barbarously executed American copy of an ancient bronze coin of Evia, depicting the face of the gorgon Medusa on one side, and (a travesty of) the head of Hercules on the other side.

There can be no doubt that this is a deliberate "minting" in

America, probably originating in Ohio where it was found, of a token coinage based on that of the home town from which Ohio Celtiberians came. It probably is to be dated to at least 200 B.C. This is absolutely incontrovertible evidence that Iberian coinage was not only known to the ancient Iberians of Ohio, but actually imitated as a locally circulating "coinage-of-necessity," in the lack of an adequate supply from abroad. All colonists at all ages have been compelled to resort to such subterfuges, as the motherland never supplies enough coin for the developing colony, and has no impetus to do so. The rest of the information on this and related finds Professor Alrutz plans to publish at Denison. I am also indebted to James Whittall for obtaining for me from Portugal necessary numismatic literature to permit the solution of this problem, and also for bringing a large-scale replica I made of the inscription to Portugal for Portuguese specialists to study; for it appears that the American version of the words *Odakis Ebiom* is written in a script a hundred years older than the version so far known from the coinage of Evia itself.

In my opinion, the archaic script, and the extraordinarily barbarous style of this object implies that it is the oldest known American coin, probably to be dated to the early third century B.C., or late fourth century B.C. In view of the archeological insults to which it has been subjected it is indeed fortunate that it has survived the ignorance by which it was condemned as a worthless Hebrew fake, when in fact it is a priceless "first" in American native numismatics.

Yet another token coin of American manufacture—this time Libyan—was noticed by James Whittall in an engraving illustrating Thruston's (1890) *Antiquities of Tennessee*. As Jim plans a report in the *Bulletin* of the Early Sites Research Society, I will merely give the illustration and translation of the Libyan text: "The Colonists will redeem." The dialect is west Libyan—that is to say, essentially Arabic—and evidently the stone disk is a token coinage. It probably dates from sometime before 100 A.D. It matches Iberian *wheel-money*, mentioned in a later chapter, and also the corresponding wheel-money found in the Spiro Mound of Ohio. Nothing is known of the purchasing power of these early massive token coins, but we do know that an Iberian Celt

Above: Coins of four Roman emperors of the fourth century A.D., from the Beverly wreck. Upper left Valentinianus I (364–375 A.D.); upper right Gratianus (367–383 A.D.); lower left Valens (364–378 A.D.); lower right Constantius II (337–361 A.D.). The coins were found together within a square yard of beach. James Whittall collection. *Photo Malcolm Pearson.*

Below: Several Roman lamps of this pattern found by Doug Davis on Coosa River, Alabama (Commander Gene Andress collection). *Photo Peter J. Garfall.*

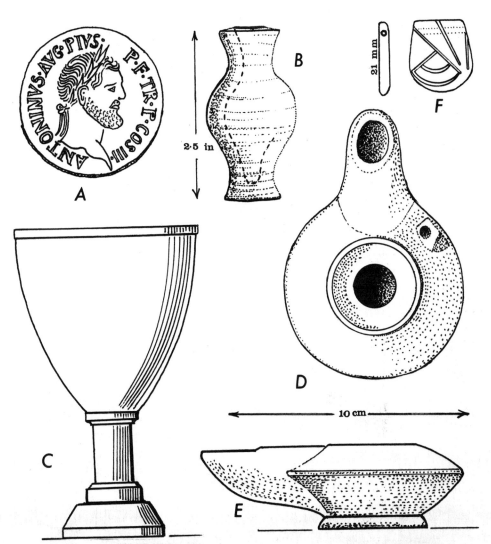

Various antiques from North American sites, mainly of Roman date. A, coin of Antoninus Pius (138–161 A.D.); the first American specimen of this emperor's coinage was found in 1819 at Fayetteville, Tennessee, 5 feet below the surface in soil that had carried 300–400-year-old forest trees. B, perfume vial of ceramic and D, E, oil lamp, probably of Pompeiian manufacture before 79 A.D., found at Muscogee Roman site on Coosa River, Alabama, by Gene Andress and Doug Davis in 1942 (Commander Gene Andress collection). C, Roman goblet of Pompeiian type found by James V. Howe in 1946, 18 inches below the surface on his farm at Clarksville, Virginia. F, blue glass bead found by the Baker River near its confluence with Stinson Brook, Rumney, New Hampshire (collection of Lynn Chong).

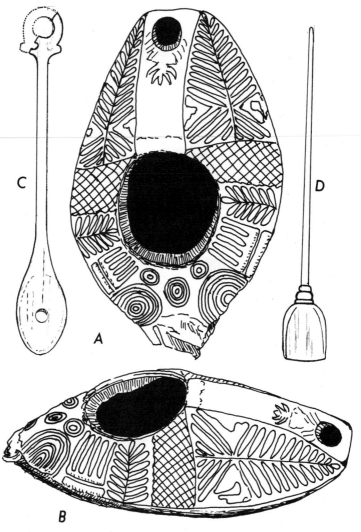

A, B, tracings made by Gertrude Johnson from photographs of the Roman oil lamp found in Connecticut by Frank Glynn, the archeologist who, according to Professor Cyclone Covey and historian Frederick Pohl, did not care to make the find public for fear of ridicule. Instead, he sent it to the Archeological Museum at Cambridge University in England, where it was identified as late Roman, east Mediterranean in origin. The whereabouts of the lamp itself is not now known. (*Information from Gertrude Johnson et al.*) C, British Museum example and D, example found in Tennessee mound, of bone spoons; the former Roman, the latter possibly Roman.

Roman coin found in garden in Columbus, Georgia, by Minna Arenowitch in 1945. Tentatively identified as Antoninus Pius (138–161 A.D.) by Professor Norman Totten. *Photo courtesy Gloria Farley from Douglas Braithwaite and Joseph Mahan.*

Coin of Constantine the Great (306–337 A.D.), reverse showing *Sol invictus* (Sun-god Unconquered) design. This example is from an uncertain Massachusetts source, but a similar coin has been reported from an Indian mound in Texas, or, according to another report, from the vicinity of a mound. During the nineteenth century Roman coins were reported to occur commonly in mounds, but detailed records were not kept. *Photo Malcolm Pearson.*

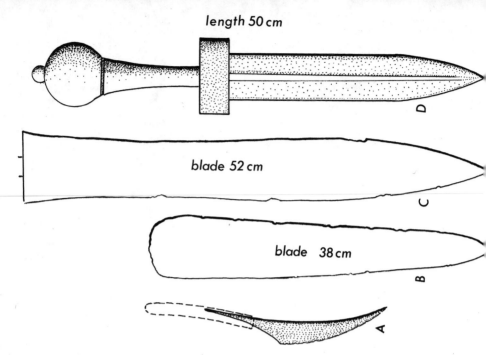

length 50 cm

blade 52 cm

blade 38 cm

A, bronze knife and B, sword blade, from ancient Michigan site (Museum of the American Indian). C, Roman sword blade from London (British Museum) of iron or steel, and D, Celtic (Galatian) sword, Pergamum.

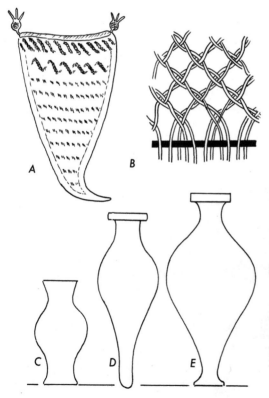

A, North African style of money wallet, known from Coptic examples, depicted upside-down in the Moneta inscription of Wyoming (page 149) and apparently indicating its use in North America during the Roman era. B, Sprang weaving technique found in ancient and medieval American textiles (Bucky King, 1975), and also employed to give stretch to moneybags of the Moneta petroglyph type. C, perfume vial from Coosa River, Alabama, and D, E, vials from Libya, probably imported from a Roman factory, unglazed pottery.

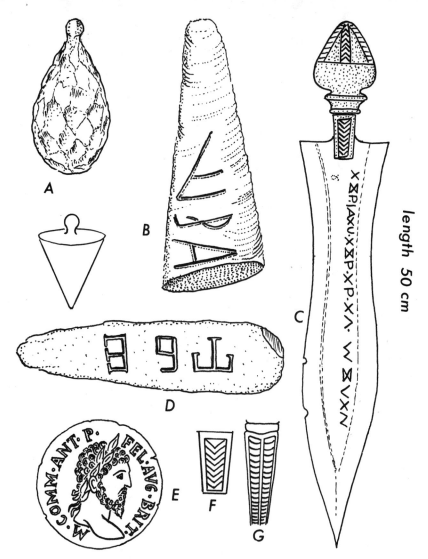

length 50 cm

A, stone artifact of uncertain use, representative of many found in Massachusetts, variously reported as fishing sinkers or plumb bobs; below it is a Roman metal plumb bob from Britain. B, inscribed fossil squid shell, employed as a phallic talisman and bearing the Iberic letters S-Q-A (Arabic, *saqa* to arouse sexual ardor) from Arkansas, *Gloria Farley*. C, Iberian iron or steel sword with wood pommel (possibly restored at later date than blade), found by Lyman R. Fellows during excavation of foundations of railway station at Concord, New Hampshire, about 1870, now in possession of his descendants in California. See following illustration for text of inscription. D, small engraved stone phallus from excavation at Lackawacksen, Pennsylvania, inscribed in Iberic script S-B-H ("prick"), found by Middlebury Archeological Research Center (Salvatore Trento). E, coin of Commodus (180–192 A.D.), an emperor whose coinage was first reported from four feet below the surface on formerly forested land near Fayetteville, Tennessee in 1819. F, pommel decorative carving of New Hampshire sword C, and G, similar pattern on British Celtic metal fibulae.

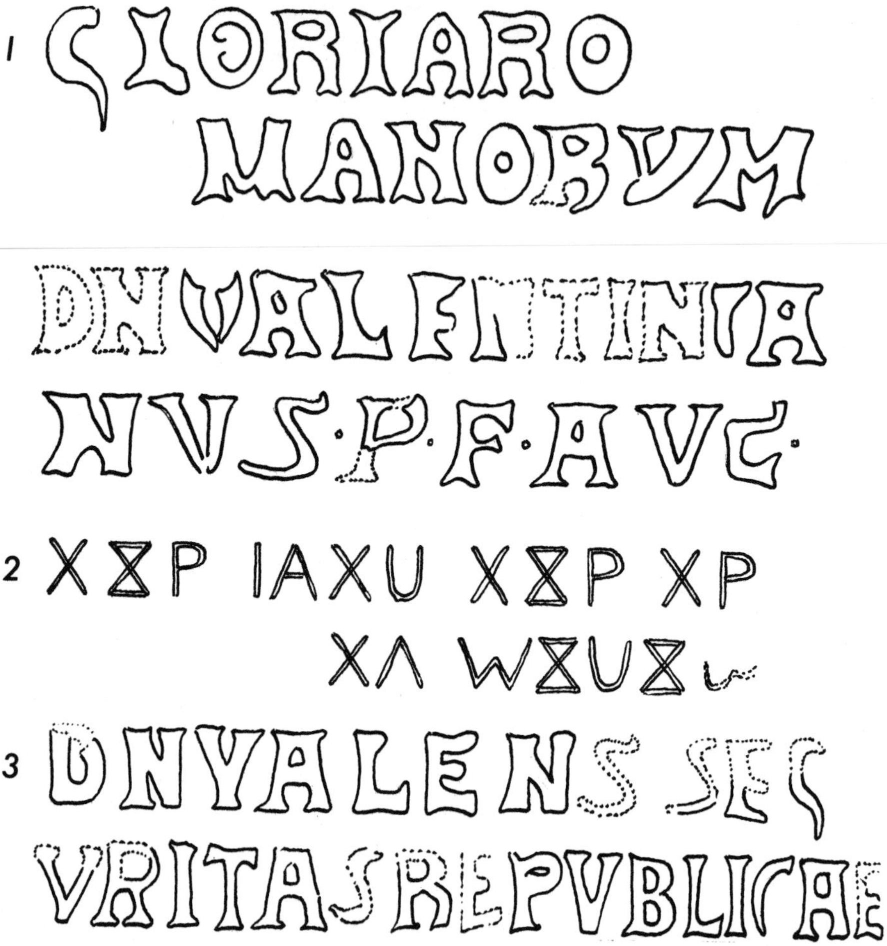

1 CLORIARO MANOBVM

DN VALFNTINIA NVS·P·F·AVC·

2 XƧP IAXU XƧP XP
XɅ WƧUƧ ◡

3 DNVALENS SFC
VRITAJREPVBLIrAE

Styles of lettering on Roman coins found at Beverly, Massachusetts. 1, Gloria Romanorum (Glory of the Romans); D(ominus) N(oster) Valentinianus P(ius) F(elix) Aug(ustus) (Our Lord Valentinian: Dutiful, Happy, Revered). 3, D(ominus) N(oster) Valens; Securitas Rei Publicae (Our Lord Valens, The safety of the Republic). 2, Iberic inscription on sword from Concord, New Hampshire, "Handwrought steel, death-dealing steel, able to cut through (?armor)."

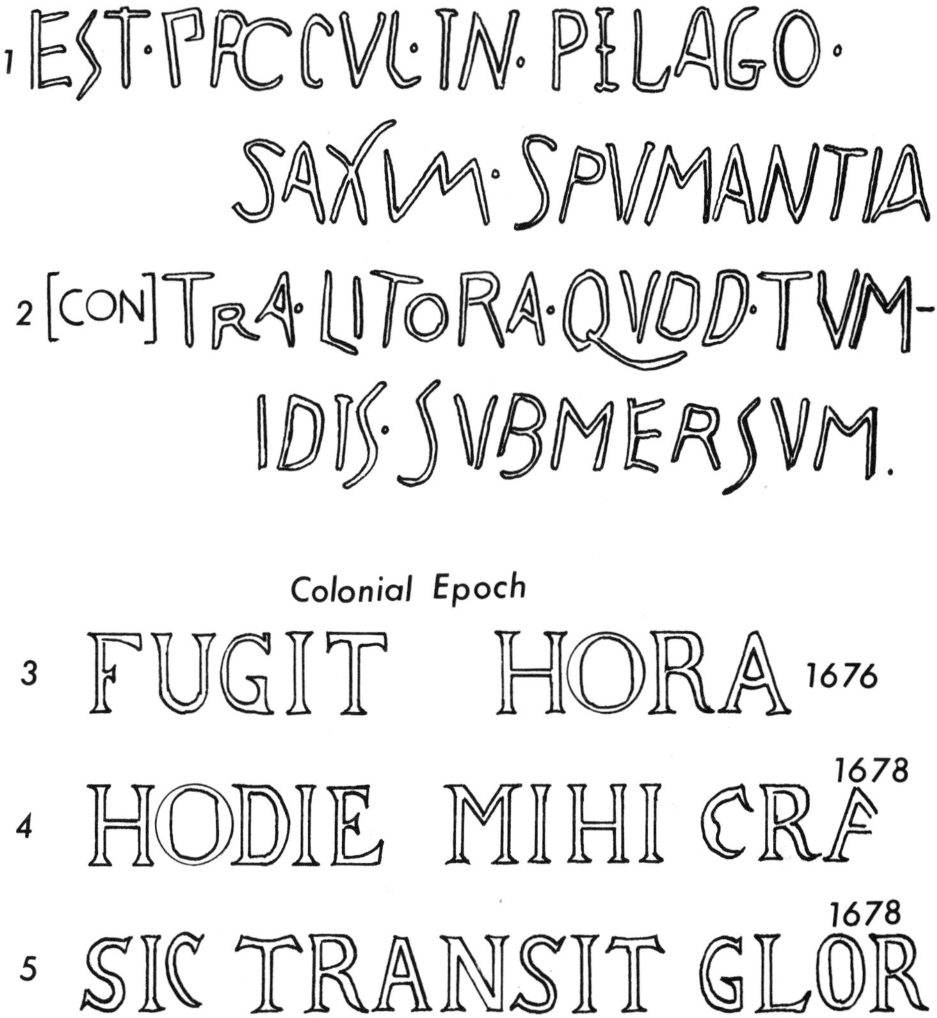

1 EST·PRCCVL·IN·PILAGO·
SAXVM·SPVMANTIA
2 [CON]TRA·LITORA·QVOD·TVM-
IDIS·SVBMERSVM.

Colonial Epoch

3 FUGIT HORA 1676

4 HODIE MIHI CRÆ 1678

5 SIC TRANSIT GLOR 1678

Latin inscription cut on rocks at York Harbor, Maine, from Virgil's
Aeneid Book 5; the script is believed to date from about the fourth or
fifth century A.D.: "There is a foam-decked rock far out at sea opposite
the shore which is covered by the waves in rough weather." Traces of
the third line here omitted. The reference is to Boon Reef, now marked
by a lighthouse. Early Colonial examples of Latin script from New
England graveyards are shown below for comparison; the York Harbor
text employs a style of lettering not used by the Colonial masons, but
similar to Iberian Latin texts of the late Roman period.

Above, coin of Septimus Severus (193–211 A.D.), found by Mrs. Curtis Robie in soil at Grafton, Massachusetts, presumed to be of ancient American provenance, but the coin had been placed in a crude brass locket during Colonial times. Below, coin of Maximianus Herculius (284–305 A.D.) found on plowed field near Maxton, North Carolina by the Cherokee landowner Jerry Maynor in 1951. *Photos: upper, Malcolm Pearson; lower, Peter J. Garfall.*

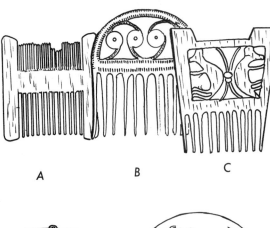

A   B   C

D   E

Roman society was fascinated when a Spanish aristocrat, the lady Plotina, was summoned to Italy as Trajan's empress in 98 A.D. Within the year women all over the Western world adopted the high Iberian comb as worn by the empress and depicted on coins, E. A, from Roman Britain; B, an earlier Bronze Age style from Denmark; C, North America (Iroquois); D, Danish (bog burial).

reported that they were rejected in Ireland, where they were denied currency value and declared illegal. His comments are given in Chapter 9.

In 1977, just before I left for North Africa, Colonel Robert Vincent, a numismatist of Cherokee descent who had collected ancient coins in Turkey, invited me to examine his Byzantine series of bronze coins and other interesting items he had acquired during his tour of duty in the area of Ephesus and other Ionic cities. This work was interrupted by my Libyan journey and resumed on my return. Thus I became familiar with the sequence of bronze coin sizes associated with the extensive Byzantine issues of the period from about 500 A.D. onwards to medieval times. In all these bronze issues, the largest value (called a *follis*) is about the size of a half-dollar, and bears on the reverse side a large capital M. Next comes the half-follis, distinguished by a capital K. Next comes the quarter-follis, marked E, written in the Greek manner (Epsilon), and lastly the smallest bronze piece, the one-eighth follis or "bit," marked with a V. This information did not seem particularly important to me at the time, and I paid more attention to the interesting Byzantine portraits of the emperors and empresses, and also of Christ, found on the obverse sides of these coins.

Fortunately, before these facts had become blurred in my memory, I had occasion to study Professor E. B. Renaud's important series of reports on the pictographs and petroglyphs of Colorado (University of Denver, 1935–1940). The apparent heraldry of the patterns on the supposed circular shield designs depicted in these petroglyphs aroused my interest. When I began to classify them, I found that the largest circular design carried a pattern dominated by a large capital M, the next largest size by a K, the next size by an Epsilon-E, and the smallest by a V-shaped arrangement of dots. As I still had the Vincent collection of Byzantine *folles* in my study, I compared the designs with the coins. There could be no doubt that the resemblances were more than an accident, and that in fact the supposed shields were in all probability a public notice setting out the relative sizes, values, and recognition symbols of the whole Byzantine bronze coinage. This was a significant step in establishing that ancient Americans were familiar with the very bronze coins of Byzantine minting that we find in American soil, and on the New Jersey seashore, to this very day. I hastened to call Bob Vincent to share this information with him. We wondered aloud at the hand of fate that had led an American of Cherokee descent to wander through the ruins of Ionia, picking up ancient coins of Byzantium destined years later to solve a vexing mystery in his far-off homeland. Page 147 illustrates the features mentioned.

Now I was sufficiently alerted to begin deliberately looking for ancient pictures of coins among the thousands of petroglyphs recorded by professional archeologists from the various states in the Southwest, where petroglyphs occur in the tens of thousands, usually associated with evidences of desert oxidation, or "desert varnish," allowing the petroglyphs to be classified as ancient, and not modern "intrusives"—like the numerous initials that vandals see fit always to cut on rocks that have been decorated by Indians in ancient times.

As I thumbed wonderingly through the standard volumes of reports on these ancient petroglyphs of the Southwest, I soon perceived that nearly every circular design is actually a representation of an ancient coin, reduced to its bare essentials in the same manner as the Celtic imitations of ancient Roman coins, but accompanied by enough detail, such as the more conspicuous letters of the original inscription, to permit identification.

Thus, in parts of Nevada and California, I found easily recognizable depictions of ancient Chinese coins of the Han and Sung dynasties, accompanied by Chinese inscriptions giving the value, or other details appropriate for a foreigner to know, when dealing with Chinese currency. Again, in Colorado, I recognized designs taken from the obverse faces of Byzantine coins, and also Byzantine religious designs continued along the West Coast northward into British Columbia, where they mingled with Celtic and Norse coin designs. These will be discussed and illustrated later in this book.

There is one more site: the great pictograph and petroglyph location called Castle Gardens, near the town of Moneta, in cental Wyoming. Dr. Don Rickey, chief historian of the Bureau of Land Management, Department of the Interior, was one of my first visitors a few days after *America B. C.* was published at the end of 1976. He had been struck by many features of the book that appeared to throw possible light on problems of American epigraphy and early history. His own responsibility lies in the discovery, identification, and protection of all historical antiquities, including inscriptions by explorers and other early visitors. He perceived that many sites might well carry inscriptions falling within his area of research, but dating from a much earlier period than had hitherto been thought to fall within the time span of American history. Unlike my critics in some archeological institutions, he came to see for himself what basis there is for my conclusions and, after a pleasant and profitable two days of work and discussions, we resolved to cooperate in the future. He began by referring to me various reports in his files at the Bureau of Land Management dealing with unexplained petroglyphs. One of the reports dealt with the Wyoming site mentioned above—the finest petroglyph location in Wyoming, remarkable for the almost universal circular form of all the designs depicted on a series of rock faces that dominate the site.

Some of the designs I recognized at sight as well-known Celtic patterns, used on disk-shaped bronze harness trappings of Celtic kings in Europe (see page 156), and also occuring in the Spiro Mound in Oklahoma, together with other evidences of Celtic designs (Chapter 9). But the great majority of the circular patterns cut into the cliffs at Castle Gardens were not familiar to me when I first saw them. They seemed so dissimilar to Indian shield patterns that it was hard to relate them to these either, and in fact at first I was as bewildered by the whole series of inscriptions as had been the archeologists who first placed them on record. These men—notably David Love in 1931, at that time still a student at the University of Wyoming; Dr. E. B. Renaud of the Department of Anthropology of the University of Denver (whom Love escorted to the site); Ted C. Sowers of the State Archeological Survey of the University of Wyoming (who reported on the site in 1941); and Arthur G. Randall of the Wyoming Geological Association together placed on record a fine report dealing objectively with the finds, and illustrating them. This material became the basis of the Bureau of Land Management reprint dated 1961, which Don Rickey now submitted to me for study.

As readers who are familiar with my earlier book *America B.C.* will recall, the ancient Celts frequently employed a peculiar alphabet whose letters look like tally marks, called Ogam. For convenience, the alphabet is also illustrated in this book (page 305). Some of the petroglyphs at Castle Gardens comprise Celtic designs but neither Don Rickey nor I could locate any Ogam lettering that might have supported this identification or thrown light upon the purpose of the whole extraordinary collection of circular petroglyphs. However, reports from various correspondents in the northern states of the Midwest and Far West did make it clear that scattered Ogam inscriptions are to be found along a belt extending westward from New England.

For nearly two more years, the Castle Gardens file remained an insoluble mystery. In the interim, I located an Amerindian community still using a creole Celtic dialect, in the upper Fraser Valley of British Columbia, and reported on their language (1976). During 1977 Ruth Knudsen Hanner, honorary librarian of the Epigraphic Society and epigraphic explorer of Hawaii, visited British Columbia and began to send me reports dealing with the petroglyphs of that region. Among the material, notably that discovered and illustrated by John Corner (1968), I was excited to discover unrecognized Ogam inscriptions, both with and without vowel signs. Obviously, this was Celtic, and of a much later vintage than the New England Ogam, in very good preservation and easy to decipher. This material is discussed in Chapter 13; what is relevant here is that some of the designs found by Corner are circular and resemble the circular petroglyphs of Wyoming.

One more link in the chain of clues that finally led to interpretation of the mysterious circles now came from Oklahoma. In the southern part of that state, Gloria Farley obtained latex impressions of a remarkable inscription discovered by Barbara Jean Woodward at Ardmore. It proved to be a tribal boundary marker, written in Gaelic Celtic—*using alphabetic script*. This was a notable first, for until now only Ogam script had come to my attention at any Celtic site. The discovery of an obviously later and more sophisticated type of Celtic inscription, employing vowels as well as letters that anyone could recognize as such, was an important clue as to the later history of the Celts in America. It meant they were still around at the time when alphabetic writing began to be adopted by the Celts of Europe, early in the Roman era. It was more than that: Celtic scholars who visited my laboratory, such as Professors Gareth and Janet Dunleavy, University of Wisconsin, Milwaukee, could now see convincing evidence of inscriptions of a kind more familiar to Celtic students in Europe.

Several times James Whittall mentioned to me that a Latin inscription has long been known to occur on a coastal rock in Southern Maine; but I had thought it probably must be the work of some seventeenth- or eighteenth-century Harvard student on vacation, since it is a quotation from the *Aeneid* of Virgil. However, as the evidence of the coins began to mount, and we realized that ancient Romans were no strangers along the historic New England coast, I remembered the *Aeneid* exercises that had been found engraved by Iberian schoolboys learning Latin during Trajan's reign. Might this Maine inscription be a verse memorized by some Iberian mariner of long ago, an officer on shore leave in the Epeiros?

One beautiful day not long before this book went to press, my old friends Malcolm and Myra Pearson drove Jim and me to the site. I was prompted to remind Malcolm that he had witnessed the whole development of the present view of American history, from the day that he first led William Goodwin to Mystery Hill to see the "stone-works." The inscription lies in a setting of great beauty, an inlet in the coast near York Bay. It was obviously cut with a metal tool, and certainly long ago, for the erosion has destroyed much of it, and the lettering is in an ancient style. Several Classical scholars who have seen it are of the opinion, which I share, that the text dates to about the fourth or fifth century A.D. But we can not yet be sure. It remains as just one more of the New England relics that tease us out of the present and into a shadowy past. The lettering is shown on page 131. Molds were taken on the occasion of our visit and these will be the subject of close study in the year ahead. Until then we are left wondering what manner of man made this poetic epigraph, and from whence he came.

Did the Romans, or their Iberian Latin-speaking subjects, merely trade with America, without thought of any more far-flung extension of their sea roads? Did those learned ancients, well versed in the geography of the world as a globe of known dimensions, ignore the logic of their own knowledge of geography, which told them that China and India must inevitably lie beyond that western Epeiros that we call America?

No, they did not. Around the sixth decade after Christ, when Nero's extravagance was imitated by the wealthy families of Rome, a torrent of gold coin swept eastward to India to finance the insatiable demand of the Roman matrons for silks and spices. Such were the conditions of the trade across the Indian Ocean, and the levies made by intermediate authorities and the profits of middlemen, that the cost of these items increased one hundredfold between the act of lading the cargo on board in India and its ultimate sale in the markets by the Tiber.

That philosopher-naturalist-economist Pliny the Elder fretted over the financial ruin of Rome that he saw looming ahead. He complained bitterly that annually, in his day, no less than one million pieces of gold were sent east, never to return. The gross unbalance of trade brought inflation and accelerated the flight of gold to the East.

Pliny's complaints were heard by Seneca, the Spanish philosopher and tutor of the young Nero, and later principal minister in Nero's administration.

Seneca commented that a cure for these financial misfortunes was not far off. He himself had become immensely wealthy, and from the comment he made, I believe that the Iberian trade may well have been the source of much of that wealth, soon to arouse Nero's cupidity. Seneca said: "Spain will soon be linked with the Indies across the Atlantic Ocean." The comment has aroused little interest among Classical scholars—but surely it is highly significant.

I believe that Seneca was well aware that the Pacific Ocean lay beyond the West Coast of the American Epeiros, and that on that same West Coast were traders from China and India. Since the world is a globe, that very trade, so wasteful of Rome's treasure by the route across the Indian Ocean, would soon be diverted across America (or across the Panama Isthmus), and thus reach Europe by a route where no grasping middlemen or greedy Oriental might exact the hundredfold tolls that so disturbed Pliny. Apparently, Seneca's dream was not fulfilled—but the germ of the idea was already planted in Iberian minds fourteen centuries before Columbus put it to Their Catholic Majesties as a lure to finance his voyage. In him Seneca lived again, and an old Iberian dream came true.

Arrival of the Iberian Bankers

For some time, Gloria Farley and I had been aware of some obscure evidence she had discovered in a cliff overhang shelter in west Arkansas implying that some kind of financial transaction had occurred. The fragmentary inscription, in Iberic, seemed to say something like ". . . lent the Chief," and on the cave wall were signs that we knew signified money: the well-known *ingot* symbol. Professor Norman Totten, a leading numismatist, visited the site with Gloria (page 144), and among ourselves we jokingly referred to the site as "The West Arkansas Branch of the Grand Bank of Iberia"—but the evidence was so disjointed that it did not seem worth publishing a paper at that time.

The missing clue, mentioned in the previous chapter, actually lay in the Ardmore Gaelic inscription. But as that inscription merely delineated a tribal boundary line, its relevance for coinage studies was not at all obvious. The final solution to the Castle Gardens mystery came like this:

After the match between the Byzantine bronze-coin series and the supposed "Indian shield" series of Colorado petroglyphs was discovered, I remembered the mysterious suite of circular "shield" patterns of the Wyoming site, and once more got out Dr. Rickey's report from the files of the Bureau of Land Management. This time I did indeed begin to recognize, one by one, designs that resembled ancient coins I had once seen. Some matched Roman Republican coins in my own collection. But the most important piece of evidence I had not understood when first I examined the materials Don Rickey had sent—it lay in a line of Iberian letters. These I had read originally, expecting Iberic language (i.e., early Classical Arabic) but found they made no sense, and gave up trying to decipher them.

But now, on this second turn around, the situation was different. We had now seen American Celtic—Spanish Gaelic—written in alphabetic letters instead of the Ogam which had been all we had known before. Furthermore, hints from many quarters now suggested that the Castle Garden site in Wyoming must have something to do with money.

Once more I read the Iberian letters of the Castle Gardens inscription, and realized that the very first word—M-N-D-R—is the Gaelic biblical word *monadoir,* used in the New Testament for *moneychangers* (whose tables Jesus overthrew on the Temple steps). A check showed that Dinneen's Gaelic Dictionary traces the word back to an early Celtic manuscript, and that the root word m-n-d is the same word as Latin *moneta*—money. Still more interesting is the fact that the nearby township in Wyoming, where the Castle Gardens petroglyph site is located, carries the name *Moneta*—as if the name is remembered from Celtic times. It was clear that the Iberic letters were spelling out a Gaelic (Celtiberian Gaelic) text, not recognized on my previous attempt to read them, as I had been expecting Arabic language similar to West Libyan. Indeed, one of my earlier decipherments of Spanish material had shown that the supposed Iberic inscription of Pujol is Catalan Greek written in Iberian script (later confirmed by Professor Linus Brunner). Thus it was not really surprising that Celts of Spanish origin should also choose to write in an Iberic alphabet. The rest of the decipherment is shown on page 149, reading the modern word *banker* in place of the old biblical *moneychanger*. Part of the text is a rebus in Greek —probably the same Catalan Greek as the Pujol text, for we know Greeks settled in Catalonia. The rebus depicts a moneybag pouring coins into a dish, but the signs also spell the Greek slogan "Phthaei"—"it was the first to come"—from the verb *phthaomai.*

What we had found, then, at Castle Gardens, is the banker's shingle, giving the trade name of the bank—roughly equivalent to our modern "First National."

The numerous circular designs could now be recognized as depictions—not so much of the Roman Republican coins that they

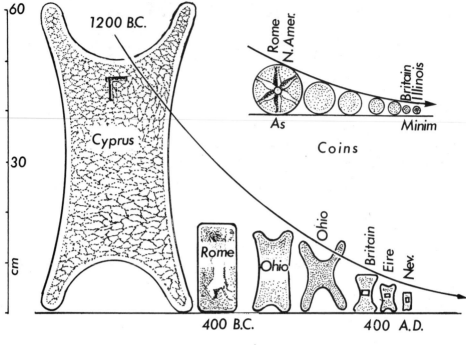

Ingots

Over the past 3,000 years currency, initially ingots of copper or bronze in the shape of a stretched bullock's hide (*pecunia*), and later circular disks bearing marks of certification (*nummi*, coins), have become progressively smaller in step with the ceaseless rise in prices, inflation. American coinage reflects the universal trend; the final inflationary steps result in replacement of copper ingots by wood ingots, and coins are replaced by bone disks, thereafter used only as gaming jettons, without currency value.

Opposite above: Replicas of early forms of money. Upper left: miniature broadsword, placed in Scandinavian Bronze Age burials after it became too expensive to bury a warrior's sword with the body. Rest of upper row: copper ingots of Europe, and (the two to the right) America, from burial mounds; the one on the extreme right was used as a pectoral or chest ornament. Lower row: casts of (left) the first Carthaginian coin recognized in America, from west Arkansas, the inscription eroded away, but the horse head on the reverse showing its origin; and a coin of Nero found in Heavener, Oklahoma. *Photo Peter J. Garfall.*

Opposite below: Replicas of the wood ingots and bone disks used by northeastern Algonquin tribes as gaming jettons. *Photo Peter J. Garfall.*

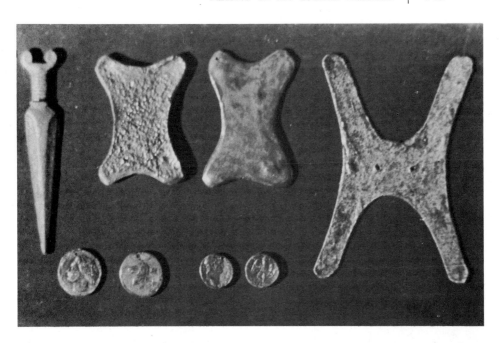

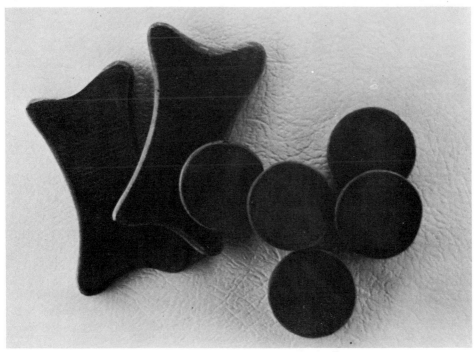

Symbols of money: an ingot to the right, inscribed on rock wall of a cliff overhang in west Arkansas; the locality was jokingly referred to by Gloria Farley (left) as the West Arkansas Branch of the Grand Iberian Bank, but later it became evident that the name was not so farfetched after all. To the right Professor Norman Totten. *Photo Mark Totten.*

Opposite: Engraved representations of coins: A, C, on Iberian tombstones of the Roman period; similar designs (*numoglyphs*) appear on British Roman tombstones and, as a consequence of the revival of interest in Classical themes in the seventeenth century, also on early Colonial tombstones in New England. B, D, E, F, G, early Roman and Etruscan bronze coins from which the numoglyph designs are taken. The numoglyph apparently symbolizes the "Penny for Charon," originally placed between the teeth of a corpse before interment, as in H, to provide the deceased with the fare to pay the ferryman across the Styx. Roman burials in Britain are often found with the coin, as in H, but this has not yet been observed in America.

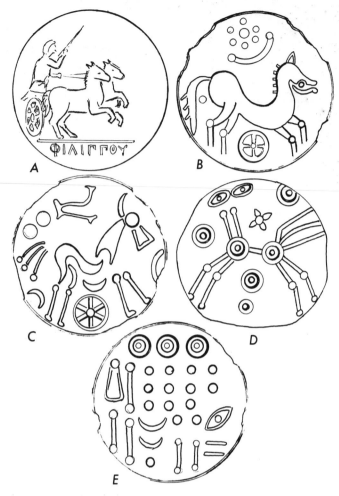

Picassoesque British Celtic versions of a Greek coin design, or "The Disintegration of a Chariot." Five stages by which the charioteer design of Philip of Macedon was converted to spare parts by Celtic artists in barbaric Britain. A, original gold stater issued in Macedonia in the fourth century B.C., and circulated in large numbers in Celtic Europe. B, Celtic imitation produced in order to maintain the coin in circulation after supplies from Greece ceased; the charioteer has disappeared as a cloud of dots, and one wheel has rolled under the horse that survives. In the next minting the horse explodes, C, and the shower of fragments assumes the disordered arrangement of D. The final artist, E, found this arrangement displeasing, and tidied up the resultant anatomical spare parts so that the skull and long bones are set out in orderly rows, the joints are similarly organized, one eye and two ribs are placed on the lower right, while three wheels are stacked neatly at the top. Until the entire sequence had been reconstructed, British numismatists and archeologists were at a loss to understand the meaning of the peculiar patterns on ancient British coinage. Only after extensive collecting and cross-comparisons was it realized that the coinage had been derived from ancient Greece. Similar Picassoesque disasters befell Roman coin designs at the hands of early American artists.

"Shield designs" (right-hand column) of decreasing diameter found at petroglyph sites N.M. 50, N.M. 233, on the upper Rio Grande in Colorado. On the left are the sixth- and seventh-century copper coins of the Byzantine emperors, issued in Alexandria and other cities, arranged in order of decreasing size and value. The symbol M signifies 1 folle, K a half-folle, X a quarter-folle, and V is one-eighth part of a folle. It is obvious that the North American designs are directly based on these low-value copper coins of Byzantium, and that such copper coins probably were in circulation in the Libyan settlements in the Southwest. In all likelihood the petroglyphs do not represent shield designs, but are relics of onetime public notices (or schoolmaster's diagrams) explaining the relative values of the coins. (Data recorded by E. B. Renaud, 1936–1940; interpretation by Fell.) Some coins by courtesy of Colonel Robert Vincent, Oklahoma.

Spiro Mound stone disks, ca. 4 inches in diameter, originally covered by copper foil.

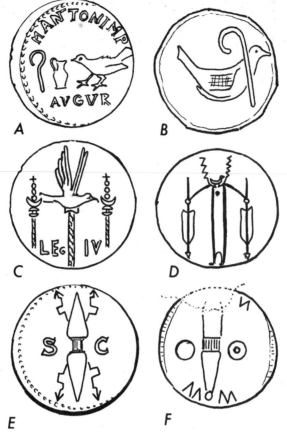

North American reflections of the Roman civil war and the triumph of Octavian. More of the coinage illustrated by petroglyphs at the Wyoming Iberian Bank, near Moneta. The hitherto inexplicable "shield petroglyphs" shown on the right are recognizable as simplified renderings of three Roman coins in circulation during the years 50 B.C. to about 20 A.D. The upper two, on the left, are issues of Mark Antony, A, depicting the insignia of the office of Augur (which he held while also Imperator, or Supreme Commander), C, depicting legionary standards. In B, the Wyoming artist retains the crook-shaped *lituus* (with which the augur designated the part of the sky to be watched for auguries given by the flight of birds) and also retains the bird, but discards the ceramic vessel as something irrelevant to the nomadic life of a fur trapper–voyageur, who would carry liquids in a leather bottle. In D, the Wyoming artist is baffled by the whole composition, which he renders as a supernatural figure whose head is replaced by the Roman eagle. E is an early issue of Augustus, depicting Jupiter's thunderbolt, the letters SC signifying a bronze issue approved by the Senate. F is the Wyoming artist's interpretation; the S and C becoming O's, while the lightning zigzags of the model are mistakenly rendered as V's and N's. These are the latest issues shown at the Wyoming site, and presumably relate to the actual date of the establishment of the Wyoming Branch of the Iberian Bank.

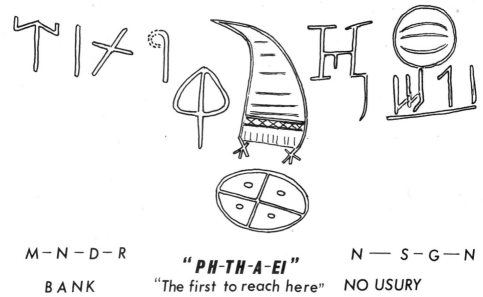

M – N – D – R

BANK

" PH-TH-A-EI "

"The first to reach here"

N — S – G — N

NO USURY

The business sign or tile engraved at the Wyoming site near Moneta. On the left the Iberic letters spell the old Gaelic word for *moneychanger,* or, in modern parlance *bank.* On the right, the word intended apparently is Old Gaelic for no interest—or perhaps, rather, no usury (i.e., not more than 12–1/2%). In the center Greek letters phi, alpha, theta, and eta form a rebus in which a moneybag discharges coins onto a dish. The word spelled means "[It was] the first to come here," resembling the modern use of the word "First" in bank names.

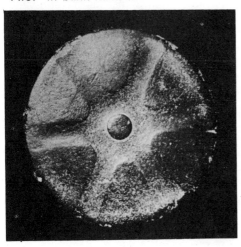

Ceramic disk found in plowed soil at Clintwood, Virginia, impressed with design of Iberian or other European bronze circular ingot of *Aes grave* type, presumably used as token wheel-money. Elvin Goodwin collection, *Photo Michael Paul Henson.*

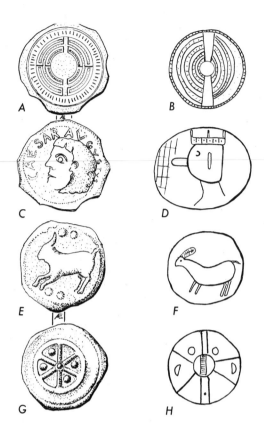

The enduring influence in North America of the Celts of Portugal is apparent in these issues, exhibited at the Moneta site of the Iberian Bank. The historic Celtic city of Eviom, which had already provided the model for the first American colonial tokens minted in Ohio (see page 157) in the third century B.C., changed its name to Salacia after the Roman occupation. During the reign of Augustus (27 B.C.–14 A.D.) the Celts of Salacia struck an interesting series of bronze coins bearing, in addition to the customary somewhat crude portrait of Augustus with his titles on the obverse, a highly distinctive reverse design depicting an ancient Celtic sun temple, or druidic circle. These are shown in A, C, drawn from Iberian examples of the coins. At the Moneta site of the Iberian Bank in Wyoming, the corresponding petroglyphs are shown in B and D. The design of B, or some similar version on other coins of Salacia, seems to be the prototype of the numerous sun circles of "medicine wheels" of Wyoming and adjacent regions of Canada and the United States. The "portrait" of the emperor, as rendered by the Wyoming engraver, is in keeping with the time-honored Celtic tradition of Britain and Iberia, namely to convert Classical busts into ludicrous caricatures as a first step to metamorphosis into some quite unpredictable end form. The archeologist who first reported on D described it as "a sort of sun symbol with a phallic design," the phallus being the emperor's nose. The other two coins and their Wyoming renderings are part of the Italian series of bronze, demonetized after the Second Punic War; like all the others depicted at the site, these would have reached North America by way of Iberia.

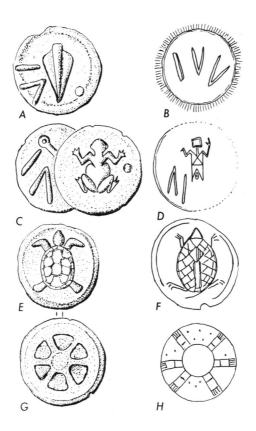

Historic Italian coinage depicted at the Moneta site of the Wyoming Bank. As the Second Punic War drew to an end about 205 B.C., the Romans placed two armies of occupation in Spain, which now became a Roman colony. The troops were mainly Italian conscripts from Campania and other districts of Italy formerly dominated by the Etruscans. Issue of the new silver *denarius* as the daily pay of a Roman soldier meant that the old heavy bronze *aes* coinage was undervalued, for ten of the bronze pieces nominally equaled one denarius. By Gresham's Law, the undervalued Italian coinage was driven out of circulation and sold as bronze bullion to the Iberians. In Iberia these pieces, or smaller imitations of them made in Spain and Portugal, now became a subsidiary colonial currency whose purchasing power was determined by local conditions. The petroglyphs on the right side, part of the advertising material at the Castle Gardens (Moneta) site in Wyoming, show that the Iberian Bank of Wyoming had introduced the discarded Italian bronze coinage into North America, where each *as* (or penny) now was equivalent to two ermine skins. On the left are shown examples of the Italian bronze coins that served as models for the Iberian coins, and their American counterparts. Traces of the original Italic inscriptions are seen in the examples B, D, from Wyoming, based on A, C, coins of the Italian city of Iguvium. It is known that the Celts of northern Italy also cast crude imitations of the Italian coins at this epoch, and it is possible that some of the models for the Wyoming petroglyphs may have been such coins. The language spoken by the customers of the Moneta Bank was Celtic, so it is conceivable that some of the colonists may have been Italian Celts.

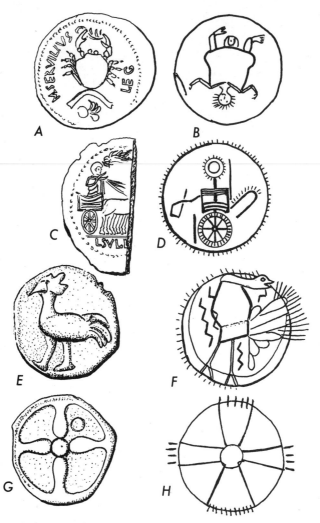

Bewilderment was the Wyoming artist's reaction to certain themes featured on the Romano-Iberian coinage. In B, the crab of the Roman model A, unknown in mid-continent, is rendered as an obese person executing a handstand. In D, a half-chariot becomes a mysterious sun god; for where no horses exist, there can be no wheeled vehicles. In F, the Old World cock of an Italian bronze piece becomes a turkey, experiencing great difficulty in fitting its ample proportions into the confines of a circular flan. In H an Italian chariot wheel becomes a cross-pattée. All designs on the right side are petroglyphs from the Moneta site of the Wyoming Iberian Bank. Those on the left side are drawn from Roman Republican and Campanian coins; Iberian examples are commonly bisected to yield lesser denominations, or "bits," as shown at C.

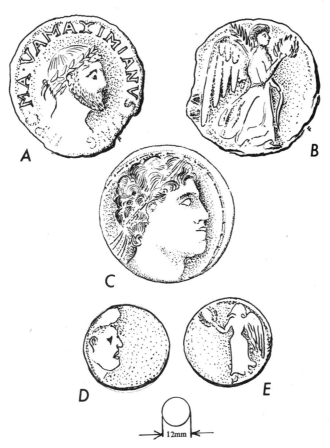

Greek, Roman, and Celtic coins found in American soil. A, B, tetradrachm of billon (a copper-silver alloy), 19 mm. diameter, struck by the Roman emperor Maximianus I in Alexandria, Egypt, in the year 288 A.D., found in a plowed field on Cherokee land in Robeson County, North Carolina, in 1951 by Jerry Maynor. The obverse, A, shows the emperor; the reverse, B, the goddess Nike (Victory) and the two signs to the lower left read "year 4" (of the reign), signifying 288 A.D. C, Bronze tetradrachm of the Greek king Antiochus IV (175–164 B.C.), struck in Syria and found in 1882 in farmland in Cass County, Illinois. The local doctor sent it to Professor F. F. Hilder, who identified it. D, E, the obverse and reverse faces of the Celtic minim, in imitation of Roman coinage, struck in Britain near the end of the Roman occupation or just after the Roman occupation, when metal was in short supply. It was found in Champaign, Illinois, in 1885, under 4 feet of undisturbed clay, during city reconstruction of a street. (Specimens submitted by Colonel Robert Vincent (A, B), and Gordon Price (D, E); determinations by Professor Norman Totten (A, B), Professor F. F. Hilder (C), and the author (D, E).)

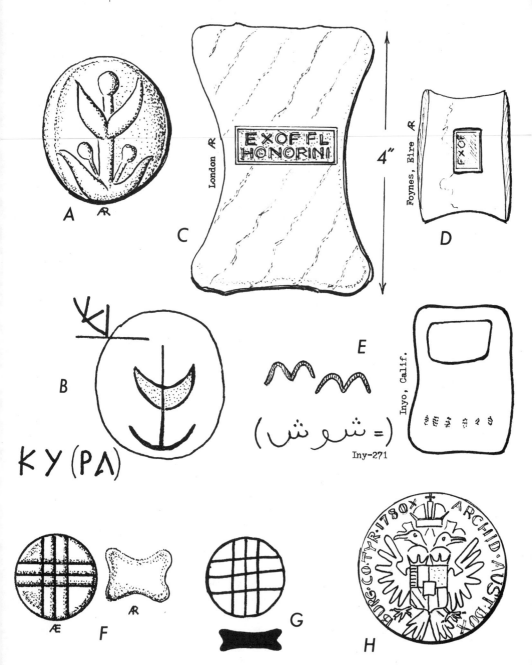

A ℞

London ℞

C

E X O F FL
HONORINI

4"

Foynes, Eire ℞

E X O F

D

B

E

Inyo, Calif.

γ

Iny-271

KY (PΛ)

(= شوش)

Æ   F

℞

G

ARCHID · AUST · DUX
BURG · CO · TYR · 1780 X

H

A ℞

C London ℞

EXOFFL HONORINI

4"

D Foynes, Eire ℞

FXOF

B

KY (PΛ)

E

Iny-271

Inyo, Calif.

F Æ ℞

G

H

Long before the flood of Roman and Iberian bronze coinage began to spread across North America to meet the demands of the expanding fur trade, Libyan explorers and colonists had settled California and Nevada, bringing with them the famous silver tetradrachms of Cyrene, in eastern Libya, on which the silphium plant was depicted, an example (from Libya) being shown here at A, dating from the fifth century B.C. The same coin appears in a Nevada petroglyph at University of California site Hu-7, near Paradise Valley, Humboldt County, as shown in B; this petroglyph carries the monogram of the Greek letters *kappa* and *upsilon,* standing for KURA, the abbreviated form of the name Cyrene, as it is given on coins. However, the Libyan settlers soon discovered the mineral wealth of Nevada, and exploited the silver mines, as the petroglyphs show. The resultant inflation drove out any bronze coinage, replaced by ingots of cast silver, as shown at E and G, both from University of California site Iny-271, Inyo County, California.

Ingots of silver, unlike those of bronze, had to carry the rectangular stamp of the assay office, as seen in the Roman example from London, shown at C, and an ancient Irish example from Foynes, shown at D. The rectangular mark appears on the Inyo petroglyph, E, and beside the carving of the ingot appear the two letters of the Libyan (and Greek) alphabets Š-Š, pronounced in Libyan Arabic as *sh-sh* (the vowel omitted). In modern Arabic, *shishi-* is the root word meaning assay-sample, and *shush* is still used in Saudi Arabia as the name of the silver Maria Theresa taler, shown at H. The Maria Theresa taler is of pure silver, and is recognized in Arabia as a universal stable currency, since it is in effect an assayed ingot. The modern Arabic rendering of *shush* is inserted at E, below the two corresponding Libyan letters.

Modern mints in London, Rome, Brussels, Bombay and—by a remarkable coincidence—San Francisco, still strike the *shush,* always bearing the date 1780, as shown at H, for use in trade with Arabia and Ethiopia. Thus, engraved on the rock of Inyo County, California, is the 2,000-year-old ancestor of the same silver coin that is occasionally struck at San Francisco to this day!

The site at Iny-271 carries other representations of coins, as shown at G, an ingot and a circular coin marked with a grid of two sets of intersecting lines, three to each set. As shown at F, the identical pattern appears in the Romano-Iberian coinage of the first century B.C. (A, drawn from the collections of the Tripoli Museum; C, in the British Museum, Romano-Celtic; B, E, G from Heizer and Baumhoff, 1962; D, after Macalister, 1977, *Archaeology of Ireland;* H, from Arabian specimens in Fell collection; F, from Victor Catala collection, after Malaquer de Motes, University of Barcelona, 1969.)

Coins and coinlike objects from Iberia, Britain, and North America. a, early Iberian coin of about the first century B.C., imitating the design of still-earlier Celtiberian "wheel-money." b, Roman Iberian coin repeating the same pattern. j, gold disk with the same pattern recovered from Upyon Lovell Barrow, England. c, d, e, g, h, i, patterns of stone disks, originally covered by thin copper sheet to simulate wheel-money, from Spiro Mound, Oklahoma. f, petroglyph in Nevada depicting wheel-money.

Ceramic imitation of coin of Evia, found in Ohio in the 1880's, and long thought to be a forgery of a "Hebrew holy stone." The inscription is given in the next illustration. Information courtesy Professor Robert Alrutz, Denison University, identification Fell. *Replica, photo Peter J. Garfall.*

Coins of Evia, A, C, D, with North American imitation in ceramic, B. In each case the inscription reads ODACIS EVIOM (currency of Evia), but the Iberian example of true origin from Evia is lettered in Latin and retrograde Iberic, whereas the Ohio copy is lettered in retrograde Greek. Below, E, carved stone token money from Tennessee (Thruston), reading in Libyan script W-F-Y-Y, L-J-W (Arabic *wafi y'aya laji'w,* Colonists pledge to redeem). F, inscription on stone disk-money, found at 4 ft depth, Cranston, Rhode Island, by Robert Renzulli, 1978, reading right-to-left H-L-N (Arabic *hulwan* money, gratuity). The script is North Iberian.

EVIA

Series 1   oo = 2 = sextans

$\Psi\, \Psi\, \Xi$ = i v E

   Cₒ = 6 = semis

Series 2
Roman   Cₒ = 6

ODACIS = currency

Celtic copies

1. Portugal

castings

2. America
Ohio

ceramics  ξΙΥΛς SIKDO

ΓΤℭΙꝯξ MOIBE

Possible sequence of coinage at Evia, in southern Portugal, with Celtic copies minted in Portugal and Ohio. Marks of value in the Iberian system of numerals, later adopted in Nevada, indicate 2 unciae—sixth part of an *as* (the sextans), and 6 unciae (half-as or semis). The *as* was the ancient Roman penny, and weighed 12 ounces before inflation during the Punic Wars led to a drastic reduction in weight.

resemble, but rather of the cruder Iberian copies of such coins, minted (with approval of Rome) for the use of Spanish and Portuguese (Lusitanian) subjects of Rome, after the Roman conquest of Spain, and the disruption of the Carthaginian empire around 200 B.C.

Numerous Iberian examples of these crude copies of Roman coins are now known from excavations in Spain and Portugal. Each of the Celtic and Iberic cities that had previously minted their own crude coinage (copied from Etruscan or Campanian models of Italy) was authorized to continue to do so under the Roman governors, for the very good reason that Rome herself was utterly unable at first to produce the flood of coins now required to meet the needs of her burgeoning empire. As the conquest of Spain and Portugal continued, during the first century B.C., Augustus renewed the minting privileges, stipulating however that the coins bear his own portrait (or a barbarous version of it carrying the words CAESAR AUGUSTUS, to identify what might otherwise be taken to be something less august). Soon afterward, Rome took over most of the minting, and Caligula canceled the minting privileges of the Iberian towns. Later, when Roman veterans established new towns in Spain, privileges to strike coin were granted again. The coins depicted at the Castle Gardens site are of the earlier vintage, of about 20 B.C., which is probably the date of the establishment of the First National Bank of Wyoming. The exchange rate is shown on one of the designs: two ermine (weasels) equal one *as* (a bronze penny). The other designs denote the equivalence of many different coin designs, mainly the large bronze *as*, and its later replacement based on the Roman *denarius*.

These pictorial presentations of current coin in ancient America were evidently intended to familiarize the fur trappers and others doing business with the Iberian banks as to the relative values of coins in terms of one another, and in terms of skins. They may be compared with the tables of relative values issued from time to time by governors, or others in authority, in nineteenth-century colonies, where foreign coin was the only currency available, apart from homemade bills of exchange. For example, in Hawaii in 1867 (when the future state was called the Sandwich Islands), the following rates of exchange were in operation:

Napoleon or 5-franc piece of France is valued at	1 dollar
Gold doubloon of Bolivia and Chile	15 dollars
Eagle of the United States	10 dollars
Sovereign of England and Australia	4.75 dollars
20-dollar piece of California	19.5 dollars
5-dollar piece of California	4.5 dollars

In this same year, various comparable tables were issued by the then independent authorities of Nova Scotia, New Brunswick, Newfoundland, and the various island administrations of the West Indies. Even at that late date, silver dollars were so scarce that Mexican pieces of 8 reales were used in their place in islands and provinces where either U.S. or British currency was legal coin of the realm, and island administrations were obliged to continue the practice of cutting the Mexican coin into halves, quarters, or one-eighth parts, to yield silver in smaller denominations or "bits." In the British islands of Jamaica, Antigua, and others, the fragmented slices of dollar were known as "bills," and as many as 9, 10, or 12 bills went to the dollar, depending on the particular island and its degree of coin-starvation.

We may infer that similar problems arose in ancient Spain and America. The Iberian soil has yielded up many examples of Roman coins cut into halves, and the designs depicted in some American pictographs comprise only one-half of a known Roman coin pattern. It is evident that the problems of currency deficiency have remained the same throughout the ages of all newly established colonial regimes. If the newly legalized Roman currency of Iberia was in severe short supply in the first century of the Roman occupation, after the expulsion of the Carthaginians in 203 B.C., as the bisected coins and other emergency tokens imply, the problems were compounded across the Atlantic. For here the Celtiberian colonists were experiencing a rapidly growing demand for their furs from a Roman market suddenly grown rich and luxurious with the spoils of conquest. Iberia, itself short of coin, was the sole source of coins for emigrants who had settled the Iberian colonies in North America. Further, as cultural and trade contacts increased between the native Amerindians and the Iberian colonists, now in process of integration with them, a further need was felt for currency to aid internal trade within the American settlements.

We know from surviving records of court cases pleaded by Demosthenes that the ancient Greek banking houses operated the system called in England, in the Middle Ages, "bottomry"; that is to say, a banker would advance the funds needed by a trader to set out on a voyage of promising, but uncertain, prospects; in return the banker was entitled to one-half share of all profits. If the voyage was a failure, or the ship was lost, the banker lost his investment. The many court cases concerned knavery on the part of skippers who would endeavor to land their cargo at some other port, and so avoid paying back the bankers' share, or who would pretend to have lost their ship when they had sold it at another port. The international maritime law to curb such malpractices that grew up between the Greek states was inherited by Rome, whose banking houses continued the system of financing ventures by bottomry. Evidently Catalan Greeks introduced bottomry to Iberia, and finally established branch banks in the American colonies of Iberia.

In southeastern Spain, ancient Greek colonists had settled Catalonia and parts of Valencia. In *America B.C.* I have already cited examples of the kind of trade agreements that Greek and Iberian merchants, bankers, and their lawyers contrived. With the passage of time, and the transfer of power from Carthage to Rome, it appears that Greek banking houses now began to take an interest in the prospects of mercantile ventures in America. At all events, it seems significant that on the oldest banker's tile so far discovered in North America, although the language is Celtic, the actual name (or slogan) of the bank is given in Greek—as if the mother house of the firm were some Catalan Greek establishment, while the customers on the other hand were Gaelic-speaking Celtiberian trappers. North America became, in effect, a group of self-administered colonies of Iberia, on the Greek model.

It is clear that the customers of the Wyoming Bank used Gaelic (Celtiberian Gadelic) as their main language, otherwise the advertising would not have been in that language. But it is equally clear that most of the customers could not read; otherwise the notices of coin equivalence would not have been set out pictorially. I believe that both native Amerindians, Celts from Portugal and Spain, and descendants of the earlier Celtiberian settlers of New England, with their Amerindian wives and families, formed the ancient community of fur trappers who met at Moneta to do business with the bank. The situation seems to be essentially that of the early nineteenth century, after the Oregon Trail was opened up; and fur trappers could come from all directions to meet once a year at a fur market in Wyoming, whence their skins would be dispatched abroad by the dealers.

When Lewis and Clark reached the Pacific in Oregon, they found that the local Indians knew a number of (rather colorful) English words and deduced that they acquired them from English-speaking traders in furs who, according to the Indians, arrived periodically by sea from the southwest, purchased all the available furs, and sailed off in the same direction. Dr. John Bakeless, the authority on Lewis and Clark, deduces that the markets for these furs were in China, where the dealers exchanged the Oregon cargo for silk, and then took off for Europe to sell the silk.

It is significant that circular petroglyphs found in California and Nevada depict the designs found on ancient Chinese coins of the Han dynasty, which was contemporary with Republican Rome and the early Roman Empire. They also depict later Chinese coins, as of the Sung dynasty. It seems very probable, therefore, that the entire economic structure of the western fur trade in Classical times paralleled very closely that which it had in the nineteenth century. Bankers financed the dealers who shipped the furs both West and East, destined for markets in the Mediterranean and in China. The demand was strong: houses were not generally well heated, and wealthy Romans—and Iberians—liked comfort. The Chinese winters are severe in regions where the ancient and modern capitals were established, and China itself could not meet the demands for furs from native hunters. Imports were needed, and America provided the goods.

Our whole idea that America was an unknown continent 2,000 years ago is false. It was a busy trading area, with shipping on both coasts. Its major exports were furs and skins for the leather trade.

Castle Gardens, the first ancient banking site to be identified, was obviously not alone. In all probability the west Arkansas site that Gloria Farley and I had jokingly called the Grand Bank of Iberia was indeed just that—the inscriptions are too fragmentary to do more at present than identify the site as a banking location. It is significant that west Arkansas has already yielded one Carthaginian coin to the searching antenna of Jesse Ray Kelley's metal detector. Possibly the west Arkansas site may have been a yet earlier Carthaginian bank. The Colorado petroglyphs that match Byzantine coinage probably mark the presence nearby of a bank that dealt with Levantine currency, during the Middle Ages, both Arab and Greek; for, as shown in later chapters, Byzantine Greek and Islamic inscriptions abound—all of them hitherto mistaken for Indian "curvilinear" signs.

By following the trail of the mysterious Roman coins across America I have overshot the course of history by leading into the West Coast sites where the Libyans had founded a maritime community, settlements of sea dogs who traded with the kingdoms of China and India, and who had done so since the third century B.C., as their coinage tells us.

Before resuming the West Coast story, which requires, by way of introduction, an account of how the West Coast came to be discovered and settled, there are also some omissions on the Atlantic coast that need attention. Coins do not deliver themselves, nor do bankers appear spontaneously without some evident form of transmission. More needs to be said about what others were doing while Rome was conquering the Western world. Conquests imply displaced people and land-robbed farmers, often also a hungry native population whose crops have been seized by the conqueror. Such displaced people often form the reserve of labor for distant colonies, whose founders beckon encouragingly to those in bondage, offering a bright vision of freedom to any who will dare to join them across the sea. The forebears of nearly all Americans felt the urge to escape to a New World. I now examine such evidence on this matter as antiquity affords.

8

Refuge America

For over 2,000 years America has served as a place of refuge for Old World communities driven from their homes by conquest or persecution. A situation only too well known in modern times, it would appear to reflect a historic role of the New World through much of recorded history. Not without justice does the Statue of Liberty bear the immortal lines penned by Emma Lazarus as she watched the immigrants stream ashore in 1903:

> Send these, the homeless, tempest-tost to me,
> I lift my lamp beside the golden door.

A curious clay tablet found in a rock crevice near Big Bend, Texas (page 165) apparently tells us that Zoroastrians, followers of Mithraic sun worship, came once to America, seemingly from Iberia, though whether as refugees or not we cannot tell. More striking are the evidences from Tennessee and Kentucky, where the combined efforts of Dr. Henriette Mertz, Professors Cyrus Gordon and Cyclone Covey, and Dr. Robert Stieglitz, have given us the outlines of an immigration there of homeless Jews after the several pogroms of Antiochus in Syria, and Nero and Hadrian in Rome. Evidently some Hebrews were already here in 69 A.D., when the First Revolt of Jerusalem against the Romans occurred. Josephus, who took part in the revolt, tells us that through the year 69 A.D. a great comet hung like a flaming sword over Jerusalem. The Zealots took it to be the sign of the coming of the promised Messiah and rebelled. Astronomers say that it was the regular return of Halley's Comet. A stone excavated from a burial mound in Tennessee at Bat Creek tells us that Jews in Tennessee recognized the sign and inscribed the stone "The Comet for the Jews." Scattered

In 1962 in a rock crevice in Big Bend National Park, Texas, Donald Uzzell discovered this ceramic tablet (sunbaked, not fired) in eleven fragments. It is written in a variant of Libyan alphabetic script, except for the repeated refrain in line 6, which uses first Lycian, then Lydian letters to repeat the word given in Libyan on line 5 (D-U-A, "Heal us"). The upper section reads left to right, the part below the horizontal broken line is written in boustrophedon, each line reversing its direction. The approximate translation is: (1) Why this suffering (2) Oh, what anguish (3) A call to prayer, 29th (4) December, Year 6 (5) Heal us (6) Heal us, Heal us. (7) "The faithful are beset (8) by sorrows. Guide, O Mithras (8) Show forth (9) thy strength and (10) promise of aid (11) as revealed by (12) Ahuramazda." The lower section appears to be a quotation copied from some other document written in boustrophedon. This evidence of Mithraism is of interest in view of the apparent Mithraic religion of the lower Mississippi tribes as described by early French travelers. *Photo Charles and Bernice Nickles.*

Historian Professor Cyclone Covey of Wake Forest University, who has drawn attention to evidences of Old World connections in various parts of North America by way of inscriptions and coins, and references in Chinese manuscripts. *Photo McNab, Wake Forest University.*

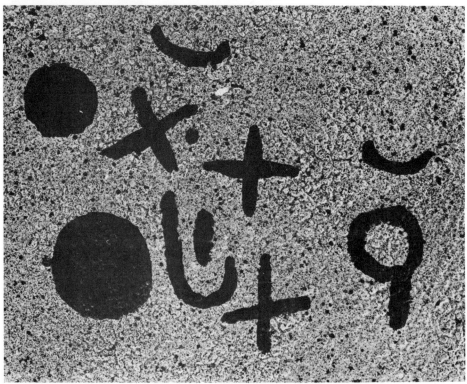

Abbreviated version of the Ten Commandments written in a form of Phoenician or early Hebrew script showing Greek influence. It is inscribed by scraping off the dark desert varnish, to disclose the lighter bedrock beneath, and has changed little if any during the past century. It is located at Las Lunas, near Albuquerque, New Mexico, and has been the object of study by the late Professor Robert Pfeiffer of the Semitic Museum, Harvard University. To left, Mark Totten. *Photo Professor Norman Totten.*

Opposite page: This ancient Andean inscription was collected and published without decipherment by Dr. Hans Disselhof, Berlin Museum of Ethnology. The script is early Iberic, in which the cross symbol is read as D (instead of T, as in Phoenician or Hebrew). The text is (1) '-D-D Shamas (sun-symbol) (2) Q-D-SH Shamas (sun-symbol), and translates as "God is the Sun, Sacred is the Sun." As the word *qodesh* (sacred) is usually regarded as Hebrew, it is possible that the Black circular sun-symbol is a mystic sign for Yahweh, in which case the inscription is to be regarded as Iberian Hebrew.

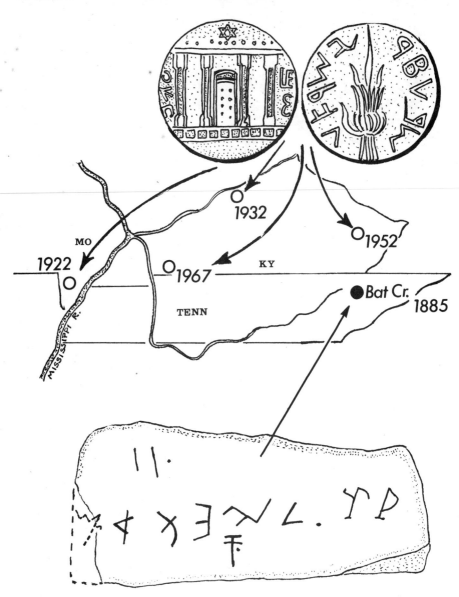

Above, the silver shekel of the Second Revolt of Israel against the Romans, 132–135 A.D., reading *Simeon* on the obverse (left), and *Deliverance of Israel* on the reverse. Reported find sites for this and related coins are shown for Kentucky and east Arkansas. Below, the Bat Creek stone from Tennessee, supposed by the Smithsonian finders to be Cherokee, but recognized by all Hebrew scholars who have studied it as a Hebrew text of the first century A.D. Dr. Robert Stieglitz of New York reads it as "A comet for the Hebrews," with reference to Halley's Comet, which "hung over Jerusalem like a flaming sword" in the year 69 A.D., during the First Revolt, begun in 68 under Nero. The evidence suggests that Kentucky and Tennessee became havens of refuge for persecuted Hebrews after the various revolts against Syrian Greek and Roman oppression. Dr. Joseph Mahan is investigating Hebrew religious ceremonies found among the Yuchi Indians of the Southeast.

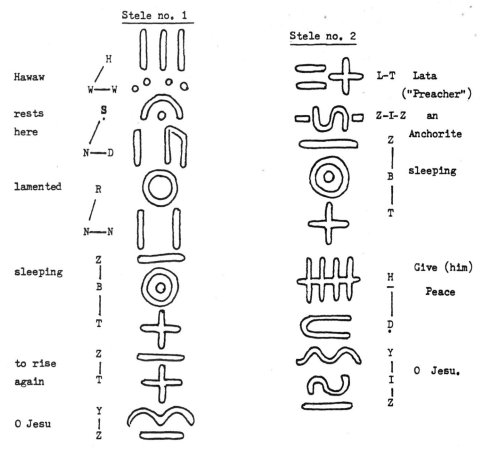

Stele no. 1

Hawaw
H
/
W——W

rests

here

S
.
/
N——D

lamented

R
/
N——N

sleeping

Z
|
B
|
T

to rise

again

Z
|
T

O Jesu

Y
|
Z

Stele no. 2

L-T   Lata
       ("Preacher")

Z-I-Z   an

Z   Anchorite

|

B   sleeping

|

T

H   Give (him)

-    Peace

D
.

Y
|
I   O Jesu.
|
Z

Inscriptions on two memorial steles of early Christians collected at Rabat, Morocco, by Professor Norman Totten. The script is Libyan, the language Libyan Arabic, antedating the Moslem invasion of the seventh century A.D., after which Kufic script was adopted.

Following left: Fifth-century inscription in Libyan Arabic at Figuig Oasis, east Morocco, recording the flight to find refuge in North America of Christian monks persecuted by the Vandals. (Inscription received from James Whittall, decipherment Fell.)

Following right: Continuation of the Figuig inscription.

(a,b)   L—q—(b)   z—w—y   m—l   s—t—t

In the name of the hermitage of the fraternity now dispersed abroad,

l—q—(b)   r—b—b—n   s—r   t

(b,c) and in the name of the Cross of the Divine Sacrament, by oath sworn

b—1   R—z   t—w—i   B—1   Y—Z—H—S

(c) to Christ the Lord, of the world emperor crowned   Lord   Jesus:

w——z   h—y—h   1—y   b—r

(d) The Testimony of an eye-witness who has returned home   (e)   by ship

z—r   T—th   t—g—r   w—t—n   t—n y—d

(e,f) that put in to Teth(wan) sea port; now in his homeland a second time,

f—n—y   t—a   m—h—1   h—n   z—1—b

(f,g) ended are the years of trouble; filled with compassion for the havoc wrought

Z—r—r—w—1   m—y—y—z

(g) by the "Trousered-Men" (i.e. Teutons) of that distinguishing characteristic;

q—r   h—1—1—q   q   W—n—t—1   z—r—y

(h,i) We were struck by total ruin in the shape of the Vandals, a contemptible

Note: On account of the shape of the rock face the scribe is compelled to change direction from horizontal to vertical, and back to horizontal lines. This, in accordance with Libyan rules, causes the signs for w & l, z & n, to interchange, and other signs change their form.

d—n—n—z—y   M—h

(i) race of no consequence.   They destroyed

n—r   w   y—d—s

(i) by fire Oh how much! (j) robbing property

z—t   m—n   1—q—y—a   g—r

(j) and stores   (k) an affliction as unbearable as the cutting edge of a sword.

+ — ooo ||| ⊥　　　◯　　　　O — — o ∨
t — z q—h—f　　　　　　　　R— z— z — i — ḍ

(k) The misery engulfed the whole world.　(l) Followers of the True Faith

E ΙΝ ᵒₒᵒ　　　　�〜 —卅— 　||| +
th— y　k　　　　　Y—Z—H— Z　　H—T !

(l) as good as fled into exile,　(m) O Jesus, grant them thy Peace!

〜 × ≣ ≡　　　　— ooo ᴗᴗ ᴗ ≡　　　O — — ooo
B— t　h—l　　　(A) Z— Q S̆ —M—L　　　r—z — z — q

(n) They decided to sail away to Asqa-S̆amal (North-Land) to seek a livelihood

O ||| + — ||| ◌　　　　Ш ⌐ooo ᴗ /〜ᴗ—
r —h —t　z—h—r　　　　Th—d q— m—n y—m—z

(n) where the sun sets in the evening.　(o) They prepared suitable dried fruits

X ᴜᴡɰᴏᴜ ∩　　　　ᒋ ⊔ ≡　　　〜ᵅ +
t— m y—th—r—m—d　　N— m— l　　　y—f—t

(o) to last a long time.　(p) They calibrated with numbers a plaque (?Cross-staff)

ooo 〜 —　　+ ooo　— ᒋ　　　O
q— y—z　　t—q　z—n　　　r

(q) for measurements　exact　of the elevation　of the sun.

⤫ O ooo ||| X　　≡ —　　　ਠ ooo　ooo ||| oo
T—r—q h—t　　l—z　　　f—q　q— h—w

(r) Sailed away from the coast the united company, (s) trying to curb their appetite:

+ ooo ||| oo + I ᴎ °　°ₒ　— ⊺ O Ш ooo
t—q h—w t—n—y w　　w　z—t r　th—q

(s,t) Carefully they counted also how many times the sun rose and shone (i.e, days).

⊤ ᴗ ||| (elision) ⌐　　+ ooo　　ooo oo
T—y—h　　h'—g　　t—q　　q—w

(u) Across the trackless wastes their Chief precisely directed (v) the helmsmen

O ⊔ —　　　— ooo o O　　O ⊥ ≡
r—m—z　　z—q—i—r　　r—h—l

(v) by his secret calculations (w) on the correct track. (x) They journeyed on

(x) contented with their lot, far away (y) to that land, inspired with zeal.

(y) They reached their destination and into the wilderness ventured. (z) The void

(z) of surging waves they had overcome by adhering to their plan. (A) Pray for

(A) our friends, each one. Bless them (B) O Jesus!

Conclusion of the Figuig inscription.

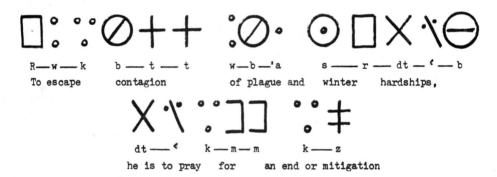

R—w—k   b—t—t   w—b—'a   s——r—dt—ʿ—b
To escape   contagion   of plague and   winter   hardships,

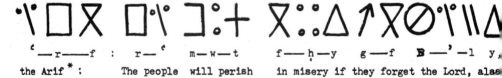

dt——ʿ   k—m—m   k——z
he is to pray   for   an end or mitigation

ʿ——r——f : r—ʿ   m—w—t   f—h—y   g—f   B—'—l y,
the Arif* :   The people will perish   in misery if they forget the Lord, alas

*Arif - precentor in charge of a small congregation lacking
an ordained priest of the North African Coptic Church.

Early Christian inscription in Libyan script, Libyan Arabic dialect, found
at Oak Island, Nova Scotia in 1803. The engraved stone was mistakenly
thought to mark the position of hidden treasure. (Decipherment Fell,
copy of inscription received from Phyllis Donohue.)

"Yasus ben Maria" (Jesus was the Son of Mary), a petroglyph recorded by Professors Heizer and Baumhoff from a site discovered by Professor Julian Steward at his site 41, in Inyo County, California. Although the inscription refers to Jesus, the phrase "Son of Mary" is found in several surahs of the Koran, so the text may be Moslem. A Christian might be expected to have written "Mary was the Mother of Jesus," or "Jesus was the Son of God." This text, deciphered by Fell and confirmed by competent Arab scholars, has been dismissed by one archeological journal as "an obvious attempt (by Fell) to appeal to the religious." But in fact neither the antiquity of the inscription, nor its translation, is disputed by leading archeologists. The style of Kufi script implies a probable date of about 800 A.D. Replica, after Heizer and Baumhoff. *Photo Peter J. Garfall and Dr. F. Julian Fell.*

Kyrie eléison

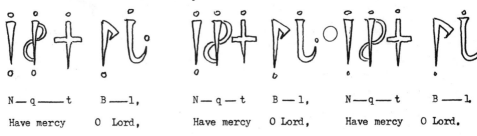

N — q —— t	B —1,	N — q — t	B — 1,	N—q— t	B ——1,
Have mercy	O Lord,	Have mercy	O Lord,	Have mercy	O Lord.

Wooden slats, about a foot long and 2 inches wide, engraved with symbols, were found to be in use as "Prayer sticks" among the Kikapu Algonquians by George Catlin, in 1831, and one of his portraits of that year shows Chief Mashina in the act of praying, holding one of the sticks. A specimen of a Kikapu prayer-stick, now in the Smithsonian Institution, was examined by Oliver La Farge, president of the Association of American Indian Affairs, and he commented in May 1957 "Its highly simplified symbols suggest that the Kickapoos had made important steps toward developing a system of writing." In actual fact, the inscription (illustrated above) proves to be the *Kyrie eleison* of the ancient North African Christian mass, rendered in dextral script of the late Punic language of Carthage. Inscriptions in this alphabet and language can be found in Libya, where the Carthaginians fled after the destruction of the city. The presence of Carthaginian coins in American soil at widely separated localities, and some Punic inscriptions cut on rock, make it virtually certain that the *Kyrie* was imparted to the Kikapu tribe by Carthaginian Christians in ancient times. The dots are probably decorative, as in Libyan Islamic texts. Ancient Libya had become Christian (in the cities) by 200 A.D., but the persecutions under Diocletian (284–304) witnessed Christians being thrown to the lions in the arena in Leptis Magna, where Punic inscriptions are now to be seen. Perhaps refugees from North Africa at this date came to find peace among the Kikapu people of Wisconsin.

Where ancient American Christians once celebrated the mass according to the order of the North African Church. The four key phrases in Libyan script, Arabic language, are (1) *The Consecration* (of the Host), (2) *The Elevation* (of the Host), (3) *The Communion*, (4) *are the Ritual of the Mass.* This inscription was found at Kelso Valley, Inyo County, California, by Campbell Grant (1968). Unlike some other references to Christian beliefs shared by Moslems, this text by its explicit Arabic-Christian vocabulary, was the work of early American Christians, probably contemporary with the priest Paladis of Colorado, second half of the first millennium A.D.

Memorial stele in slightly illiterate North African Greek of the Byzantine period, found at Cripple Creek, Colorado, recording that: "Herein is the last resting place of Palladis, the servant of God." The use of an omega (long o) for the definite article, instead of omicron (short o), is a peculiarity found in Coptic Greek. *Replicated from tracing supplied by Gloria Farley. Photo Peter J. Garfall, Dr. Julian Fell.*

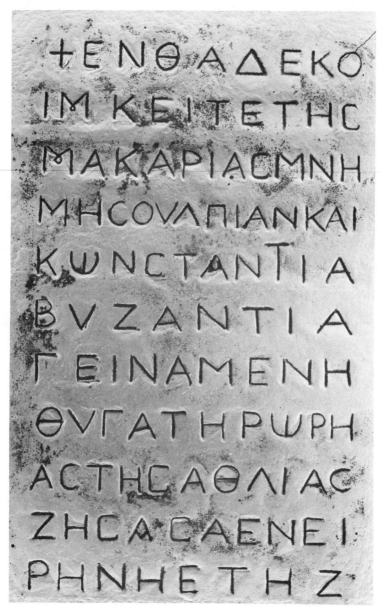

+ΕΝΘΑΔΕΚΟ
ΙΜΚΕΙΤΕΤΗϹ
ΜΑΚΑΡΙΑϹΜΝΗ
ΜΗϹΟΥΛΠΙΑΝΚΑΙ
ΚⲰΝϹΤΑΝΤΙΑ
ΒΥΖΑΝΤΙΑ
ΓΕΙΝΑΜΕΝΗ
ΘΥΓΑΤΗΡⲰΡΗ
ΑϹΤΗϹΑΘΛΙΑϹ
ΖΗϹΑϹΑΕΝΕΙ
ΡΗΝΗΕΤΗΖ

Memorial stele inscribed in North African Greek, using similar phrase-ology to that of the Colorado stele, recording the last resting place of the seven-year-old daughter of Ulpian, born in Byzantium and who died of an illness in Constantine. *Photo Peter J. Garfall.*

Nevada Greek and North African Greek show similar epigraphic peculiarities. After the coming of Islam to North Africa, the Greeks of that region not infrequently adopted the Arabic convention of writing from right to left, the individual letters being reversed. A, the name Zachariou so written on a Coptic embroidery of sixth to eighth century A.D., in the Victoria and Albert Museum, London. B, short inscriptions frequently had the letters in a disordered sequence, as in the name Isaac, here spelled with an extra A and placed sideways on a tapestry of the fourth to fifth century A.D. from Egypt, now in the Cooper Union Museum, New York, and depicting the sacrifice of Isaac. Note the triplication of the letter A. C, the epigraphy of this Bawit mural of the eighth century A.D. shows disregard for upper- and lower-case distinctions, long o (omega) and short o (omicron) are confused, e is used where i should occur, in spelling the name of the saint or monk MAKARIOS. This semibarbarous style of writing North African Greek is reflected in west American inscriptions, where similar derangements become apparent.

D, From a fragment of a lesson on map projection given at Lagomarsino site St-1, Storey County, Nevada, the phrase E Polo (from the pole). E, Early Christian art in Douglas County, Nevada draws its inspiration from Byzantine coinage, as shown by the inscription to the left IC XC (Iesos Christos). F, The abbreviated Greek word Leipso (waning) superimposed upon the figure of a crescent moon, at Lagomarsino site, Nevada. G, At the same site, Lagomarsino, Nevada, the same inscription again accompanied by a crescent moon, but this time the word LIPS-OPHOSS (waning-moon, for Greek Leipso-phos) is spelled in part from right to left, and in part from left to right. Site data from Heizer and Baumhoff (1962), decipherment by Fell.

A North African Greek-speaking Christian of the Byzantine era finds refuge in Oklahoma. One of the outstanding field discoveries of Gloria Farley in the 1978 season is the fine inscription on the Cimarron cliffs, written in the vernacular North African Greek in vogue in cities like Cyrene and Constantine. The abbreviated text is to be read as AIT(OMAI) EMILI(A)NU(S) TMĒD (ĒN). It translates as "I, Emilianus, lay claim by [right of] cutting this inscription." Emilianus was a Christian, as shown by the manner in which he has cut the letter T to form a Greek cross (which is the letter T in Punic script of Carthage). Disregarding any pre-existing Amerindian claims to this piece of Oklahoma, he is exercising the ancient common-law right of claiming ownership of something found, apparently ownerless, by cutting one's name on it. This ancient law is still invoked in northern lands, as when, for example, a whale is washed ashore dead, or a valuable tree trunk. The first finder may claim it. The British and Federal governments acknowledge the legality, and invoke the same law if the claimant fails to remove the object—he is then liable for the full cost of removal as if, for example, the whale decays and becomes a public nuisance before the claimant has extracted the oil or baleen.

The manner in which the letter L is formed (of two parallel bars) shows that the script of Emilianus is that of a Libyan Greek. And the double dots on the letter I show that he lived in the Byzantine era. The reversal of the letters N and D reflect the inconsistent style of the Dark Ages, when scripts tended to revert to the crude styles in use before the rise of Classical civilization. The Moslems changed all this. Believing that the Koran was the sacred word of God Himself, the Islamic schools trained the finest epigraphers, and soon after the mid-seventh century, North African inscriptions assumed a very beautiful and decorative form—but, the script and language was now Arabic. Gloria Farley's original tracing from this inscription is 5 feet across; the words are arranged in a single line, each letter about 3 to 4 inches high. To fit the page, here the words are arranged in three lines.

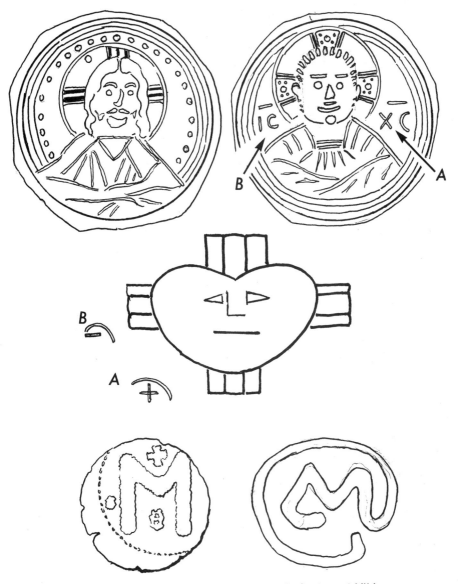

Byzantine coins were widely circulated by both Arab and Viking users. Those depicted are (upper left) Constantine VIII, 1025–1028 A.D., and Alexius III, 1195–1203 A.D. The latter piece, of debased silver, or one similar to it must have served as the model of the Nevada petroglyph, shown below, located 2 miles east of Genoa, Douglas County, engraved on granite boulders. The discoverers, Elsasser and Conreras, omitted to note the Byzantine Greek lettering on the petroglyph, marked A and B, corresponding to the Byzantine coin, and identifying the portrait as Iesos Christos. These, and similar matches between Islamic coin designs and North American petroglyphs, make it probable that either Arab or Viking mariners brought medieval coinage to western North America. Below, Byzantine *follis* (a bronze coin), and right, Nevada petroglyph apparently based on it.

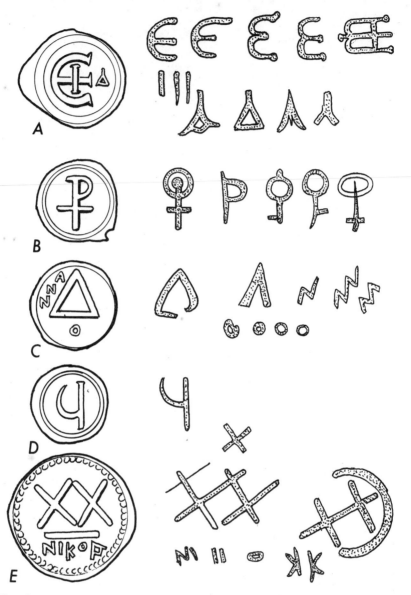

Five Byzantine copper coins appear to be the source of a great part of the repetitive "curvilinear" signs reported by Heizer and Baumhoff (1962) from the single site Grimes Ch-3, Churchill County, Nevada. The symbols are in fact all letters of the Greek alphabet, or conjunct (double) forms as used on ancient coinage. To the left, from above downward: A, 5 nummia piece of Constantinople, Justinian I, 527–565 A.D. B, One nummion, same emperor. C, Three-quarter follis, Constantinople, Heraclius, 610–641 A.D. D, five nummia piece of Phocas, 602–610 A.D. E, half-follis, same emperor. Thus all the associated signs at the Grimes site are consistent as to date, derived from coins that were circulating in the early part of the seventh century, prior to the Islamic era. Data in part from Byzantine coins lent by Colonel Robert Vincent, Oklahoma, and from Heizer and Baumhoff (1962), interpretation Fell.

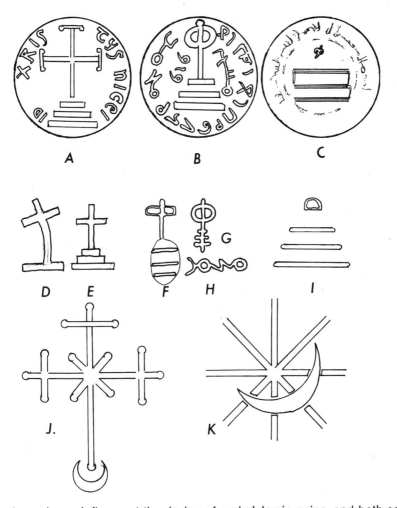

Byzantine coinage influenced the design of early Islamic coins, and both coinages, in turn, influenced the petroglyph artists of western North America. A, coin of the Byzantine emperor Leo IV, 775–780 A.D., showing a popular cross-on-steps motif; the lettering reads "Christ conquers." This coin was used by both Viking and Arab traders, and also became the model of B, issued by Arabs at the end of the eighth century, the cross being now converted to a different shape to avoid Christian connotations; the inscription in Kufic reads "God is One: Mohamed: minted at Manbij." C, dirhem of Khalif Harun-ar-Rashid, 786–809 A.D., in which the Kufic script has assumed the form of the motif. Below are North American petroglyphs that match these. D, Grimes site, Nevada (Heizer and Baumhoff), E, Texas, (University of Texas). F, Inyo–267, University of California. G, Valley of Fire, Nevada, Atlatl Rock. H, name Mohamed, sometimes written across the motif, as at G. I, Cimarron cliffs, Oklahoma (Farley). J, During the reign of Basil II, 976–1025 A.D., a new motif occupied most of the flan of Byzantine silver coins, a chi cross super-imposed on the cross-crosslet, the whole supported by a crescent moon. K, Cor-responding motif from site N.M. 50, Colorado (Reynaud), the crescent moon now transferred to cover the chi-cross. These American developments may be com-pared with analogous trends in early Islamic epigraphy as discussed, for example, by Norman Totten in *Origins of Islamic Coinage*, Monograph of the India-Asiatic Numismatic Society, 1973.

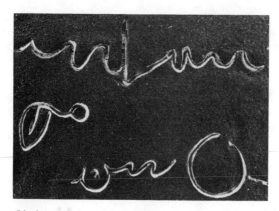

Shaitan maha mayan, Satan is the fount of lies, reads this Classical Kufi Arabic inscription, some two feet across, on a boulder on the west slope of Boundary Peak, in the White Mountains near Benton, on the border of Nevada and California. The style of script indicates a date after the seventh century A.D., and the unknown scribe was a Moslem. The inscription was discovered in 1951. It is probably to be associated with Gladwin's Red Pottery people, who entered the Plateau from the south around 700 A.D. Inscriptions of this type point to a second incursion of Arabic speakers, arriving from the Middle East by way of a trans-Pacific crossing. *Replica, photo Peter J. Garfall.*

Opposite page above: When Christianity came to the New England peoples, early in the Roman Imperial era, some of the old pagan stone temples were taken over by monks. This inscription, on the wall of a large chamber in Vermont shows the Christogram overlying (and therefore post-dating) the older pagan Celtic sun-grid (see *America B.C.*) The Christogram is made from a combination of the Greek letters Chi and Rho, standing for Christos, and in the early form shown here the sign resembles a capital P with a cross bar. Below, to the left is A or Alpha, and to the extreme lower right are traces of an Omega. Between the Alpha and Omega are the Greek letters IC XP (Iesos Christos). Above is the Greek word ANTP, standing for *Antron* (grotto or cavern). Following the example of Saint Patrick in Ireland, the New England missionaries engraved the sacred monogram on heathen stones and buildings, thus purifying them for use for Christian worship. Traced from cast of original, discovered by Fell and John Williams, 1976.

Opposite page below: Inscriptions that are relics of the earliest Christian phases in New England are widespread. All examples shown occur in Connecticut, generally on or near sites where the old pagan stone chambers occur. a from near Groton, and b-f from the New Haven area (exact locations omitted on account of the risk of vandals until official protection can be put into effect). The abbreviations used are: IC (Iesos or Jesus); XP (Christos, as in figures c and f, the so-called Chi-Rho monogram); M and MA (Maria); and in f we see the combination IC XP Alpha and Omega. The custom of burning candles in honor of the Virgin Mary and other Christian saints was fostered by the Emperor Justinian early in the sixth century A.D. In the examples b, c, d, e, f, the letters are formed from cupules cut into the horizontal surface of large rocks, and it appears obvious that they either held candles or served as small oil lamps, so that the sacred monograms were illuminated during the services. The Festival of Candlemass (February 2) is the modern survival of these ancient customs. As some of the cupule patterns from

pagan times form outlines of the stars of the polar constellations, it would now seem reasonable to infer that they, too, held candles, thus displaying illuminated depictions of the stars above. The use of Greek lettering by the earliest Christians of North America does not mean necessarily that Greek missionaries were involved. Rather it is an American reflection of the situation in Roman times in Iberia and in Britain, where the Chi-Rho and other Greek symbols also were employed, possibly as a means of avoiding drawing too much attention in a Latin official environment while Christians were still liable to persecution. a, found by David Barron; b-f, found by Frederick J. Pohl and John Gallagher, identifications by Fell.

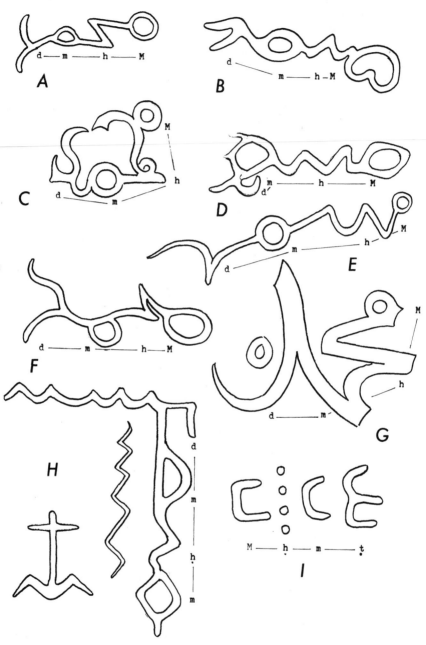

Various epigraphic renderings of the name of the Prophet Mohamed. A, El-Ain Lahag (Morocco). B, East Walker River, Univ. Calif. Site Ly-i (Nevada) C, Formal decorative Kufic, El-Merj Mosque, Barqa (Libya), ca. 925 A.D., D, E, Churchill County, University of California site Ch-71 (Nevada). F, El-Haji Mimoun, El-Ain Sefra (Morocco). G, Decorative Naskhi style, Ceramic painting, purchased El-Suq, Tripoli. H, Cottonwood Canyon, site Mi-2 University of California, Nevada. Name of Prophet combined with rain symbols and praying man. I, In Tifinag script, southeast Algeria, near Libyan border (Mission Lhote).

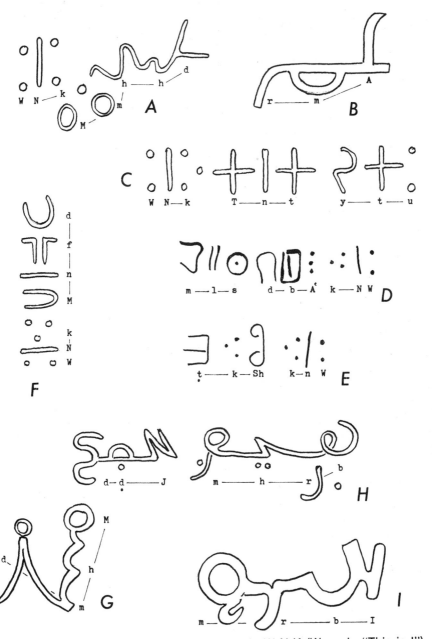

Berber autographs, all beginning with the formula W N-K (Wa nak, "This is I"), followed by the actual name. A, Wa Nak Mm-hh-d (This is I, Mohamed, misspelled), Garfield Flat, Nevada, University of California site Mi-4, Heizer and Baumhoff. C, Wa Nak Tanat Yatu (SE Algeria, near Libyan border). D, from letter, reads right-to-left, Wa Nak 'Abdeslem (Algerian Berber). E, (from letter) Wa Nak Shikat (Algeria). H, Road from Ashla to Shelala, Gery, Morocco, Kufic, Ibrahim Jedhdi. (G. B. Flamand). F, reads vertically upward, Wa Nak manfad (This is I, Manfad), Wad Sufait, SE Algeria, Mission Lhote. B, Amr ("Chief" or "Captain"), Grimes Site University of California Ch-3, Nevada Heizer and Baumhof. G, Mohamed, in Naskhi script (cf. Fig. G.) Same site as F. I. Ibra(h)im, Hidden Cave, Churchill County, University of California site Ch-6, Nevada Heizer and Baumhoff.

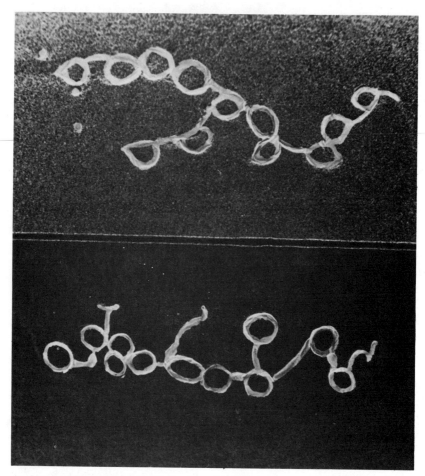

In North Africa illiterate Bedouin tribesmen engrave petroglyphs that comprise chains of connected circles, sometimes intermingled with Libyan or Kufic inscriptions. It is self-evident that the chains of circles are imitations of the most conspicuous letters of the Kufic alphabet, namely the letters M and H, and that the petroglyphs are simulated writing. The upper portion of the figure shows such a chain of circles from Bu Lariac, Sahara, after Catalan et al. (1974). The lower part of the figure shows a corresponding petroglyph, recorded by Heizer and Baumhoff from the East Walker River site in Nevada (University of California Berkeley site Ly-1) (1962). Classified in the American nomenclature as "Curvilinear type 10, Connected Circles," the name may well be retained, since it does not in fact conceal any alphabetic writing as is the case with most other of the Curvilinear series. *Photo Dr. Julian Fell from replicas in the Epigraphic Museum.*

Dr. Ali Khushaim, Islamic historian, vice president of UNESCO, and Professor of Education in the Libyan Studies Center of the University of Tripoli, on one of his visits to the Epigraphic Society and National Decipherment Center. *Photo Peter J. Garfall.*

"Ismi Allah," In the name of God, the opening phrase of every chapter of the Koran, and a favorite subject for Islamic epigraphy. Above, as engraved on Nevada bedrock, and decorated with hieroglyphs depicting the mountains (center, above), lakes (above, right) and cactus (above, left). Beneath, Ceramic plate decorated with Libyan ornamental script "In the name of God," and with numerous additional strokes of purely decorative function, from the market in Tripoli. *Photos Dr. Julian Fell.*

Slightly restored inscription engraved in large Kufi letters at the entrance to the Nevada petroglyph site discovered by Professor Julian Steward, and named by him "Lost City." The Kufi reads W-R-D L-B-Y, "Newcomers from Libya," to the right decorative Tripolitanian rosettes. *Replica, photo Peter J. Garfall.*

Hebrew shekels dating from the Second Revolt in 132 A.D. occur in various parts of Kentucky and a nearby district of Arkansas. These are surely the records of American immigrants from Judea. Dr. Joseph Mahan is presently researching these matters in the context of the language and traditions of the southeastern tribes.

Christian relics are widespread in America, as the illustrations to this chapter explain. But we also find records of Christian flight to the New World among the inscriptions on the rocks of North Africa. A notable one is the very long text (pages 170–172) engraved by a Christian monk who actually *returned* to Morocco from America, leaving his comrades behind in the wilderness; they had fled to escape the attentions of the Vandals in the fifth century of our era. Other texts from Nova Scotia, Connecticut, and places on the west coast of Canada and the United States tell us that small colonies of Christians had come here at various times. Traditions of apparently ancient Christianity have been recorded among the Cherokees by Chief Alvin O. Langdon of the eastern Etowah Cherokees; although such traditions require further research before we can safely regard them as ancient, the epigraphic evidence of ancient Christians in North America is unimpeachable. The religion did not survive into modern times, but it did influence the generalized sun worship of many American Indian tribes, and our earliest explorers noticed reverence for the cross among several tribes.

Christianity was introduced separately on a number of different occasions, at varying dates. For example, the arrival of the Byzantine Greeks in Colorado is to be associated with petroglyphs where the portrait of Christ or of saints can be found with Byzantine Greek abbreviated lettering, similar to that on North African surfaces where the old Coptic or Byzantine Church once held sway, before the coming of Islam.

Islam itself was brought to west America, probably very soon after 650 A.D., when the Moslems swept across North Africa to Spain. Relics of Islam are among the most easily legible of our Kufic Arabic inscriptions, and arouse the wonder of Arab visitors to America. Examples are shown in this chapter.

Later, the Norsemen brought first paganism, then on still later visits, Christianity. They built the oldest surviving church on American soil, the lovely old Romanesque tower at Newport, Rhode Island (pages 362–365). As explained in the captions to the illustrations, Norse runes declare the origin of the tower. And I let the pictures tell the rest of the story.

Christianity Comes to the American Celts

A few years ago, a colleague in Britain, W. Edmund Filmer of Surrey, came across a peculiar document—or, more correctly, an eighteenth-century engraving reproducing the document, that had once formed part of a collection of early Irish manuscripts. It was written in a script unfamiliar to Irish investigators, and had been supposed by some to be Phoenician, and apparently enough could be read of it to indicate that it had some connection with law. Mr. Filmer sent me a copy of the document with an invitation to determine the language if possible. On examining it, I saw that the script was quite similar to one known to us from some schoolboys' slates, carrying exercises such as handwritten passages of the *Aeneid,* set by an ancient Iberian schoolmaster who once taught in the Spanish city of Italica, in the days of Trajan (himself the scion of a family of Italica). One can imagine the pride of the youngsters as they approached the study of Latin, knowing that one of their own home town now ruled the empire; the master probably had no great difficulty in coaxing his charges into the foreign tongue.

The surprise in the document from Britain lay in the fact that when the text was read as being this Italic script of the Guadalquivir Valley, the language it delivered was like some strangely misspelled dialect of Gaelic. What we had, evidently, was a long consecutive sample of the hitherto unknown Celtiberian language. It could be read without undue difficulty, using an Irish dictionary.

In reading Julius Caesar's account of the ancient Britains, one gathers that the Romans were greeted, upon landing in Britain, by an onrush of naked savages brandishing weapons, and that they

192

lived in relative simplicity in dwellings that we in America would equate with wigwams. There is no mention of more substantial buildings, or of anything so sophisticated as, for example, a mint striking an official coinage. Consequently, one gains a rather misleading impression of Britain before the Romans came to civilize the inhabitants, and the lavish jewels and breathtaking art of the ancient Britons (obviously pre-Roman, since it is martially oriented) is bewildering. Something evidently had been omitted from Caesar's conspectus of Britannia!

As for the Irish (never conquered by Rome, and hence taken little note of save as vaguely eligible for future conquest, and prone to appear in British ports on board ships of their own contrivance), Roman historians were not enlightening.

Thus the O'Connor manuscript presents a new aspect of the ancient Irish scene, for it proves to be a fragment of an account written by a Spanish Celt—more precisely a Spanish Gael (for such is his language)—dealing with aspects of Irish law such as would be of interest to other Spanish Gaels who might intend to visit the country. Certain references in the document to *wheelmoney* and to Etruscan coins and Tyrrhenian "Bulls" (i.e., coins of Italy and Sicily on which bulls are depicted) show that the document is itself a second-century copy of a much older document that must have been written in the third century B.C., when such coins were in circulation. Filmer suggests Galicia as the source of the original manuscript.

Thus the document seems to present a portion of an account of the Irish Celts at a much earlier date in their history than we hitherto have known them. It appears to me that the material would apply equally well to the Celts who came to America from Iberia, for the Irish admit to an Iberian origin. It refers to Tanistry, by which is meant administration of law by deputies of the king. Here it is:

(43)   *On the Origin of Tanistry*

(44)   To infer that it was in Eire itself that this system of government arose would be both false and an affront to history.

(45)   In the obscurity of the mists of olden time a desire would
       arise [we may guess] to replace armed combat by arbi-
       tration.

(46)   And it would seem a desirable thing that land boundaries
       should be fixed without recourse to moats.

(47)   At first certain of the kings and commoners

(48)   and the wisest sages, the worthy yeomen of long ago, and
       poets

(49)   and bards and druids, each initially coming to this con-
       clusion individually,

(50)   conscious of the advantage that would accrue to the
       people in matters of justice and equity,

(51)   in grief and misfortune. Such could have been the be-
       ginnings of a system of government in Eire.

(52)   Under circumstances such as this, it would seem, the
       Dicta of our elders would then be conveyed from here
       [Iberia] to that island.

(0)   *A Sample of the Legal Declarations of Eire*

(1)   Henceforth cases involving wrongdoing are to be made
       over to the wisest men.

(2)   Any case is to be brought to judgment without delay.

(3)   Henceforth in any case involving false utterances let
       amends be paid in compensation for the harm.

(4)   Henceforth if a complainant be merciful, let the judges
       also be merciful.

(5)   If any slave commits a great nuisance by reason of his
       lusts and is called upon to answer for his offense, then

(6)   let him be charged on the day following: and as punish-
       ment

(7)   for the wrongdoing let the slave wholly expiate the offense
       by transporting burdens on the shoulder-beam

(8)   on his master's estate. And let him suffer the discomfort
       of the shoulder-beam for so long as his lusts are im-
       moderate.

(9) If any slave dares to escape, to go into hiding or to roam as an outlaw

(10) and is espied from afar off, he may buy his freedom by paying gold in proportion to his worth.

(11) But if he persists as a fugitive, and enters a village

(12) to hide, then the people there are to lay hold of the villain, and to put him in fetters.

(13) If a malicious man utter lying words that another declares to be slanderous

(14) to the measure of his tongue-loose recklessness shall he transport heavy burdens for the other man

(15) and be constrained to work the shoulder-beam for so long as the lawmen shall determine.

(16) Any person may enter or depart from Eire if he be Gaul, Scot, or Iberian.

(17) Etruscan coins and also "Bulls" [Italic coins bearing the image of a bull] are preferable to others.

(18) "Wheel-money" [rondels] is not legal. Iberian disks [rondels] are reckoned worthless.

(19) The common people may eat corn, together with game birds, but they may not

(20) hunt bears. They may kill stags, goats and red deer.

(21) It is their own misfortune if heavy rains cause scarcity or famine in Eire.

(22) If any person insults a priest in the temple or beside a sacred well, or grossly

(23) blasphemes during the chanting at the high altar, his case shall be brought to judgment, and his fate announced without delay.

(24) And no man shall be put to death except by judgment of a court summoned for him

(25) and for the injured parties, all of whom are to be summoned by name

(26) to the high altar, to attend the trial for the duration of its session, distance notwithstanding.

(27) Under roof, or a spacious cavern, they are to assemble together, facing the decision-making Tanists,

(28) each head of a household bearing arms, by nines arranged,

(29) and conforming to the two feuding sides, the challenger's and the deedsman's.

(30) The prosecutor is to make his complaint in a loud voice on the criminal act of violence, and asking

(31) whether the crime be one of malice aforethought, or an unpremeditated act of passion, summoning each freeman by name

(32) to the altar to give his opinion in the presence of the assembled people, protected by them, and facing them.

(33) Then he is to inquire the learned opinion of the Tanists. And if the reply is an unfavorable verdict, let the condemned man thereupon be bound

(34) to the picket to be slain in retribution, his body cast down from a high cliff top.

(35) But if on weighing the case, one and all having heard the complaint, they declare a verdict of not-proven,

(36) then let the picket be hewn down as needless, for there is no guilt

(37) of manslaughter on his part. Thereupon straightway the assembly shall march rejoicing to any of the well-known sacred springs, and to the oracle there

(38) let a donative be given larger than is customary, for the sake of the acquittal. And thereupon they are to immerse their man in the depths of the spring.

(39) And the oldest of the sages is to make known the verdict to the assembled people, declaring that all men should know that they may expect justice in misfortune in these precincts,

(40) and that whether it be fraud that is the cause of a dispute,

(41) or be it lust, or malice aforethought, or the death of a slain man, or a boundary line

(42) that is under survey, crime will be countered by justice moderated by clemency.

Thus ends this noble document, a fragment of some larger work, but one of which any Celt may well be proud. It must surely be the oldest written code of laws in northern Europe.

Since the author—whose name is unknown to me—implies that the laws of Eire derive from those of Iberia, it must follow that the Celts of New England, and their descendants across the continent to their later homeland in British Columbia, Washington, and Oregon, would bring this common law with them to the New World. From them it would later be imparted to their Creole descendants and probably would have much influence on the legal systems of such neighboring Amerindian tribes as might have friendly relations with the Celts.

I wish now to refer to the language of the Iberian Celts in America. At the time when I sent the manuscript of *America B.C.* to the publisher, it seemed that this tongue had wholly disappeared from the American scene, save for a few relict words of uncertain provenance now found in the northeast Algonquian dialects, and some possible relict place names. These suggestions have been much criticized by some archeologists here, even as recently as May 1978. This is strange, in view of the fact that on the occasion of my Hammond Lecture in New York in 1976 I presented a general outline of the vocabulary and grammar of the Takhelne language of the Fraser Lakes area, in British Columbia, showing it to be a Creole Celtic tongue related to Gaelic, and derived from Gadelic (or Old Gaelic). The report was printed in volume 4 of the *Occasional Publications* of the Epigraphic Society in 1977. I give here a brief extract of representative vocabulary, but this is not the place to go into detail or to discuss grammar. According to a recent Smithsonian publication (Goddard and Fitzhugh, 1978) "No American Indian language is derived from an historically known Old World language," and "No loan words of Old World origin have been found in any North American Indian language." Although I am not aware of Celtic publications by these critics, and they obviously are not aware of mine, I hope that a revised assessment may seem reasonable.

Representative Vocabulary of the Takhelne Language of British Columbia.

English	Gadelic	Gaelic	Takhelne	English	Gadelic	Gaelic	Takhelne
old	senos	sean	shan	elder	koini	caoin	qan
asleep	sofnio	suain	sesthi	bad	tegu	tiug	tio
bright	ghel	gel	yel	colored	bendi	bendi	pintai
crooked	ser	serh	zerh	dark	mer	mug	mek
fluid	tulia	tuile	telle	good	su	su-	zu
gray	gher	gris	kres	hairy	rani	roin	rai
thin	tanais	tana	ten	many	lenu	lin	lane
red	kin	geann	ken	arrow	keras	corr	kra
building	tegos	tigh	tih	chief	mogtios	mochtae	mutih
chip	kasr	casnaid	qas	cough	kwes	casad	khwes
hook	ser	serh	zerh	daughter	auge	oigh	eacha
day	dijas	diugh	dzin	libido	ewyll	aill	eyel
disgrace	nagro	naire	nerh	duck	eti	athi	tetai
father	pater	athair	pa	foot	koxa	cas	khe
food	bivoton	biad	bed	footprint	ong	eang	yan
hand	lama	lamh	lla	head	togio	tuigse	tsi
height	altus	allt	tlata	skin	pellis	peal	pel
honey	rem	renor	re	jaw	ito	ithin	eyeta
laughter	tloq-	tlachd	tlo	leaf	tanais	tana	ten
life	bitu	bith	bitsi	light	svel	solus	sa
man	dunjos	duine	dene	raft	ram	ramhach	rhenyes
roof	spen	(—)	pen	spit	sugo	sugh	so
sky	aer	aier	ya	summer	samo	sam	shin
sun	sulis	solus	sa	whole	holos	uile	ul
word	rhetor	radh	rhetih	water	udskio	uisge	uskha
to be	tajo	tha	ta	not to be	ni con	cha'n	qennih
become	svel	sel	selli	burn	kai-	kaio	kaio

In my original report, I noted words in the Takhelne language that referred to sports resembling those of the Gaels—hurling the caber, for example—and to something that sounded like Ogam writing. I suggested that a search be made of the rock inscriptions of British Columbia to see if Ogam occurs. It does, and in fact had already been discovered and recorded by John Corner in 1968, eight years earlier, but as he had not recognized his finds, they remained untranslated. In this book I have referred the British Columbia inscriptions to the chapter on going to school in ancient

America, for they seem mostly to comprise school lessons. Similar inscriptions also occur in Oregon, Nevada, and California.

The artistic work of the British Columbia Celts initially resembled that of the New England Celts, and therefore also that of Europe. Examples given in this chapter will illuminate the matter better than words. But there is a notable difference from New England in the subject matter of much of the epigraphy of British Columbia and the nearby states of Washington and Oregon. These western Celts were evidently in occupation much later than their New England cousins, and, in fact, were in all probability the direct descendants of the New England Celts. For if the Celts vanished from the East, they surely reappeared in the West, and a transcontinental migration seems to be the explanation. To this day, a language recognizably Celtic in much of its vocabulary, and some of its grammar, is still spoken by a few surviving Takhelne in the Fraser River lakes region.

The later aspect of the western Celtic inscriptions is shown by a change in the art style, which now reflects the Irish passion for mirror-image patterns, for rendering the skeleton visible in living creatures, and later still a profound feeling for Christianity. Here, as in the case of the peoples already discussed in foregoing chapters, coins introduced from the Old World conveyed much of the artistic fashion of the day to the New World. The work of the British Columbian Celts provides us with constant reminders of what their cousins were doing in Ireland. It seems clear, therefore, that the legendary voyages of the Brendan era of the Irish Celts actually did occur, and Irish thoughts and art were brought here by the voyagers. Here I leave the reader to contemplate the illustrations and their explanatory captions.

◉ swords
battleaxes
0 burials
inscriptions
R runestones

Celtic Americans from the New England region appear to have spread across North America in the latitudes of about 40° to 50° N before Roman times. Their later distribution is at times difficult to distinguish from the Norse settlers on account of the close affinity of Celtic and Norse art. Later Celtic immigration came principally from Ireland and brought Christianity to the erstwhile pagans.

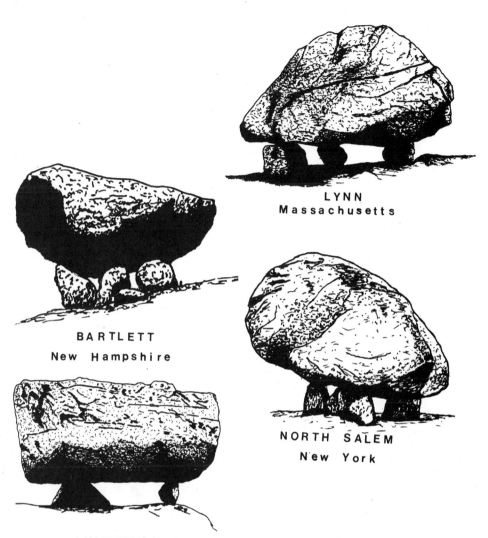

LYNN
Massachusetts

BARTLETT
New Hampshire

NORTH SALEM
New York

KINNELON
New Jersey

DOLMENS

EASTERN NORTH AMERICA

Whittall

More giant dolmens have been recognized since the publication of *America B.C.* In this selection drawn by James Whittall, two recently charted examples, each with fifty-ton capstones, are shown from Lynn, Massachusetts, and Kinnelon, New Jersey. North Salem, with its ninety-ton capstone remains the largest known example from America. *James Whittall.*

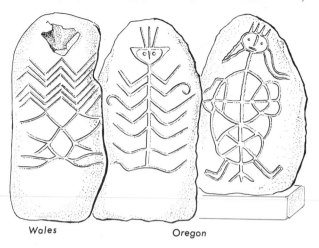

Wales   Oregon

Transcontinental migration of the New England Celts occurred so early that they carried with them to Oregon the most primitive Celtic art, usually called in Britain "megalithic" but, as shown in *America B.C.*, no distinction can be drawn in America between early Celtic and megalithic. The example from Wales occurs at Barclodiad y Gawres in Anglesey, the two Oregon examples are from the Dalles region (described by Beth and Ray Hill, *Indian Petroglyphs of the Pacific Northwest, Hancock,* 1974), and are represented by casts in the Museum of the Oregon Historical Society.

The giant dolmen of Lynn, Massachusetts, known since Colonial days as Phaeton Rock, but only recently identified by Whittall as a dolmen. *Photo James Whittall.*

Portion of sculpture executed in native bedrock, originally at Searsmount, Maine, from which this massive head was removed to Sturbridge Village Museum, Massachusetts, the location of the torso now being unknown. The swamp-oak leaves and acorn on the diadem suggest Druidic connotations. Irish Celtic art is suggested by the widely staring eyes and the shaped curves of the nostrils. *Courtesy of the Sturbridge Museum, photo Malcolm Pearson.*

The more stolid stone sculpture of the French Celts is suggested by the heroic head, twice life-size, discovered in 1811 at a depth of 10 feet when foundations were dug for the cellar of a house at Essex, Massachusetts. It is now in the Peabody Museum, Salem. *Photo courtesy Peabody Museum Salem, James Whittall.*

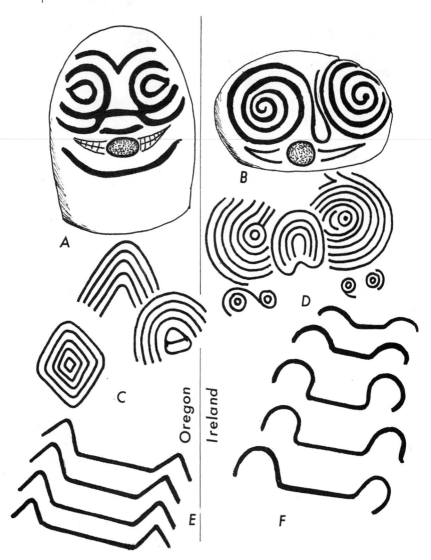

Typical so-called megalithic art of Ireland (right side) compared with corresponding petroglyphs of Oregon (left side). Distribution details are given by Beth and Ray Hill (1974).

Celtic goddess from Portugal now in the Whittall collection. *Photo Malcolm Pearson.*

Gloria Farley with the Celtic boundary stone at Ardmore, Oklahoma. The inscription reads in alphabetic script AOS NOUG, FIRID, AILC. The language is Gadelic, very close to modern Irish Gaelic.

Four Celtic alphabets. A, Italica (Spain) ca. 100 A.D., Vergil *Aeneid*. B, Ardmore (Oklahoma), boundary stone. C, O'Connor Tanisteachd manuscript, Celtiberian. D, Book of Kells (Ireland) ca. eighth century A.D. The D, reversed F, R and L suggest affinity between the American and Kells styles.

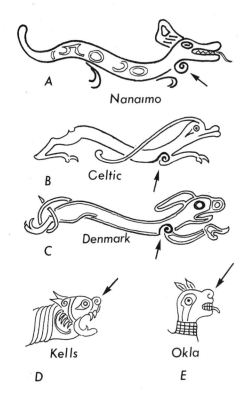

A
Nanaimo

B
Celtic

C
Denmark

D
Kells

E
Okla

Celtic dragons found in districts where Celtic inscriptions or living Celts occur, also adopted as carved art form by Vikings. A, Nanaimo, British Columbia (Beth and Ray Hill). B, in Celtic manuscript at St. Gallen, Switzerland (a former Celtic city). C, Viking example from Mammen, Denmark. Note details, such as the spiral by the shoulder, that are purely arbitrary conventions and cannot have been independently developed. In British Columbia today a Celtic Creole language is still spoken by the Takhelne people, and Ogam inscriptions are now being recognized. Similar spiral treatment can be seen in the nostrils of the beast in the Book of Kells, Ireland (D) and in a Spiro Mound, Oklahoma, engraving (E).

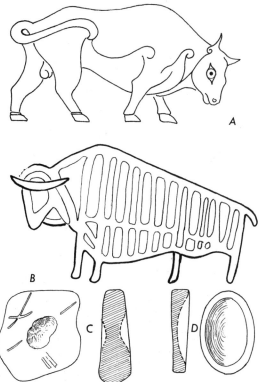

A

B

C

D

Celtic art in Portugal, Ireland, and Scotland devotes much attention to stylized bulls. A, as rendered in the Book of Kells, and in several petroglyphs of Scotland. B, skeletonized version found by Gloria Farley in Colorado in 1978. Attention to internal organs, especially bones, is also an ancient feature of Celtic art. C, D, Celtic touchstones, intended to avert evil by rubbing the thumb in an oval depression when danger threatens; C, from southern Illinois, found by Professor Halsey W. Miller, originally a glacially-transported pebble, the natural striations being mistaken by ancient Celts for divinely-formed Ogam; D, modern touchstone (or "worry-stone") from Connemara, Ireland, of polished green serpentine, collected by Renée Fell.

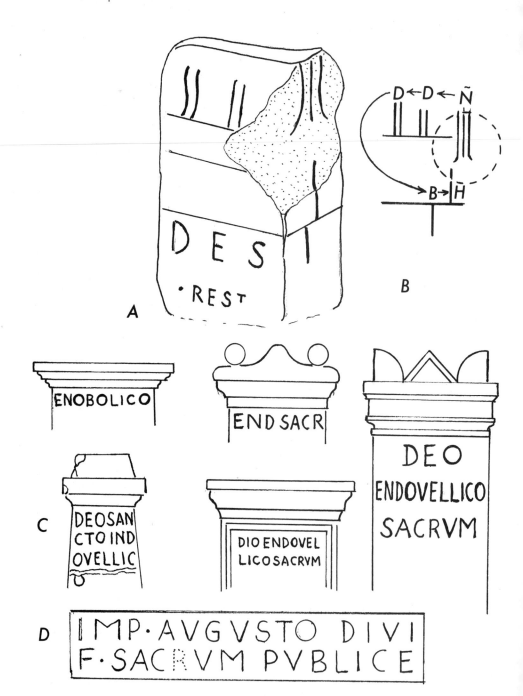

A

B

C

D

ENOBOLICO

END SACR

DEO
ENDOVELLICO
SACRVM

DEOSAN
CTO IND
OVELLIC

DIO ENDOVEL
LICO SACRVM

IMP · AVGVSTO DIVI
F · SACRVM PVBLICE

A bilingual Ogam-Latin altar dedication from Portugal, the Ogam section antedating the Roman occupation, the Latin section and the restored portions of the Ogam dating from about the time of Augustus (first century B.C. to first century A.D.) A, the altar stone, one of a series of over twenty examples from the ancient Celtic site now known as San Miguel de Mota. By comparing this stone with others of the series (shown at C, below), Professor Scarlat Lambrino of the University of Lisbon was able to demonstrate that the Latin letters D E S stand for DEO ENDOBHELICO SACRUM (Sacred to the god Endobellicus). The letters REST beneath signify RESTITUTUM, meaning that the altar had been damaged, and was restored and reinstated in Roman times. The style of the lettering matches that of the dedication to Augustus found at San Miguel de Mota, and shown at D below, hence the restoration was carried out in all probability at the same time as the other steles were set up. The damaged altar stone, A, is evidently the oldest of the series. The Ogam text, some of the letters recut or repaired when the Latin text was added, is deciphered at B, to the right. It gives, to the extent that vowelless Ogam is able to do so, a shortened form of the god's name (E)ÑDD(O)BH, and is the only known example of a rendering in Celtic script of this Celtic god's name.

The existence of such vowelless Ogam monuments in Portugal and Spain was predicated in *America B.C.,* and soon after publication, examples were discovered—notably this bilingual text. The evidence is conclusive that vowelless Ogam of the American type was used in Celtic areas of Portugal and Spain, and that the script is in fact of Iberian origin, or at all events was used in Iberia centuries before the oldest dated examples from Britain. The claim that "Ogam was invented in London no earlier than the fourth century A.D. by a person who had studied Latin" (Smithsonian Institution *Statement on America B.C.,* May 1978) is apparently based on one of several theories that were current a quarter of a century ago, when Etruscan origins were also advocated, as well as the Arabic origin postulated by Brash, the leading Ogam authority of the nineteenth century. Later theorists also overlooked the fact that both Brash and his colleague Bishop Graves, and Sir Samuel Fergusson all reported examples of Irish Ogam from which the vowels were omitted. James Whittall has republished these examples, now in museums in Ireland, and has pointed out that they appear to be indistinguishable from similar phallic inscriptions found in America, and reported in *America B.C.*

Skeleton birds feature largely in the art of both countries, but whereas the British kind might sport two heads, the west American Celts compromised by using a bird with eyes in both the front and back of its head. A, from the Book of Lindisfarne, simplified; B, Kitselas Canyon, British Columbia, after Edward Meade, *Indian Rock Carvings of the Pacific Northwest* (Grays, 1971). C, D, of dual Irish-Norse affinity, are from Dublin tokens.

Art motifs Ireland (two lower left figures) compared with typical motifs of the Spiro Mound series, Oklahoma. Early Celtic Ogam occurs in Oklahoma.

A

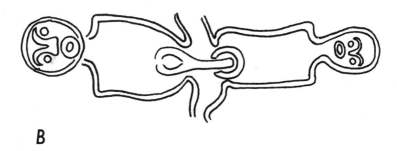

B

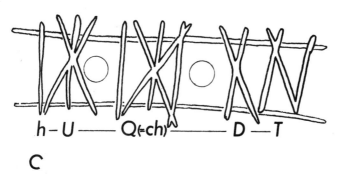

h – U ———— Q(=ch) ———— D – T

C

By the eighth century A.D. Gaelic artists were fascinated by the mirror image. Art had become more complicated in Ireland; in America it remained explicit. A, from the Book of Kells, simplified; B, petroglyphs at The Dalles, Oregon, on the Columbia River and copulating couple at Clo-oose, Vancouver Island, discovered and recorded by Beth and Ray Hill, in *Indian Petroglyphs of the Pacific Northwest* (Hancock House, 1974).

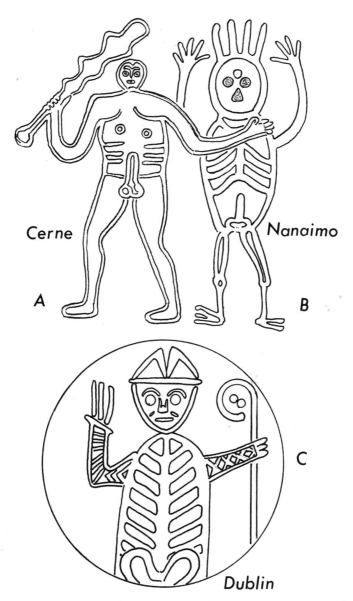

Cerne

Nanaimo

A

B

C

Dublin

Skeletonized art crosses the boundary from pagan times to enter Celtic Christian art, as in the case of the Irish bishop, probably Saint Patrick, shown at C on a Dublin medieval token; here the pelvic bones replace the phallus of earlier styles, as the Cerne Giant, A, discussed in *America B.C.*, and the similar (but much smaller) Nanaimo figure recorded by Beth and Ray Hill (1974). C is an example of pewter tokens recently discovered in Dublin, thought to date from the twelfth century A.D.

Comparable motifs from Ireland (left) and the Pacific Northwest (right), the latter after Beth and Ray Hill (1974).

Roman heraldry adapted to an American public. When Julius Caesar defeated Ptolemy XII, in 47 B.C., he celebrated the conquest of Africa by issuing a denarius bearing the image of an elephant trampling on a serpent. In due course the coins brought word of the event to the Colorado settlements. A Glen Canyon artist, conscious of American susceptibilities, took care not to offend the serpent worshippers by transforming the snake to a spiral, playfully tossed in midair; he then added a mountain goat for good measure and, in the Celtic mannerism, attached it to a double spiral. Coin from Fell collection, pictographs from Glen Canyon, *after photograph by Utah Museum of Natural History.*

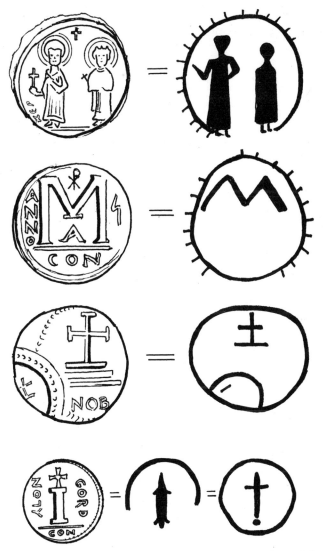

As Byzantine coinage reached western North America (possibly in part on Arab vessels, and in part brought by the Byzantine Greeks of Colorado) the Celts of the Northwest were selective as to the designs they employed in numoglyphs. Whereas in Colorado the whole range of values appear as the so-called Indian shield patterns (Chapter 7), only those designs that can be interpreted as Christian appear in the British Columbia numoglyphs and pictographs. Thus the large M of the follis is selected, since it can be understood as symbolizing Maria, but the K of the half-follis is rejected, having no Christian connotation. On the left, typical Byzantine coins of the early Middle Ages; on the right, corresponding petrographs collected by John Corner (*Pictographs in the Interior of British Columbia,* Vernon, B.C.: Wayside Press, 1968) from sites along the Fraser River. This area, as shown by Ogam inscriptions, was formerly occupied by the Takhelne people of the upper Fraser Valley lakes, whose present language is largely of Celtiberian derivation (Fell, 1976).

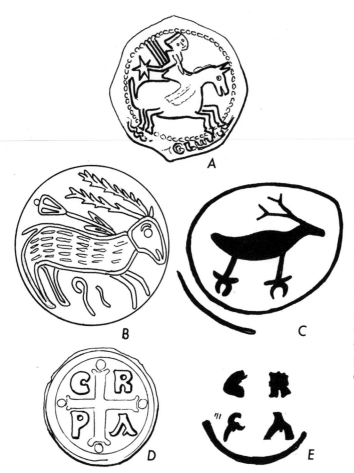

A

B

C

D

E

Coinage issued by the Crusader princes and their successors in Greece, and Turkish imitations, A, served as a model for the Dublin token, B. The latter in turn appears to be the model for the British Columbia petrograph C, collected by Corner (1968). Similarly E, also observed by Corner, appears to be the British Columbia derivative of the Byzantine coin D, issued 1067–1071 A.D. by Romanus IV, during the Crusader years when such coins flowed into northern Europe and especially Ireland.

Opposite page: Motifs on Danish coins (which circulated in Ireland) from the era 900 to 1000 A.D., upper four rows, and their apparent British Columbian derivatives. The bottom row shows British Columbian derivatives of an early Islamic coin (left) of the seventh century A.D. and of a Norman penny (right) of the twelfth century A.D.

Jefferson's Lost Manuscripts

In addition to his other interests and skills, President Thomas Jefferson was endowed with a natural interest in languages. He is said to have been acquainted with nine, including three of the Amerindian tongues. Like all men of his caliber, he was impatient with academic conservatism, though this in no way diminished his respect for universities, one of which he founded. He wrote to his grandson, a student at Columbia, advising him not to waste time taking courses in Greek—the young man could easily acquire Greek by devoting a couple of hours to study of the language by himself in the afternoon. Jefferson added "I know of no better teacher than a good dictionary." He also advised the boy to take courses in "Fluxions" (differential calculus)—but not to do so if the professor of mathematics insisted on wasting time with a prerequisite course on geometry.

Jefferson was intensely interested in the American Indians and in the philosophical problem of how these people had come to America. He realized that in their language there might be found important clues to the matter, and during his presidency he instructed Lewis and Clark to make careful lists of words used in the languages of the various tribes through whose territory the explorers were to pass. Jefferson himself, when on a visit to Vermont, was fascinated to observe that the Abenaki people wrote on pieces of the smooth inner bark of the birch trees, and he himself wrote several letters to his daughter on birchbark during his journey.

In a letter written to John Adams in 1812, Jefferson mentions that his interest in the American Indians began in his boyhood:

> In the early part of my life I was very familiar and acquired impressions of attachment for them which have never been ob-

218

literated. Before the revolution I was very much with them. I knew much the great Outacity, warrior and orator of the Cherokees. He was always the guest of my father on his journeys to and from Williamsburg. I was in his camp when he made his great farewell oration to his people, the evening before his departure for England.

The moon was in full splendour, and to her he seemed to address himself in his prayers for his own safety on the voyage, and that of his people during his absence. His sounding voice, distinct articulation, animated action, and the solemn silence of his people at their several fires, filled me with awe and veneration, altho' I did not understand a word he uttered.

In his *Notes on the State of Virginia*, published in London in 1787, Jefferson shows that the then ruling passion among the landed gentry of Britain for opening ancient burial mounds in search of antiques or other relics of the onetime inhabitants and predecessors of modern peoples had also spread to America, where Jefferson himself had superintended the cutting of a section through a Virginia mound. He referred to this early interest again in 1797 in the course of an address to the American Philosophical Society, of which he had just been elected president.

Jefferson's interest in languages never flagged, though it was only in enforced idleness during periods when he was out of office that he was able to indulge his taste for the extinct tongues. Like all educated men of his time, he had acquired Latin in school, and he knew Greek. Anglo-Saxon came to his notice accidentally, while investigating the etymology of some English words. He became so interested in it, and in Middle English, that he wrote a syllabus for instruction in both languages at the University of Virginia. Then he was called to the highest office in the Republic, and perforce had to put linguistics behind him for a time.

The war against the Barbary pirates occurred during his presidency. A little-known aftermath, as I gather from papers copied for me by James Whittall, was that when consular offices were established in North Africa by the State Department, the diplomatic officials seem to have been selected on the basis of their linguistic ability. As late as 1823 we find that William Shaler, consul of the United States at Algiers, was submitting a learned series of reports on the Berber language for publication by the

American Philosophical Society. In one communication he recommends that a young man competent in languages be trained in Arabic in Paris, and then join his consular staff in order to investigate the Berber language. At this time, Jefferson was in his old age, though he still held office as a member of the Council of the Society. The vocabularies Shaler supplied resemble those that Jefferson had asked Lewis and Clark to prepare, and I think we see in them the hand of the Virginian scholar.

With such careful gathering of linguistic materials under Jefferson, and his incipient feeling (as it would seem) that North African languages might be relevant to the study of American languages, why, then, did nothing eventuate from these studies? Jefferson's biographer Thomas Fleming has given a succinct answer to this question in his book *The Man from Monticello*. Fleming writes:

> What Jefferson hoped to make the great intellectual work of his retirement was destroyed by a scoundrel. In a trunk shipped from the White House to Monticello were notes and observations he had accumulated over fifty years, on Indian languages and dialects. He planned to write a definitive book on the Indian languages, which would help trace their origins, by comparing their basic linguistic patterns to those of other cultures. With his knowledge of Anglo-Saxon, Greek and half a dozen other languages, Jefferson was superbly qualified for the task. But a thief broke into the ship while it was enroute to Monticello, and stole this irreplaceable trunk. Finding nothing salable in it, he threw it into the James River. Friends managed to fish out a few of the manuscripts that drifted to shore, and sent them to Jefferson, mud-smeared and illegible. But all hope of doing a comprehensive work was gone.

But scholars continued to investigate the Berbers, and about the same time as Shaler was submitting his vocabularies and grammatical notes to the Philosophical Society, Dr. Walter Oudney made a journey along the coast toward Tunis, in the course of which he noticed that wherever he found communities of Berbers, the adjacent rocks were seen to be freshly engraved with signs "that resembled European letters to some extent." After making inquiries, he learned that these were indeed writings of the Berbers, and from the sultan at Ghraat he acquired a table of sound values

Thomas Jefferson, from Rembrandt Peale's portrait painted in 1805. At this time, communications with the United States consular representatives in Tripoli and Algiers, in consequence of the war against the pirates of the Barbary Coast, probably drew to Jefferson's attention the possibility that some linguistic relationship might exist between the North African tongues and those of North America. He encouraged the collection of vocabularies by the consuls in North Africa, and also by American explorers such as Lewis and Clark who were encountering Amerindian tribes not previously known. His planned research on the subject during his retirement was frustrated by the theft and destruction of linguistic records he had accumulated during much of his life.

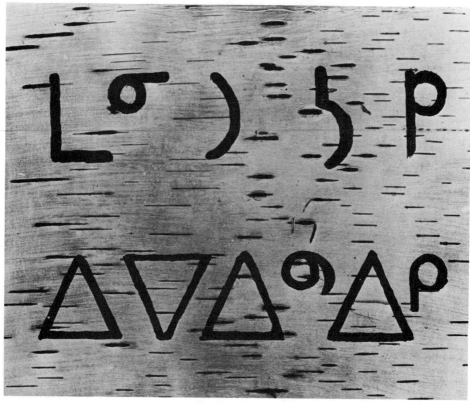

In the early part of the nineteenth century, missionaries working with the Cree and other Algonquian tribes in Canada found it convenient to adapt a native alphabet to render the Christian message in a form attractive to the Indians. Signs that represented consonants in the original script are evidently derived from one of the early Iberian scripts. James Evans, a Wesleyan teacher who worked with the Western Cree in Ontario and Manitoba from 1840 on, assisted by William Mason, adapted the script to indicate vowels (by rotating the letters into any one of four positions), and then translated parts of the New Testament. At first they used birchbark in place of paper, as the Indians did. This example is probably from the hand of a young Indian student. Along the top line it reads, left to right, *Ma-ni-to sa-ki* (God is Love), and the bottom line reads right to left *Ki-i-chi i-a-i* (The Great Spirit). Both the script and the vocabulary match Classical Arabic roots of similar sound and meaning, showing that the writing system can not have been a modern invention but, like that of the neighboring Micmac tribe, must have been brought to North America in an earlier era of North African voyages. *Epigraphic Museum, Photo Peter J. Garfall.*

In *America B.C.* the hieroglyphic system of writing used by the Micmac Indians of Nova Scotia was attributed to influence from Egypt, and the similarity of the signs to hieratic letters was illustrated in tables. Since the Micmac writing was already in use in Nova Scotia a century (at least) before Champollion first deciphered ancient Egyptian, this was taken as evidence of an ancient contact with Egyptian writers of the ancestors of the Micmacs of modern times. More recent studies have led to the conclusion that the Micmac contact was not so much with ancient Egyptian writers directly, as rather with eastern Libyans, from the border of Egypt and Libya: this region was once the home of the Adrymachid tribe who, according to the ancient Greek historian Herodotus, had "adopted Egyptian manners."

Herodotus also records that the Libyans of the Siwa Oasis region (now part of Egypt) spoke a language that was a mixture of "Phoenician and Egyptian." Micmac signs have also been observed on a bilingual proclamation of a Libyan king of the second century B.C. Thus Micmac script is probably to be attributed to east Libyan influence. Here Bernard Francis of the Micmac tribal Cultural Center in Nova Scotia discusses with Fell a handwritten copy of portions of the hieroglyphic version of the Catholic mass, translated by the Abbé Maillard in the eighteenth century. *Photo Peter J. Garfall.*

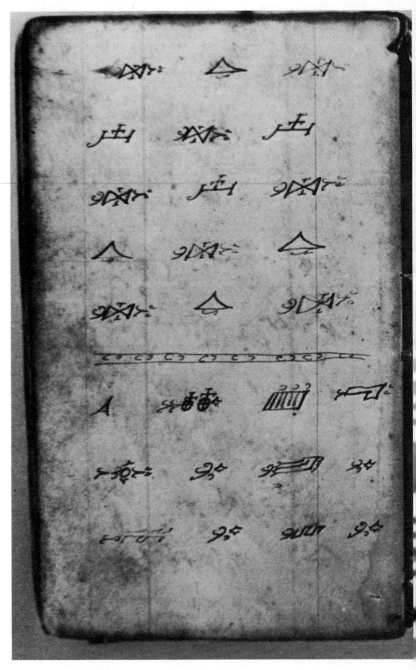

A page opening of the hieroglyphic mass book shown in the previous illustration, one of several handwritten copies known still to exist. The section on the left-hand page, at the top, is part of the *Kyrie eleison*, the first five lines reading as follows: (1) have mercy, Lord have mercy (2) Christ have mercy, Christ (3) have mercy, Christ (4) Lord have mercy, Lord (5) have

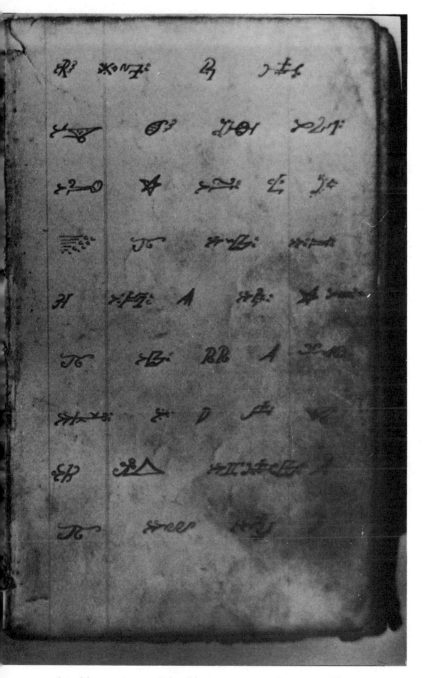

mercy, Lord have mercy. It is relevant to note that on a Kikapu prayer stick in the Smithsonian Collection occurs in Carthaginian script, three times repeated, the phrase "Have mercy of Lord," the word Baal being used for Lord.
Photo Peter J. Garfall.

Dr. Mohamed Jarary (left) points to the first Kufic inscription to be recognized in North America, the words *Shams* (Arabic, sun) found with a red ocher representation of a sun-disk, replicated to half scale from the find site in Texas. Discovered in 1935, it was originally reported as a black worm-shaped marking accompanying what appeared to be a sun-disk, and its true nature was first noted by Fell at a lecture to the University of Maine in 1976. This first visit to Harvard by Drs. Jarary and Ali Khushaim (right) in 1977 led to closer collaboration between North African and American investigators, and thus to the discovery of numerous Kufic inscriptions in other parts of North America. *Photo Peter J. Garfall.*

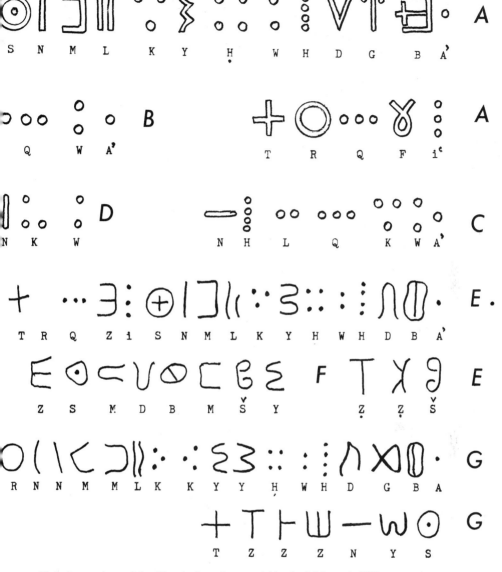

Alphabets shared by North America and North Africa, 1. Tifinag alphabets of North Africa and North America. A, Tamahaq of Ahaggar (Algeria), Gospel of St. John in the Berber language. B, East Lyme, Niantic (Connecticut), so-called "cupstone" (a Libyan shipping sign), after 100 A.D. C, Al-Kahan inscription, Lagomarsino (West Nevada). D, Berber autograph, Garfield Flat (Nevada). E, letter of the Berber Shikkat (to Louis Rinn), Algeria. F, variant forms used in the same letter of Shikkat (mirror-image forms appear in lines that read alternatively from right-to-left and left-to-right, i.e., boustrophedon still employed in the late nineteenth century). G, Letter of the Berber Aggour (Algeria): forms rotated 90° occur in words written vertically (the text winding in sinuous boustrophedon).

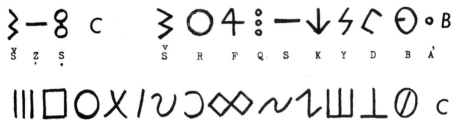

N N N M M M M Y Y Y W W W H D G B A'

U Y S̆ S̆ S̆ R R R F ?F J S

S̆ Z S̩   S̆ R F Q S K Y D B A'

ɛ R R T N M M Q Y Y Z Ḥ B

SN MKN MN MNW MA S R K N M J Ṭ W A'

Conjunct letters

Y F W S R T M K Z Ḥ G B A'

L W F J Y

S K W W D B A'

Alphabets shared by North America and North Africa, 2. Libyan alphabets in North America. A, Massacre Lake and Swan Lake Canyon, Nevada (lettering on charts of North America and Hawaiian Islands, see Chapter 12). B, Massacre Lake, plan of Kasba (Pueblo village). C, Massacre Lake, Corn harvest record, D, Hickson Summit, Nevada (Islamic text, "Ask no favors of God . . . etc."), showing continued use of Libyan script after seventh century A.D. E, Oak Island, Nova Scotia, a late Libyan Tifinag script ca. 500 A.D. F, Virgin Islands Tifinag (Islamic ?). G, Tennessee.

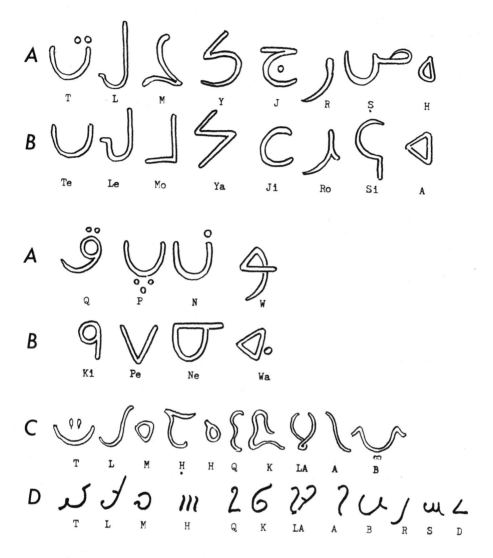

Alphabets shared by North America and North Africa, 3. A northern
Iberian script is native to the eastern and central Algonquian tribes.
Shown in A is the style of Arabic script in most general use in the Arab
world today. The letters in use by the Cree and Ojibway tribes are
shown in B, and very similar forms have been adopted by other
Alonquian tribes; about 1950 a slightly modified form was adopted by
the Eskimo of Canada. In the Alonquian and Eskimo usage, each letter
can be rotated into four positions, 90° apart, thereby signifying each
of four possible vowels to follow the consonant. C, Naskhi of El
Salvador, Pacific coast, of Indonesian origin. D, Demotic, a script used
in ancient Egypt during the later history of that country. The similarity
of the letters to those of the Naskhi alphabet of modern Arabic
suggests the probable origin of Naskhi from Demotic, whereas Kufic
is more closely related to the ancient Libyan script.

Distribution of some North African and Iberian scripts in America.
H, East Libyan Hieroglyphic (Adrymachid, Micmac). I, Iberic and west
Libyan occurring together. K, Kufic Arabic. L, Libyan or Numidian
Arabic. N, Naskhi. T, Tifinag. In addition, the Cree, Ojibway, and
Chippewayan tribes in Canada employ a special Algonquian script of
Northern Iberian origin.

for the signs. Oudney's diary, with the table and some vocabulary of the Berber tongue, were later published in French translation by E. F. Jomard in 1845.

As time went by more explorers collected copies of the strange inscriptions. Scholars began to realize that at least two kinds of alphabet are involved. One, commonly called *Tifinag*, is used by some of the Berber tribes to this day, and is relatively younger than a similar, but somewhat divergent, alphabet used in ancient times, and commonly called *Libyan* or *Numidian*. Therefore, the language enshrined in the Tifinag inscriptions is modern Berber, and can be read and translated by persons acquainted with Berber. But the language of the more ancient Libyan script remained an almost complete mystery for 150 years.

Later explorations disclosed that the Libyan alphabet had at one time been in use across the whole of North Africa, from Sudan in the east, westward to Morocco. Then examples of Libyan script were found engraved on megalithic dolmens in Spain, and on cliff faces in the Canary Islands, and then in recent times from America and some Pacific islands.

When Libyan inscriptions were recognized in America, I began to give increased attention to the problem of Libyan decipherment. Some of the texts, in the nature of short graffiti left by explorers on cliff faces as they passed by, could be read as a dialect of Egyptian, and I included some examples of these in *America B.C.* But others, both in America and in North Africa, obviously had no connection with ancient Egyptian, and remained undeciphered. The eventual solution came in 1976 and proved a considerable surprise. It was this aspect of my work that seemed most to interest scholars at the universities in Libya, and in other parts of the Arab world, and which led to the close collaboration that now exists. For the results have begun to throw a whole new light on the history of the southern Mediterranean lands, and their relationship both to the Arab world and to the Americas.

When I left Tripoli to resume work on the Libyan inscriptions of North America, I left a volume of manuscript decipherments with my colleagues at the university there, for their comment and advice and possible amendment. By the time this book appears in print, the decipherments will also have been added to the series published by the Epigraphic Society (*Occasional Publications*, vol. 6, 1979).

Jefferson died in 1826. Fourteen years later, a young Wesleyan missionary named James Evans, who had been sent to preach the word of God to the Western Cree, a tribe of the Algonquian nation ranging from Ontario to the Rockies, found that his flock was already in possession of a writing system in which signs representing consonants were scratched or painted on birchbark. Evans conceived the idea of using the Amerindian letters in his translations of parts of the Gospels, indicating the vowels by rotating the consonants into four positions, to represent in this way the vowel that followed a consonant, four alone being recognized. Thus, consonants were converted into syllabic signs, on the principle of ta-te-ti-to in place of the original *t*, sa-se-si-so in place of the original *s*, and so on. He obviously had no idea that the original script is in fact related to an early Iberian script.

The other missionaries, believing that Evans had invented the writing system, adapted it to the use of other tribes of Algonquians, so that it is now spread almost from coast to coast. In recent years, a modified form has been adopted by the Eskimos, and again on that occasion the script was misleadingly announced (by the United Nations) as a "new invention." In fact, both the script, and also much of the vocabulary of Cree and other related tribes, can be traced to northern Iberia, and there can be no doubt that the script and the loan vocabulary were brought to North America by ancient voyagers from Northern Spain. This in no way detracts from the great service performed by James Evans in preserving the ancient script and adapting it to modern uses.

Evans also conceived of the idea of a Cree press. He carved raised versions of the letters with a pocket knife. Then he made negative molds in clay from the wood models. He appealed to the agents of the Hudson Bay Company to save and collect for him the tin lining of tea chests, and with this he cast metal type in his clay molds. He then adapted a fur press to take his movable type and succeeded, in the wilderness, in printing page by page his and his colleagues' translations of the Gospels. For paper they used birchbark, and for ink soot mixed with fish oil. The completed books were sewn with leather laces, and bound in deerhide. His Cree disciples recorded the event by the saying: "The birchbark has begun to utter the Word of God." Today modern fonts enable the great work that Evans began to be continued as ordinary printed books in the Cree character.

Why have we in America been so slow to recognize the strong and widespread Iberian and Arab influence in the languages and cultures of the Amerindian peoples?

The answer is not far away. Jefferson was, in fact, far ahead of his times in turning his thoughts to North Africa and to the Arabs and Berbers of the Barbary Coast. History forced his attention upon that part of the world because American ships were subject to attack by the North African mariners, who resorted to piracy whenever opportunity offered—as indeed did the Greeks and Turks and other Mediterranean peoples, keeping up an age-old tradition of buccaneering that reaches back into the times of the *Iliad*. Homer makes frequent reference to Phoenician slave women in the households of Greek chieftains and further tells us that they were seized in the course of Greek raids upon peaceful communities. During Roman times, piracy was severely suppressed, and for several centuries law and order was maintained upon the seas; but after the fall of Rome, old habits returned. Jefferson's presidency spanned an era when American and European powers alike determined to assume the mantle of Rome, and to restore some semblance of orderly commerce and freedom to travel. But Jefferson was a thoughtful and learned antagonist, and after the Barbary States were brought to recognize America as a determined and dangerous opponent, the peace that followed brought with it a measure of understanding—or at least the desire for understanding.

But the year now was 1804. What did the Western world know of Arabs—let alone the even more mysterious Berbers? Almost nothing. An eccentric English noblewoman, Lady Hester Stanhope, had set up a kind of court in a deserted and ruined convent in Phoenicia (Lebanon), and from her orientalized manner of life came strange stories to Europe. Famous travelers such as the French poet Lamartine and the English author-philosopher Alexander Kinglake visited her. Kinglake wrote an account of his travels called *Eothen,* but it was not published until 1844, by which time Jefferson had been dead eighteen years.

Even then the Arabs were only beginning to emerge into European and American consciousness, mainly as wandering nomads, more or less kept in some semblance of order by the despotism of the Ottoman Empire.

Not until 1840 was there any translation of an Arabic literary work into English—this was Edward Lane's rendition of *The Arabian Nights,* a work that remains to this day almost the only Arab literature known to us in the West. And even Lane's efforts were frustrated by the puritanism of his age. Only when Richard Burton issued an expurgated version in 1885–1888 did British and American educators consider the work suitable for presentation to a general audience. Meanwhile, one more traveler had appeared among the English. This was Charles Montague Doughty who, in 1888, published a book of his adventures with the Arabs that was destined to take its place as one of the masterpieces of English writing. He wrote in an archaic and evocative style, reminiscent of Chaucer and the Elizabethans, with passages inspired directly by the Arabic of his hosts. He called this famous book *Travels in Arabia Deserta.* And with that, save for some inspired translations of poetry, the English-speaking peoples of the world had to be content until a young archeologist, Thomas Edward Lawrence, provided a romantic view of the Arab revolt in which he participated. His main work, *The Seven Pillars of Wisdom,* was known to my generation in school by name alone, for only 1,000 copies were issued for private distribution. A shortened and expurgated version called *Revolt in the Desert* appeared in 1927, and that was the edition that filled the minds of youth in the colleges of Britain and America with the first notions that the Arabs are indeed a remarkable and admirable people, despite their extraordinary and dangerous manner of life as presented in these few works available to us.

It was with that slim background, and almost no detailed information on any aspect of Arab life whatever that I personally first encountered Arabs in Arabia and Egypt in 1939. I was charmed by their polite manners, and mystified and fascinated by Moorish architecture and above all by the written Arabic language itself. But when I returned to British—and later to American—societies, I found little interest in these matters, and almost no reading materials in the libraries available to most people. Desert sunsets, silhouettes of pyramids and caravans, were commonly to be seen as paintings hung on the walls of English homes, but their owners seemed to have acquired them by means other than travel, and knew little if anything about the Arabs depicted in these colorful paintings.

Who could read any work in Arabic? Almost no one. What colleges taught Arabic? Few indeed, for who among the student body required such courses? Then World War II broke upon us, and in the fury of the battles in the western desert, scarcely any attention whatever was paid by any of us in those desperate days to the hopes and aspirations of the North African peoples through whose lands the Germans, Italians, British, and Americans rampaged. After peace came, it was almost with indignation that the Allies grudgingly consented to independence for the North African nations.

That, then, is the background of our slowly dawning awareness of the gifted and intelligent Arab and Berber peoples of North Africa. Certainly from such a protracted and fragmented approach to North African history and ethnology, little might be expected to emerge that might attract the attention of anthropologists and linguists studying the native Amerindian peoples of the New World. Thus our predecessors completely missed the fundamental truths only now becoming apparent; truths that are still dismissed by all too many people without adequate understanding of the matters they spurn.

11

Arabs Before Islam

For centuries, since historians began to pay attention to the Arab world, it has been almost universally assumed that the Arabic language spread to North Africa when the victorious armies of Islam swept from Egypt to Spain during the seventh century A.D. Before that time, it has been assumed that Berber, or some older dialect allied to Berber, must have been the spoken language of Libya and the lands to the west.

In parts of Tunisia and other places where the Carthaginians had built trading centers, the language would be Punic, itself a dialect of Phoenician. The Romans referred to the inhabitants of eastern Algeria, southern Tunisia, and Libya as Numidians; hence the language of the Numidians would presumably be some early form of Berber—certainly not Arabic. Presumably also, the people of Morocco, whom the Romans called Mauritanians, would also speak a language similar to Berber. These inferences were apparently supported by the fact that ancient inscriptions in all these North African countries are written in Libyan (i.e., Numidian) letters. When the Romans under Augustus found it convenient to transfer a Libyan king suddenly to a new throne in Mauritania, his Moroccan subjects accepted him as such.

All these historical facts seemed to imply that a language ancestral to Berber would have to have been used in the inscriptions cut on North African monuments prior to the coming of Islam. And when the first Berber dictionary was prepared by a scholarly committee, including the Imam Sidi Ahmed ben el Haji Ali in 1844, the fact that many Arab words occurred in it was attributed to borrowing on the part of the Berbers, after they had come under Arab influence—that is, after the seventh century A.D.

236

Thus, when it was noticed that the Berber word for a building—*benian*—is the same as the Arabic word of the same meaning, scholars said "Well, of course it is the same for the simple reason that nomads who dwell in the desert have no word of their own, because they do not make buildings." Although this seems logical, it is not; most Berbers live in adobe buildings and are farmers, not nomads.

It follows nonetheless that whatever word is used for "building" on an ancient Numidian inscription, it will not be *benian,* since no Arabic speakers were present in North Africa at that time. Therefore the word could not be borrowed.

In 1975 two of my colleagues, Professor Norman Totten and James Whittall, both had occasion to visit Morocco and, at my request, made copies of ancient Numidian inscriptions that came under their notice. These could be dated approximately to the late Roman Empire (one of the inscriptions included a Latin text showing that it was the tombstone of a legionary). I examined the Numidian texts and was surprised to notice that the phonetic transliteration of the Numidian letters yielded meaningful phrases in the very language that history said could not be present at that date—namely Arabic!

The following year the Epigraphic Society published the texts and their decipherments and translations, together with a critique of the supposed evidence that Arabs were absent from North Africa prior to the spread of Islam. Later I was able to locate a bilingual inscription, in Punic and Numidian, that had been cut on the foundation stone of a temple erected in memory of King Masinissa. The Punic language can be read without difficulty, as it is similar to ancient Hebrew, and scholars had already published the translation. But on examining the hitherto undeciphered Numidian text on the same stone, I found the very word *benian* in that part of the text where, according to the Punic version, the word *building* ought to occur. It soon became obvious to me that most of the other words in the Numidian text matched Arabic; the remainder were similar to modern Berber. Now the information given on that inscription enabled the foundation stone to be dated to the year 139 B.C. We now had complete proof that Arabic language was not only present in Tunisia some 800 years before the

Islamic invasion, but was so important that the royal scribes employed it in official public inscriptions.

These and similar decipherments made it clear why so much difficulty had attended the decipherment of ancient Libyan and other North African texts in the Numidian script. We had made the mistake of supposing that no Arabic could occur in such texts, and therefore no Arab scholars had been consulted by the archeologists who discovered the inscriptions.

This fundamental work had to be done on North African inscriptions because only there do we find the associated records that permit inscriptions to be dated as exactly as in the case of the temple to Masinissa. It could not have been done on American material because we still lack any firm dating standards in American epigraphy.

But once the answer had been arrived at on African inscriptions, it became possible to solve the hitherto refractory examples from America. As soon as I returned from Libya, I re-examined the fine series of Cimarron cliff inscriptions discovered and published by Gloria Farley. It became apparent at once that the previously insoluble texts can be read without difficulty as Arabic, using Libyan alphabetic letters, and that the men who had engraved them must have been American contemporaries of their cousins in North Africa.

These results aroused great interest in Arab lands, and during my visit, and subsequently, they have been shown and explained on television in Tunisia and Libya.

Two questions arise at once. First, why had the historians been so wrong about the date and manner of arrival of Arabs in North Africa? Second, if the Arabs did not come with Islam, when and how *did* they reach North Africa? And for us in America, there is a third and much more important question: What does it all mean for our own history?

Let me answer the first and second questions now. Not *all* historians were wrong. Rather, it depends on which history book you choose to read. If, instead of consulting such works or standard compilations as the *Cambridge History of Islam,* we turn instead to ancient authors in Latin and Greek, we learn that entirely different opinions prevailed. The Roman historian Sallust, for example, who lived in the first century before Christ, tells us that the Libyans are descended from a people who came from Asia Minor, and who were allied to the Phoenicians through the language they spoke. The Greek historian Procopius, who lived in the sixth century A.D., states that the Moroccans are descended from migrants who came from Canaan, in Phoenicia, and that they originally left their Phoenician homeland at the time of the wars of the Hebrew king David. Arab historians, such as El-Bekri and Ibn Haldun, also record similar beliefs. Evidently truth lies with these ancient writers, and the "people allied by language with the Phoenicians" were the ancient Arabs whose language we find on the old North African inscriptions.

And what of our American inscriptions? They evidently tell us that voyagers from North Africa, using Libyan script and speaking ancient Arabic, arrived on our coasts, and that some settled here. No longer is it incongruous or incomprehensible when we find Arab vocabulary in American languages that employ a non-Arab script; for we see that languages and scripts are independent variables, and any one language will borrow the script of another if the circumstances make this useful. Having now established the presence in North Africa in ancient times of both Arabs and Berbers, the two peoples who dominate the present-day populations of North Africa, it is appropriate to consider briefly how the two peoples differ with respect to those customs that we can recognize in an archeological setting. How do we distinguish Arabs from Berbers when all we have to make the judgment by are ruins of their habitations? A glance at their manner of life provides the answer.

Except for the people who live in the cities, and who have adopted modern Western manners for the most part, the population of North Africa may be considered as forming two distinct ecological groups:

(1) **The farmers,** agriculturalists who live in settled communities, generally in the more mountainous areas, and who irrigate the land to grow their crops. These are mostly Berbers, light-skinned Europoids, still speaking the Berber language in the Atlas Mountains, though Arabic has been adopted in other areas. Their villages comprise fixed dwellings, built either of dried mud (Arabic

The ancient Libyans who lived along the Gulf of Syrtis, west of Cyrene, spoke a language that appears to have been a dialect of preclassical Arabic containing many Berber loan words. This conclusion is based on the language written with Numidian characters and found on royal and civic monuments dating from the reigns of Massinissa and Mekusen, two Libyan kings who ruled over most of the North African coast in the second century B.C. The illustration shows a small portion of a bilingual stele of Mekusen, in which Punic (above) and Libyan (below) parallel texts report the same information in both languages, the former allied to Hebrew, the latter to Arabic. Epigraphic Museum. *Photo Peter J. Garfall.*

Opposite page: How the western Libyans wrote. On official inscriptions, such as those of King Massinissa and King Mekusen in the second century B.C., neatly executed texts are found employing the alphabet shown in B. After the first century A.D., certain letters changed their form, notably A, L, W, K, Q, H, all of which assumed a braille-like aspect, made up of a number of dots. This later style, called Tifinag, is illustrated below, at C. The signs marked Š represent the sound of *sh* in English. These alphabets were used alike by Arabic and Berber speakers.

However, after the conquest of Tripoli by invading Islamic Arabs from the east, in 646 A.D., most Arabic writers in North Africa adopted the Kufic alphabet, shown in A above. It has numerous variant forms, and inscriptions are sometimes very carelessly written, in other cases (especially on mosques and royal tombs) engraved with exquisite artistry, embellished with leaves and florets. The Berber tribes in some areas retained the Tifinag alphabet into modern times. Most modern Libyans and other North African Arabic speakers today use a variant of the Naskhi alphabet, in which certain letters are rendered differently from those of eastern Arabic; these special forms are known as Maghrib but, as they have not so far been recognized in American inscriptions, they are omitted here.

"It is sacrilege to scrape off an inscription; do not offend Baal." So reads the text of this ancient Libyan inscription, written in a language close to Classical Arabic, but using an ancient North African script called Numidian. It was found at Hickison Summit Pass, Nevada, and reported as Indian petroglyphs in 1962. *Epigraphic Museum replica, photo Dr. Julian Fell.*

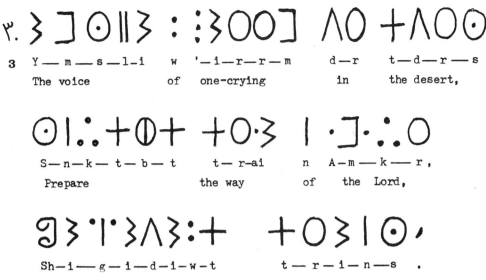

3   Y—m—s—l-i   w   '—i—r—r—m   d—r   t—d—r—s ,
The voice   of   one-crying   in   the desert,

S—n—k—t—b—t   t—r-ai   n   A—m—k—r ,
Prepare   the way   of   the Lord,

Sh—i—g—i—d—i—w—t   t—r—i—n—s .

Make straight   his paths.

Example of Tifinag script, derived from ancient Libyan, still in use among the Tamahaq Berbers of southern Algeria and northern Mali. Locally known as *T'Iullem Meden* or "They, the Iullem Tribe," it is probable that *T'Iullem* is the same word as *Tellem,* the legendary builders of the Pueblo-like cliff dwellings of the Dogon country now inhabited by the non-Berber Habbé tribe. A search for inscriptions resembling the one illustrated here might yield verification of the hypothesis. The passage cited is verse 3 of chapter 40 of *El-Kitaba en Nebi Ishaia* (The Book of the Prophet Isaiah) in Tamahaq Berber of the Air district of Algeria and the Niger region. Inscriptions in this alphabet occur along the Atlantic coasts of North America, from Nova Scotia, Maine, Connecticut, and the Virgin Islands: all date from after 100 A.D. The numerical adaptation of this alphabet was in use among the Hohokam people of the arid western states of North America (see Chapters 7 and 9).

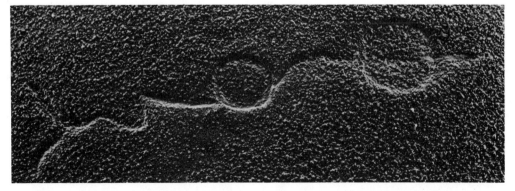

A Moslem personal name *Hamid* (Tranquil) inscribed in ancient Kufic Arabic (reading from right to left H-M-I-D), dating from some time after 650 A.D., and replicated from an engraving at the Atlatl Rock in the Valley of Fire, Nevada. It was formerly regarded as a meaningless Indian petroglyph, and classified as "A curvilinear meander, type 14." *Epigraphic Museum, photo Peter J. Garfall and Dr. Julian Fell.*

at-tobi, our word *adobe)* or of stones cemented together with adobe, forming split-level rectangular apartments, the floors and ceilings strengthened by wooden beams which may project beyond the outer walls. Tall towers of square cross-section serve as storehouses for the village community. They have small and irregularly dispersed rectangular openings that serve as windows. Those Berbers who retain their ancient customs practice chin-tattooing of the women, who do not wear the veil, even though they are now Moslems. The men, on the other hand, often cover the head and face with a scarflike cloth, showing only the eyes to strangers.

(2) **The nomadic pastoralists,** mainly Arabs, who live in the lowlands in tents, and who drive their herds from place to place in search of pasture, since the desert climate will not support a stationary pastoral life. These people do not build fixed villages, but instead carry portable dwellings of hides and props, so that camps can be pitched whenever and wherever the occasion demands. The women veil the head and face, are not tattooed, and the men do not veil the face. The language used is Arabic, the religion Islam.

Both Berbers and Arabs have schools associated with religious centers, such as the tomb of a locally revered holy man. For the Berbers with fixed habitations, the teaching naturally occurs in the village itself. For nomadic Bedouins, on the other hand, only the more advanced teaching can occur at religious centers. Most of the time, the children are obliged to move about with their parents, so a peripatetic teacher is also required.

Both the nomadic people and the agriculturalists make much use of leather. Skins of animals, tanned with acacia bark, serve as water bottles, which are portable and unbreakable. Nowadays, those who live in the cities and towns use ceramic ware, made on the potter's wheel. The excavations show that this was also the custom in Roman times. But before Roman times, the wheel was unknown to North African potters, and the dishes and bowls and other vessels of clay that they made were shaped by hand using coiling techniques. With this technique, many vessels could be shaped like animals, or even portraits of people, or free-form patterns. The pottery was hand painted in typically formal designs—often four-part symmetrical patterns of formal elements.

Herodotus reported that Troglodytes (people who live in holes in the ground) inhabited Libya. They still do! Communities may combine to excavate a circular depression in the desert rock, some 60 feet or so in diameter, and 20 feet deep. Then, out of the circular wall thus produced, individual rock-cut apartments are excavated, all opening into the central depressed circular area, the "hub" or *qaba*. This technique provides a cooler dwelling, sheltered from the sun's heat. Ventilation shafts connect the apartments with the surface of the desert overhead. This arrangement, seen in the mountainous desert to the west of Tripoli, and extending into Tunisia, may be the origin of the circular *kivas* of the so-called *pueblo* towns of the southwest United States. Similarly, the square adobe buildings of the Berber villages appear to match the pueblos of North America, while the portable tents of the pastoral Arabs seem little different from the tipis of the plains Indians. Further similarities will become apparent as the book proceeds.

But one circumstance, more than any other, served to turn my thoughts to North Africa, long before I had any inkling that the pueblo ruins of North America might have some historical link with that continent. This was the stream of field reports that came in from members of the Epigraphic Society. From Oklahoma, the Colorado border, and Arkansas, Gloria Farley brought back to her home in Heavener a remarkable series of latex impressions of inscriptions she believed to be ancient, mostly found on river bluffs and carved on boulders on the mountains or concealed in woodlands. That Gloria was correct in her assessment became obvious, for the markings were made up of Libyan letters, though often it was impossible (with the inadequate knowledge of ancient Libyan language we then had) to discover the meaning of the inscriptions. One of Gloria's finds had both Libyan and Latin letters side by side with an engraving of a nude warrior holding two spears. My attempts to extract a meaning from the inscription were fruitless until I became acquainted with the regions of North Africa where Berbers and Romans had once lived side by side. Only then did I realize that the mysterious bilingual of the Cimarron warrior gave his name in Berber and Libyan, and that both texts identified him as Mars, the god of war.

These and other incidents underlined the importance of a better knowledge of North African antiquities and languages. Without that we were like a blind man trying to read a printed book. Either he must regain his vision, or find a means of converting the unreadable print into braille.

Along the southern margin of the Sahara desert, in the state of Mali, live the Habbé tribe of some 250,000 black people whose language betrays no near affinity with Berber. Their culture, however, is very similar to that of the settled Berber farm communities, for they build square towers as storehouses for food, have multiple-storied buildings, floored by laying timbers horizontally to project through the adobe walls. Their villages are constructed like Mesa Verde, clinging to the cliff walls of a long line of escarpment called the Bandiagara. The means of access to these cliff-hanging towns is often by way of very narrow defiles and flights of rock-cut steps, or wood ladders. Their most conspicuous artifact, apart from the remarkable mud towers (usually capped by a thatch roof resembling a huge straw hat), is the universally employed basket. The baskets come in all sizes and many shapes and styles, both round and square, and made by coiling and plaiting techniques. Indeed, were these people known only from their artifacts, they would be classified in America as late Basketmaker II or III, and their ruined cliff dwellings would be called Pueblo. Like their neighbors, the Habbé make use of the Al-Kahan oracle, play wood flutes, weave in the same manner as the nomads on stake looms set in the ground, and cover the adjacent cliff faces with pictographs of mythical or religious themes. All these features occur in west America.

According to tradition (for they have no known writing system), the Habbé were driven to take refuge in these cliff dwellings by hostile Fulani, a West African tribe, around 1350 A.D. They claim to have displaced an earlier cliff-dwelling people called the Tellem, supposedly dwarfs who invented the cliff-hanging adobe towns. The archeology is obscure, but the sequence of events seems strangely reminiscent of the arid West of North America. In either area, we evidently witness the outcome of cultural influences, emanating from North Africa, and adopted by unrelated adjacent people. Just as West Africans have adopted a North African culture, so also could native American tribes when Libyan colonists reached the Americas.

The archeology of the region occupied by the Habbé has so far failed to disclose who the Tellem predecessors were, but such remains as have been examined show that they were certainly no dwarf people. Now, to the north of Bandiagara cliffs are found to this day a tribe of Berber-speaking people, the Tamaha, who still employ the Tifinag alphabet of the Libyan Berbers. They call themselves T'Iullem-meden: "They, the Iullem tribe." I believe that the "Tellem" of the Habbé legendary history must be T'Iullem, for this would be consistent with the apparent Berber origin of the architectural structures and other features of the Habbé. The matter could be resolved if a search were organized for possible Tifinag inscriptions in the Bandiagara cliffs region.

Scattered across the arid western states of North America lie the mysterious ruins of a vanished civilization. Archeologists speak of the builders as the Pueblo people but, until 1978, no one could say what language they spoke or where they came from. Seven centuries ago, they suddenly abandoned their towns and vanished.

Who were these Pueblo folk? The answer, as we now have discovered, lies engraved on American bedrock, written in ancient characters that can still be read and understood. They disclose the forgotten story of a great odyssey that began long ago on the other side of the world.

Twenty-two centuries ago, when a pharaoh still ruled in Egypt, seafarers from the city-states of North Africa passed through the canal at Suez that King Darius had built, and then sailed down the Red Sea to cross the Indian and Pacific oceans, and so discovered the West Coast of America. Here they established flourishing colonies in many places, and used their experience of desert life to good advantage in the arid regions they encountered.

These early Americans brought with them a knowledge of navigation, astronomy, and mathematics. They knew that the earth is a globe suspended in space, and they charted the coasts and islands of the seas they crossed. Their philosophers established schools of learning to perpetuate this knowledge. One of the regions they chose for this purpose lies in the high plateau of

Nevada. Here these ancient scientists remained in undisputed possession for twelve centuries. Then, almost as suddenly as their forebears had come, they vanished without trace, leaving behind a host of rock-cut inscriptions.

Until recently, no one had any idea as to what the strange ciphers might mean, or whether they recorded intelligible information. Archeologists called the markings "Great Basin Curvilinear," but when they asked the Indian people as to what they meant, the Paiute and Shoshone tribesmen of Nevada could tell them nothing, save that neither they nor their forebears had cut them.

The so-called Curvilinear is in fact writing—ancient Punic, Greek, and Libyan Arabic of North Africa—using alphabets that are proper to those tongues. Similar texts, including also Celtic, Iberian, and Hebrew, were inscribed in other parts of America, but the Nevada examples are unique for their isolation—and consequent excellent preservation—remote from the destructive hand of any later invader, and preserved by natural aridity. Here, then, the ancient history of America may be read and understood.

The population of Nevada has increased fivefold since first I visited that splendid plateau some thirty-five years ago. In those days, the state averaged only one human being to each square mile, which is the same as saying that it was emptier than the Arabian desert. It was still spoken of as the Silver State. Everywhere people used those large handsome coins called silver dollars and took pride in the fact that they were minted from metal that came from Nevada mines.

The stark grandeur of the scenery, those folded ridges of bedrock that rise so abruptly out of the desert flats, reminded me of the Yemen, and of Sinai, where I had traveled some years before. It was like Arabia, too, in the clarity of the atmosphere and the crimson glow of desert sunsets that set the peaks on fire in those last few moments before darkness falls. Named for the splendid Sierra Nevada whose snow-capped summits rim the western horizon, the entire state is a plateau suspended one mile vertically above the rest of North America—truly the roof of our continent, an American Pamir ringed by mountain walls and with

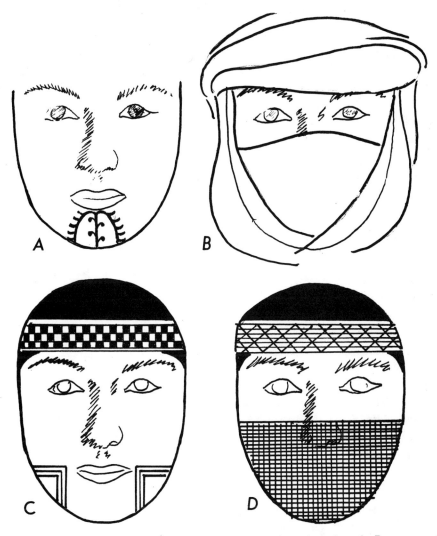

Tattoo and face-veils in North Africa and ancient America. A, B, a
Berber couple from an agricultural community in the Atlas Mountains:
A, woman with face unveiled and with chin tattoo; B, her husband,
his face fully veiled by a scarf in the presence of visitors (and no
tattoo). C, D, a Hohokam couple of the Mimbres Valley Mogollon culture
in New Mexico in the tenth century A.D. The woman, C, is unveiled
but has chin tattoo; D, her husband is veiled, and apparently has no
tattoo. (A, B from life; C, D, based on ancient bowl painting, Peabody
Museum, Harvard University.)

Adobe buildings in typical rectangular style of an agricultural
community of Berbers, Atlas Mountains, Morocco. The cultivated fields,
often irrigated, are adjacent to such permanent places of habitation.

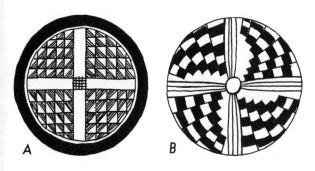

A   B

Ceramic bowls, handmade
by coiling clay without the
use of a potter's wheel,
characterize ancient
Libya and ancient North
America. In both areas
the same designs and
techniques persist to this
day. A, decorated bowl for
use at table, Libya. B,
similar bowl from the Four-
Corners area of the arid
Southwest, about 900
A.D.

Cliff dwellings at Montezuma Castle National Monument, Arizona (above), and at Mesa Verde National Park, Colorado (Wetherell Mesa longhouse) (below). The western American villages much resemble the cliff dwellings of North African peoples such as the Habbé (page 246). *Photo Professor Norman Totten.*

Stone-built dwellings with timber beams incorporated also characterize both North African towns and these American examples, the Great Kiva of the the Anasazi culture, Aztec Ruins National Monument, New Mexico (above), and the Cliff Palace, Mesa Verde, Colorado (below). *Photos Professor Norman Totten.*

The Pueblos of New Mexico present a similar aspect to that
of the abandoned hillside villages on the slopes of the
Jabal Nafusa in inland Tripolitania, overlooking the Plain
of Jafarah.

Although Libya lacks rivers, the ancient mosaics indicate a former familiarity with riverine boating scenes, including the use of the papyrus boat similar to that used by some American peoples in lake or riverine environments. National Archeological Museum, Tripoli. *Photo Peter J. Garfall.*

Boats made from large tree trunks, such as are not native to North Africa, appear in some Libyan frescoes of river scenes. They imply that Libyan colonists abroad would in no wise be constrained to seek desert environments, though they would be capable of occupying such territory. National Archeological Museum, Tripoli. *Photo Peter J. Garfall.*

Sea angling with rod and hand net two thousand years ago on the coast of the Gulf of Syrtis. Tripoli Museum. *Photo Peter J. Garfall.*

News of the American finds brought scholars from North Africa to investigate the reports. Here Dr. Mohamed Jarary (right), general director of the Libyan Studies Center, University of Tripoli, and Professor Ali Khushaim (center) of the Executive Council of UNESCO and noted Islamic historian, work with Fell (left) at Harvard. *Photo Peter J. Garfall.*

The canyons and cave shelters in wind-eroded desert plateau country of Nevada, Valley of Fire State Park, where thousands of petroglyphs occur, some of them pictographs by Indian hunters, others written inscriptions by ancient nomads who occupied the territory before the twelfth century A.D. *Photo Joseph D. Germano*

much of the air of mystery or even magic that we associate with secluded alpine terrain.

In those days, thoughtful people in Nevada had already become conscious of the fact that an aura of mystery overhangs their land. Seven years earlier, they had set aside the Valley of Fire as a permanent park, to preserve its fantastic Jurassic formations, and the myriad petroglyphs carved upon them, as an open-air museum for future generations of Americans. Earlier still, in 1925, the Californian archeologist Julian Steward had explored some of the petroglyph areas with pen and camera, to lay the foundations of decades of future research. It was he who discovered and named the enigmatic Lost City—for so he called it, though in truth there are no ruins—just hundreds of inscriptions carved upon boulders as large as buildings. His name is not inappropriate for, now that the texts can be read, we know that the site was seasonally the scene of a city of tents erected by summer visitors, only to be deserted when the winter snows came down.

At the time of my first visits to Nevada, I was already interested in ancient inscriptions. The Royal Anthropological Institute had published a paper of mine on the subject of Polynesian pictographs. But now the times were out of joint, the world was at war, and my journeys were occasioned by scientific liaison duties for the Allied forces in the Pacific theater, so inscriptions could play no further role in my affairs until the army had done with me.

The opposite had been the experience of Captain J. H. Simpson of the U.S. Topographical Engineers, whose duties as an explorer led him to the discovery of the Medicine Rock petroglyphs at the mountain pass named for him. On June 6, 1859, he reported the discovery of "hieroglyphics" on some boulders just below the summit of the pass. They include the interesting horoscope for the twenty-fifth lunar day of November (see page xv). Although the Paiute Indians later attributed this to the Modoc tribe, said to have lived there in the fifteenth century, this is highly improbable, and the astronomers or astrologers of the ancient civilization of Nevada must in fact have been the authors.

Had it been recognized at the time, this early discovery by Simpson could have initiated research into the origins of the ancient peoples of Nevada, and indeed of North America; for the astrological symbols disclose a knowledge of the zodiac that could only have come from the ancient Mediterranean in Classical times, and automatically exclude an Asian origin (for different symbols are used in the oriental zodiacs); and of course the inscription could not possibly be the "independent invention" of Amerindians.

As time went by, thousands of other petroglyphs were discovered and recorded, culminating in the establishment at the University of California, at Berkeley, of an extensive photographic file, and the publication in 1962 of the most comprehensive report on the subject. This was the book *Prehistoric Rock-Art of Nevada and Eastern California* by Professors Robert F. Heizer and Martin A. Baumhoff.

At this juncture it was not realized that ancient Mediterranean inscriptions are present in North America, and it was supposed that the Nevada and other petroglyphs could not represent any kind of writing at all. They were accordingly classified into several categories, according to whether they suggested animals or plants, or merely abstract patterns. It was this latter grouping, named "Great Basin Curvilinear" by the archeologists, that actually comprises written texts; but to anyone unfamiliar with the writing systems of North Africa, they did not look like writing. Similar inscriptions occur in other states; and in Texas, for example, the archeologists had named them "Vermiform petroglyphs," attributing no meaning to the worm-shaped markings included under that term.

In 1976, after the publication of my book *America B.C.* in which Libyan and other North African inscriptions were reported from America, Arab scholars began to visit my decipherment laboratory and epigraphic museum in order to see for themselves what basis there might be for my findings. Their response was immediate and enthusiastic. Not content with visiting us in America, they found means to enable me to work with them on related problems in North Africa. Later we rejoined forces in America, the work now going ahead at an accelerated pace. Greek and Celtic scholars also lent their skills, and with the passing of each year, we now are gaining ever clearer insights as to the past history of this continent and its peoples.

The revolution in American archeology that has already occurred depends on one single new element: we can now read many of the inscriptions left behind by our forerunners in this hemisphere. What these inscriptions are telling us is that, until now, we have been acting like illiterates, collecting the relics of vanished people and trying to reconstruct their lives without paying any attention to the written records that they have bequeathed us. Fragments of pottery have been made the basis of our interpretation of history.

Let me illustrate the point by an analogy I recently drew when discussing this matter with a leading archeologist.

Suppose we had no knowledge of eighteenth-century English history, and were dependent upon archeological research to reconstruct it. This is how we in America might have approached the problem a few years ago:

> Ongoing studies show on numerous sites in Britain that the Salt-Glaze-Pottery People continued in uninterrupted occupation of England until the beginning of the eighteenth century, when a new incursion occurred. By tree-ring analysis of trees still living in the forests near Dresden, Germany, and comparing these with tree rings visible in the house timbers of ruined dwellings of the region, we can date to the year 1710 the first incursions of the Porcelain People, a tribe believed to be of Asiatic origin characterized by their clear white glazed pottery. In England, by tree-ring dating, we detect their arrival in the London area about the year 1729. Although the Salt-Glaze People remained undisturbed on many sites, the invaders spread, and by 1759 (according to tree-ring dates) a second invading group had occupied Staffordshire. This last incursion seems to have originated in northern Italy, and their highly characteristic pottery has led to our naming them the Blue-and-White Unglazed Pottery Culture. Some of the pottery employed other colors, notably black-and-white, but all of it is immediately identifiable by the Classical cameolike style, reminiscent of Roman and Etruscan cut glass of earlier times. By the end of the eighteenth-century, the White-Porcelain People had become the dominant tribe in England. In most aspects of their culture, they seem to have adopted the manners of their predecessors, the Salt-Glaze people, but notable new features introduced by the Porcelain People include a great development of canals throughout the land, apparently to facilitate commerce, though one theory is that England had suffered a change in climate, and

that a great irrigation system was required in order to prevent the spread of deserts. Nothing is known about the racial origins or languages spoken by these peoples, but, as indicated, there are strong grounds for suspecting migrations from Asia and northern Italy.

Now, however ridiculous this travesty of English history may appear, the sad fact remains that it is in just such a manner that much of North American history has been "reconstructed." We have paid no attention to the inventive genius of the inhabitants and have failed to consider that a single people can advance from one level of technology to another without any "incursion" of strangers from abroad. Adhering naïvely to the idea that all new developments are brought from another place by some footloose wandering tribe, and that pottery styles are inviolate markers of peoples, we have created a host of different fictitious "Peoples" whose complex comings and goings fill the pages of American archeology texts, but tell us absolutely nothing about the languages or places of origin of any one of them!

In the view of our teachers, no native American might ever exhibit the inventiveness of the ceramic chemists of Dresden, or the artistry and experimentation of Josiah Wedgwood of Staffordshire. No American could ever sail abroad to bring back to his people samples of the work and wares of other nations, and hence no native American potter—or canal builder, or mathematician, or astronomer, or whatever—might ever be influenced by advances made in other lands.

The whole approach to ancient history—including medieval history—of the Americas has been based on such false premises. That they are false is abundantly proved by the *written records* left for us to read by those very Americans whose history we have presumed to deduce on the basis of their discarded broken pots! Every hour uncounted broken dishes by the ton are thrown away by modern Americans, but I hope the day never comes when the history of man in space is undertaken by investigators whose sole interest is in broken plates and Coke bottles. With all due respect to traditional archeological beliefs and practices, I am certain that whatever records remain in the future of rocket technology of our age, no contribution to the subject will be made by collectors of shattered kitchen ware, glazed or otherwise. A single surviving transistor, and the not-infrequent college graffito $e = mc^2$ will have more to say to archeologists of the future than cups and saucers ever could.

But I have digressed. As events were soon to show, we were now on the verge of finding new evidence that had eluded us for five years, relics no less of the navigations of those same Arabs before Islam. Libyans who somehow set their prows to the rising sun, to cross the Indian and Pacific oceans and rediscover the New World by sailing in the opposite direction from that followed by their predecessors under Carthage.

The Great Navigations

The discovery of the most ancient maps of America—and of the Pacific islands and coasts—came about mainly for two reasons. First, I had returned from my field work in Libya deeply impressed by the evidence of maritime superiority of the ancient civilization of that land. Second, I was always very conscious when studying the maritime mosaics in the National Archeological Museum in Tripoli of evidence in the form of cave inscriptions in the Libyan language that we had recognized in northwestern Irian (New Guinea) in 1974. These New Guinea inscriptions included star maps, navigation diagrams and even calculations attributed to Eratosthenes, and appeared to be the work of a Libyan navigator who signed his name M–W. The word *mawi* in Egyptian means a guide or navigator, but it also sounds very like the Polynesian name Maui. In Polynesian legend Maui was a great sailor who, in the figurative speech of Polynesian tradition, was said to have "fished up new lands" from the sea. His exploits, and many other mythical adventures attributed to him, are recounted on all the far-flung islands of Polynesia. He seems to have been a real person, presumably an early explorer of the Pacific.

When I recorded the Libyan inscriptions from New Guinea I made the inference that the M–W of the cave texts was indeed the same as the Maui of Polynesian legend, and so then began to investigate the ancient Libyan language in order to find out if the Polynesian language is related to Libyan. It soon became evident that this is the case, and since 1975 several scholars, Professor Linus Brunner of Switzerland, Dr. Reuel Lochore of New Zealand, and I myself, have made continuous contributions to the etymology of the Polynesian language on the basis of studies of the North African and Semitic languages.

The New Guinea inscriptions led me to infer that Maui had

entered the Pacific Ocean from the northern Indian Ocean, and had crossed the Pacific in the direction of the Americas, apparently discovering some parts of Polynesia en route. The date of the voyage appeared to be the fifteenth year of Ptolemy III, of Egypt, as an eclipse of the sun visible in New Guinea in November 232 B.C. seemed to be the same as one recorded by Maui as occurring in "the fifteenth year of Pharaoh's reign": as the year 232 B.C. was in fact the fifteenth year of the reign of Ptolemy III, this seemed to provide reasonably good evidence of the date of Maui's voyage, if indeed I had read the inscriptions correctly.

Inevitably, therefore, I had a strong intuition during my later work on the Libyan sites of North America that sooner or later we must encounter charts of the voyages of Maui or his successors. But where? I had been disappointed in Libya itself where, despite the wealth of mosaics depicting life at sea, there appeared to be no remains of nautical instruments or mosaic versions of maps of any kind.

I came back to America to see if one more winnowing of our ever-increasing resources of ancient inscriptions might yield some clue. This time success was not far off, and in fact a continuous chain of clues came into my hands that ultimately led straight to the long-sought goal.

The year before, Peter Garfall and John Furatini of Schoenhof's, Cambridge booksellers who specialize in locating foreign publications, had been scouring the New York markets for linguistic and archeological works. Among their finds were a number dealing with the mysterious Mochica culture. This was a people of unknown origin who established a lively civilization on the northeast coast of Peru over the years 200 B.C. to 900 A.D. Nothing was known of their language, but their pottery and clay figurines show an exceptional sensibility for art and humor, much of it sexually oriented. This feeling for art, combined with evident musical interests, and clothing resembling that of Classical times in the Mediterranean, had earned for the Moche the sobriquet "the Greeks of South America."

Two features struck me as I studied their art. There were faint but recognizable traces of Libyan influence—for example, painted on a statuette of a jaguar, I noticed the four Libyan letters T-G-R-S, and above these letters, what looked like degenerate Arabic letters spelling M-M. From the lettering on Libyan mosaics of hunting scenes in North Africa we know that in Libya, in Classical times, the African leopard was called not *pardus* or *leopardus*, but *tigris*. There are no African tigers, so apparently the Greeks, after Alexander's Asian campaigns, introduced this Asian word into North Africa and applied it to the leopard. If a Libyan were to be confronted by a jaguar he would certainly have called it *tigris*, which is what the Libyan letters on the jaguar statuette appeared to spell. Again, in South American mythology, the puma and the jaguar are held in religious veneration; and in the Quechua tongue of Peru, the word *mama* connotes a divine mother. So although I could not be sure of the matter, the inscription suggested to me that a Peruvian artist had painted appropriate Quechua and Libyan words on his figurine. Did this mean a Libyan contact had occurred, and if so, how?

A still more striking feature of the Moche art were vase paintings of what were obviously dragon-ships, with sailors on board casting landing gear, mooring ropes, heaving the sounding lead, with circular fishing nets laid out to dry on deck, their floats like corks around the edge of the net, and so on. Yet, to my surprise, I found that previous investigators had regarded these nautical paintings as "representations of sea monsters," instead of ships, which they obviously are.

I searched the Tripoli Museum for comparable pieces from the excavations in Libya, but was disappointed. There are cats and references to cat worship in the Libyan inscriptions at Thougga, Tunisia, as I was able to demonstrate to my North African colleagues—but we found no dragon-ship designs, and no inscriptions on pottery to match the "Tiger-Mother," if that indeed was what the Peruvian figurine did say.

After I began to work on the Nevada inscriptions, I soon encountered a clue that aroused my interest in the problem, for there were engravings of ships, including dragon-ships, and one of the ships had a caption beside it in Kufic letters F-L-Q, the old spelling of *felluqa*, which means *ship* in Arabic. So there *were* dragon-ships on the western seaboard of the Americas after all, and furthermore they were definitely associated with a Libyan colonial civilization, speaking classical Arabic.

That was clue number one, sought and found.

The next problem: Did the Arabic-speaking Libyan colonists of western North America have any knowledge of foreign lands?

For if the dragon-ships that the Moche artist had painted in Peru were visitors from California or Colorado, then the settlers of our arid Southwest, and the desert plateau, could be expected to leave some record of this fact.

Reviewing what we had already discovered, I remembered that Gloria Farley had found a fine petroglyph of a horse in the Cimarron series, and that this horse carries a Libyan brandmark. We had often wondered how this apparent recollection of a beast that lived in Africa, but not in America, could have been so vivid as to prompt a conspicuous cliff petroglyph. Now I began to wonder if it was a recollection, not of something that forefathers had passed on as a tradition of the homeland, but rather of something that the engraver himself had actually seen on an overseas voyage from America. This notion would have been laughed out of court, had I expressed it at any public lecture, so I deemed it wisest to for the time being to make no reference to it. I re-examined the various elephant glyphs to which I had already made reference in *America B.C.* From my friend Dr. Clyde Keeler I received a fine replica of a ceramic elephant figurine, with a headless oriental rider, extracted from Teocalli Mound, Cuernavaca, Mexico by Dr. H. A. Monday, together with two locally made imitations in stone, also found in the burial mound. All these suggested to me now the possibility of Americans voyaging to the lands of origin of these animals, and bringing back tall travelers' tales about them, resulting in illustrative petroglyphs or, in the case of the elephant figurine, an actual imported art object from India or China.

I now began a systematic combing of all the recorded petroglyphs from those states in search of nautical information. The ancient charts, cut on rock, and faithfully recorded by modern anthropologists as meaningless petroglyphs, thus came to my notice.

The charts carried the name of Maui. They must therefore represent the maps he himself drew in the course of his great voyage of discovery twenty-two centuries ago. But, of course, he did not actually cut the versions we now have. His far-ranging voyages would leave no time for ascending the Colorado River, and then hiking hundreds of miles through the Sierra to the hidden valley at northern end of the Great Basin.

No, the name Maui, and the attribution to him, is to be compared with any modern map that announces itself to be "Mer-

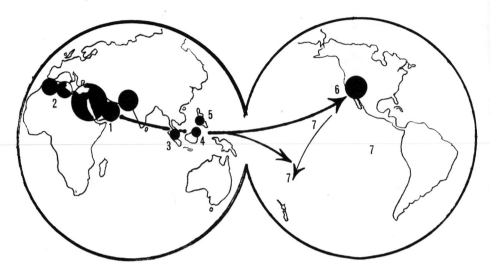

A trail of Arabic language and inscriptions, relict alphabets and fossil vocabulary curves around the globe and marks the ancient trans-Pacific sea roads to North America. 1, Classical Arabic, still extant. 2, Maghrib Arabic, still extant. 3, Malay, formerly using Arabic script, still retaining much Arabic vocabulary, mainly Moslem. 4, Dayak and Sea Dayak, with Arabic loan vocabulary. 5, Samal, Tau Sug and Bajan, in Sulu Islands, some loan vocabulary, Arabic script formerly used, Moslem or former Moslem communities and Arab Christians. 6, Hohokam Arabic, written and spoken, Libyan and Kufic Arabic alphabets, now extinct. 7, Polynesian dialects rich in Libyan and Classical Arabic, formerly with some Libyan alphabetic script, contacts partly direct via Indonesia, and partly indirect via Hohokam voyages from western North America where ancient charts of Polynesia have now been discovered.

Opposite page: While English-speaking children learned that C-A-T spells *cat,* relics of the ancient school sites in Nevada show that young Americans a thousand years ago were taught that F-L-Q spells *ship* (Arabic and Libyan *fulk,* our *felluca*). Scattered petroglyphs of stylized ships, sometimes with the Arabic or Libyan lettering (mistaken for Indian doodles) are widespread in the hunting areas of Nevada, for the boys were apparently taught by schoolmasters while the elders were busy in the hunting season, taking skins and furs for the trans-Pacific markets. This example is at Steward's site 207, in the Grimes petroglyph area of Churchill County, Nevada.

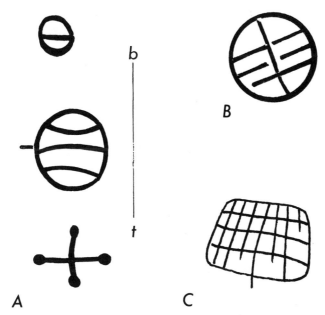

A B C

The Nevada children, probably in "summer school" (actually fall and spring were the upland hunting seasons, as Heizer and Baumhoff infer), learned that the earth is a globe (Libyan Arabic T-B, Arabic *taba,* globe), encircled by the equator and the tropics; and they learned how flat maps are related to the grid of spherical latitude and longitude established by the Libyan scientist Eratosthenes. These examples of school petroglyphs occur in southeastern California, where the Arabic-speaking Westerners (probably Hohokam) also spent time; Professor Julian Steward designated one site by his number 38, the other is number 210 of Heizer and Baumhoff's enumeration for Inyo County. The anthropologists who explored these petroglyph regions left excellent accounts of what they found, but failed to realize the significance because they did not recognize the writing.

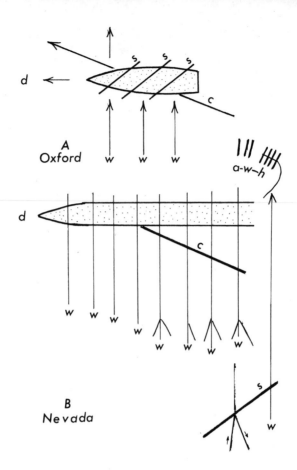

A
Oxford

a-w-h

B
Nevada

As the boys grew older, the more promising among them were sent to more advanced training at what we may recognize as America's first maritime academy, located at Professor Julian Steward's sites numbered 202 and 212, near the East Walker River in Lyon County, Nevada. In the above comparison we see the timeless truths of the sea as expressed by teachers of navigation 2,000 years apart. A, diagram presented in the *Oxford Junior Encyclopedia* (vol. 4, 1951), explaining how a sailing ship must trim her sails (s) in order to achieve a course (c) in the presence of a beam wind (w), the rudder being set to keep the hull aligned in the direction (d). B, diagram engraved on basalt boulders at University of California site Ly-1, East Walker River, Nevada, as recorded by Heizer and Baumhoff (1962), petroglyphs attributed to ancient hunters. The diagram explains how the lateen sail of a Libyo-American felucca, with its long, sleek streamlined hull, must be trimmed (s) in order to achieve the course (c) in the presence of the beam wind (w). A separate diagram (not included here) explains how the steering oar is to be set to align the hull in the direction (d). Both diagrams illustrate the effect of *leeway,* the deviation from a true course which a ship makes by drifting to leeward under the influence of wind from the beam. The keel counteracts this, and an extensive area of canvas as sails exaggerates it. In the American version, the beam wind is specifically identified by the label to the upper right H-W-a (Arabic *hawa,* wind). The letters of the inscription antedate the Tifinag style, and may date the diagram to earlier than the first century A.D.

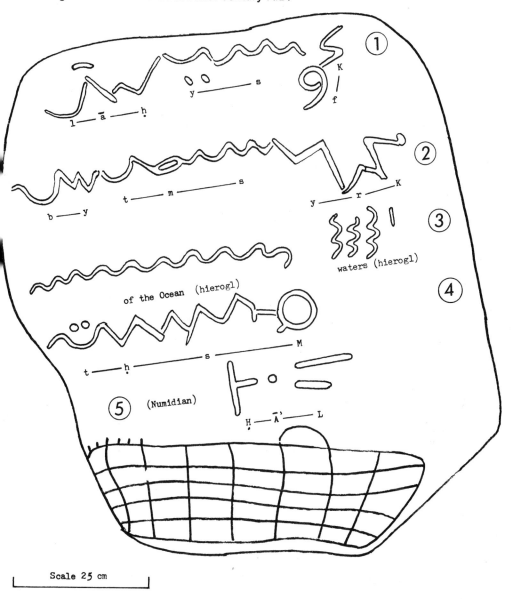

Scale 25 cm

Among other sites used for the teaching of navigation was Lagomarsino, 10 miles northeast of Virginia City, known since 1904, when it was discovered by John Reid. The site, now protected by the State of Nevada, has been investigated by Steward (1929) and University of California, Berkeley, archeologists, but no meaning could be attached to the signs. As is now evident, the purpose of the site was instruction in navigation and geography. This example reads in Kufic Arabic (1) The commensurate equivalent conversion (2) of spherical azimuths of land (3) and ocean waters (4) to plane surfaces. A Libyan text reads (5) Conversion. It is one of a series of inscriptions dealing with conic projections in mapping.

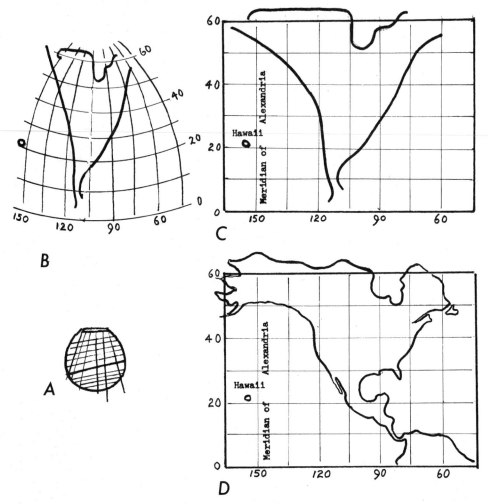

At these sites conical and rectilinear projection from spherical surfaces, A, was evidently taught. B (to which the grid has been added for clarity) could thus be converted to C, resembling our Mercator's projection, or its simplified predecessor, D. The outline of North America shown in B corresponds to that given in the Nevada petroglyph record, hitherto overlooked.

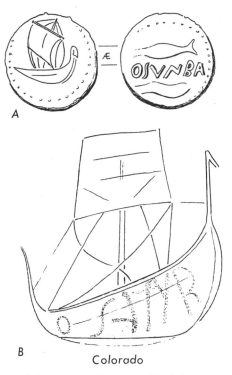

A

B   Colorado

Since their very training as mariners enabled these young graduates of the Nevada academy to sail the sea roads of the Pacific, the ships they commanded varied from one era to another, as fashions changed in the Old World. The earliest American vessel of which we have any detailed knowledge is the one depicted in the splendid Colorado petroglyph discovered by Gloria Farley and her Oklahoma team in 1978. This, and contemporary coins exhibit with grace and artistry the enchanting lines of first-century ships of Iberia. No doubt the contemporary ships of North Africa and America were similar. A, a first-century coin of the Portuguese city of Osunoba (believed to have been a port located near modern Faro), showing that Iberian ship design had already developed streamlined hull structure by that early date. The same design, rendered still more elegantly, is seen in the Colorado petroglyph, B, recently discovered by Dale Murphy, a member with Truman Tucker, of Gloria Farley's expedition to Baca County where important inscriptions are now known to occur. It is reasonable to infer that ships of the type illustrated both on the coin and by the petroglyph were crossing the Atlantic during the first century A.D., for even if the Colorado petroglyph were copied from a coin of Osunoba, a ship would still have had to deliver the coin to America. The one and only example of the Osunoba coin is now lost, and the illustration is taken from an eighteenth-century engraving made at the time when the coin was owned by Frei Manuel do Cenaculo, Bishop of Beja. Markings on the hull of the Colorado ship seem to resemble the name OSVNB. A, after dos Santos, *Arqueologia Romana do Algarve* (1971), data from James Whittall, who also is responsible for detecting the close similarity of the Colorado ship to that of the Osunoba coin. B, drawn from latex cast obtained by Gloria Farley, 1978.

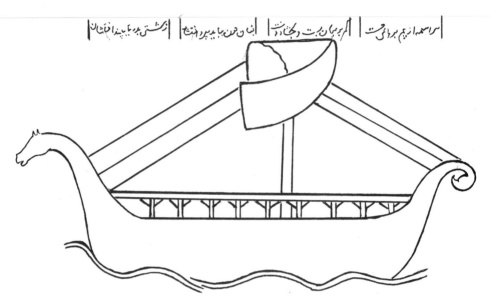

A medieval Arab manuscript from the Mediterranean depicts a Norse ship, above, with a horse's head as its prow figurehead. Seemingly, this fashion also came to North America, for a petroglyph found at the Lost City site of Steward shows a ship of this type, below.

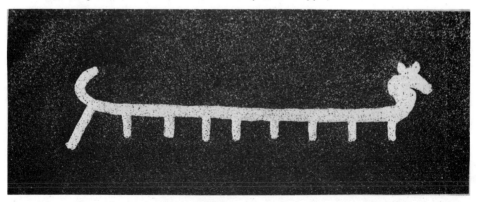

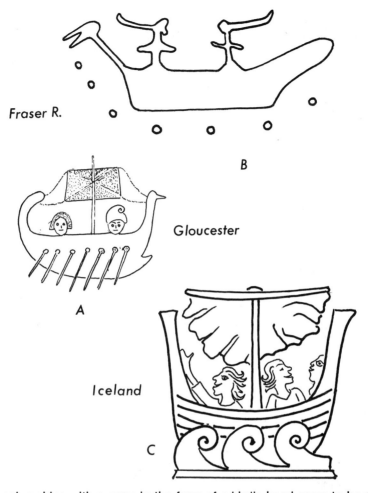

Fraser R.

B

Gloucester

A

Iceland

C

Seagoing ships with a prow in the form of a bird's head seem to be a Celtic invention, as the oldest known example is from a fourth-century mosaic at Low Ham, England, dating from the Roman occupation, and shown at A. At about this time it became fashionable for scribes to represent ships with two disproportionately large mariners, even though the bank of oars required many more. Both peculiarities are shown in the British example. A further mannerism adopted by the Celtic artists is the tendency to represent men and animals in mirror-image pairs. All the foregoing characteristics are exhibited by the British Columbia rock painting shown at A, and discovered by John Corner near the confluence of the Fraser and Stein rivers. As the district abounds in Ogam inscriptions, and Celtic speakers are native to the Fraser valley, there can be little doubt that the British Columbia petrograph is the work of a Celtic artist, one obviously acquainted with seagoing ships. To obtain the mirror-image, he makes the wind blow simultaneously in two opposite directions, to carry the sailors' hair, or head dress, to left and right. C, a comparable medieval drawing by a Norse artist, part of the decorations of a copy of the Icelandic Jónsbók in the Kongelige Bibliotek, Copenhagen, dating from the 1300s. (Data for B will be found in John Corner, *Pictographs in the Interior of British Columbia,* Vernon B.C.: Wayside Press, 1968.)

The Nevada sea lords made journeys along the American coast southward to Peru, where local Mochica artists painted this curiously detailed—yet curiously incorrect—representation of mariners coming ashore, with sounding line poised and anchoring rope ready to cast, the fishing nets (that supplied the sailors' need for fresh food) drying in the sun. But, being acquainted only with the ancient reed-boats, the artist has mistakenly assigned a reed-built hull to this fast-moving dragon-ship of the north. *Replica from Mochica bowl, photo Dr. Julian Fell.*

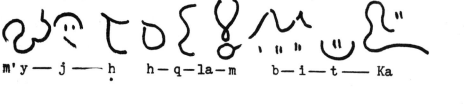

m' y — j — ḥ   h — q — la — m   b — i — t —— Ka   *1*

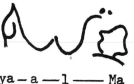

ya — a — l —— Ma   *2*

Visitors from abroad also came to America, bringing news of newer ship styles. *Katiba malaqah haji mi' Malaya*—"Record of a visit by voyagers from Malaya"—so reads this Arabic text found by Remberto I. Galicia in a cave at La Gruta de Corinto, El Salvador, and forwarded for interpretation by Maximiliano A. Martinez H., San Salvador. Beneath the Arabic text (which probably dates from the tenth to twelfth centuries A.D., when Arab voyagers were active in Indonesia) are three lines in an unknown script, evidently pictographic, and perhaps used at the time of the visit in Salvador. Arabic-speaking mariners reaching western America from Indonesia would be able to understand the Libyan dialect of the colonies established from Libya a thousand years earlier, for the intermittent contacts with the Old World (proved by the arrival of Islamic religion) would tend to stabilize the language, at least in coastal regions. As powerful Hindu kings occupied Indonesia after the third century A.D., and introduced decimal Sanskrit enumeration into Java, it is possible that the early arrival of decimal notation in North America may have been mediated by Malayan or Javanese mariners. *Inscription courtesy David J. Guzman Museum,* transl. Fell (1977).

Opposite page above: Latest of the newer types of Arab ship would be the *fulk,* already mentioned, and here shown with the parts of the vessel identified in Libyan Tifinag script. For comparison are shown also the hulls of the Santa Maria and a vessel built by the pharaoh Amenhotep (Amenophis) around 1500 B.C.

Opposite page above: These voyagers were no babes-in-the-woods in the matter of navigation. In addition to their understanding of the stars (Chapter 5), they had been in possession of the magnetic compass since about 300 B.C., as shown by this Iberian dial, the rim of a ceramic bowl made at Liria in southern Spain, in which a lodestone was floated, or a magnetized needle suspended. *Photo Peter J. Garfall.*

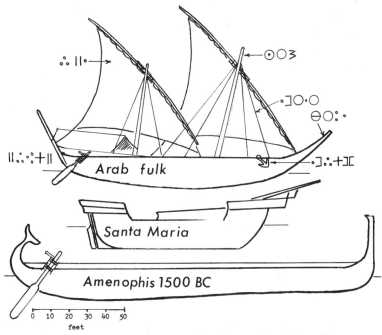

Arab fulk

Santa Maria

Amenophis 1500 BC

0 10 20 30 40 50
feet

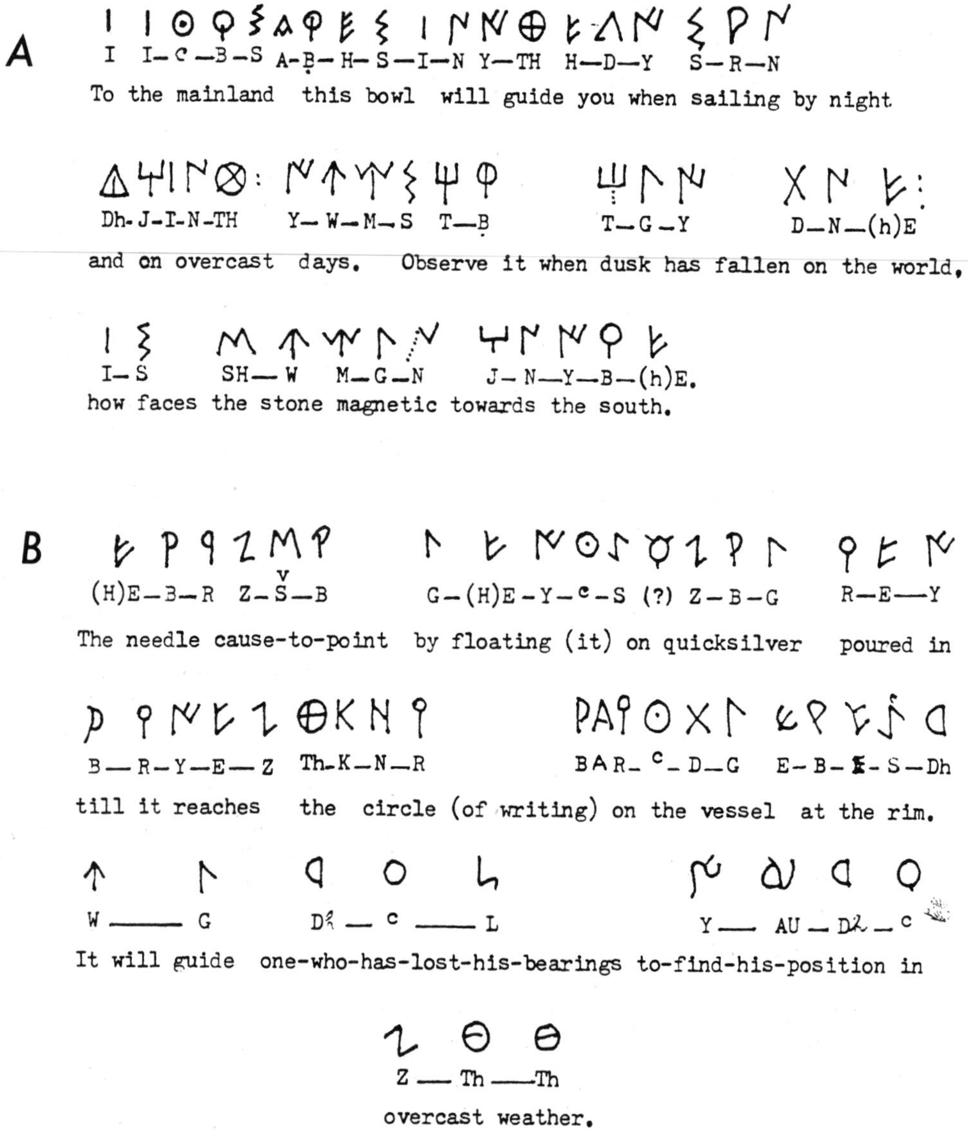

A

I I⎯c⎯B⎯S A⎯B⎯H⎯S⎯I⎯N Y⎯TH H⎯D⎯Y S⎯R⎯N

To the mainland this bowl will guide you when sailing by night

Dh-J-I-N-TH   Y⎯W⎯M⎯S T⎯B   T⎯G⎯Y   D⎯N⎯(h)E

and on overcast days.   Observe it when dusk has fallen on the world,

I⎯S   SH⎯W M⎯G⎯N   J⎯N⎯Y⎯B⎯(h)E.

how faces the stone magnetic towards the south.

B

(H)E⎯B⎯R Z⎯S⎯B   G⎯(H)E⎯Y⎯c⎯S (?) Z⎯B⎯G   R⎯E⎯Y

The needle cause-to-point by floating (it) on quicksilver   poured in

B⎯R⎯Y⎯E⎯Z Th⎯K⎯N⎯R   BAR⎯ c⎯D⎯G   E⎯B⎯£⎯S⎯Dh

till it reaches   the circle (of writing) on the vessel at the rim.

W ⎯⎯⎯ G   Dℓ⎯ c ⎯⎯⎯ L   Y⎯⎯ AU ⎯ Dℓ⎯ c

It will guide one-who-has-lost-his-bearings to-find-his-position in

Z ⎯⎯ Th ⎯⎯Th

overcast weather.

Two sample decipherments of the inscriptions written on Liria compass dials originally published (with explanation) by Fell in the *Occasional Publications* of the Epigraphic Society.

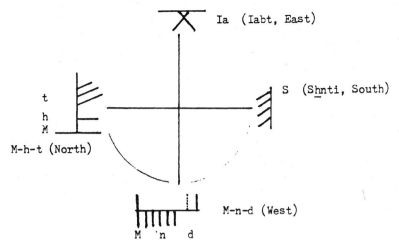

Ia (Iabt, East)

S (Shnti, South)

M-h-t (North)

t
h
M

M-n-d (West)

M 'n d

A simplified compass dial, lettered in Ogam script but employing Libyan (and Egyptian) terms for the cardinal points. Known as the Tennessee Disk, and engraved on a stone lamina, its decipherment was also published in the OPES.

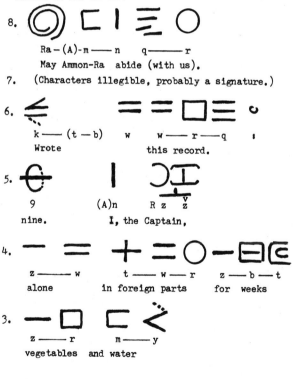

8.

Ra—(A)-m——n   q——r
May Ammon-Ra abide (with us).

7. (Characters illegible, probably a signature.)

6.

k——(t—b)   w   w——r—q   !
Wrote   this record.

5.

9   (A)n   R z z
nine.   I, the Captain,

4.

z——w   t——w—r   z—b—t
alone   in foreign parts   for weeks

3.

z——r   m——y
vegetables and water

2.

g——w——r   n—s——ꞌ—n
on an exploratory mission. We put in here for

1.

S——f——n n
Our ship is

As the Tennessee Disk would imply, voyages continued on the eastern quarter of the Americas while the western waters were under exploration. This ancient record of a voyage upon the Atlantic was found inscribed on the cliffs of the Canary Islands, at Barranco de Balos, by Antonio Beltran Martinez of the Museo Canario, Las Palmas de Gran Canaria (1972). It deciphers as Libyan Arabic, probably of about the third century A.D. (but perhaps older). The text is to be read from below upward. Decipherment originally presented at the Libyan Studies Center, University of Al-Fatih, with Naški Arabic transcript (see *Occasional Publications,* vol. 6, Epigraphic Society, 1977).

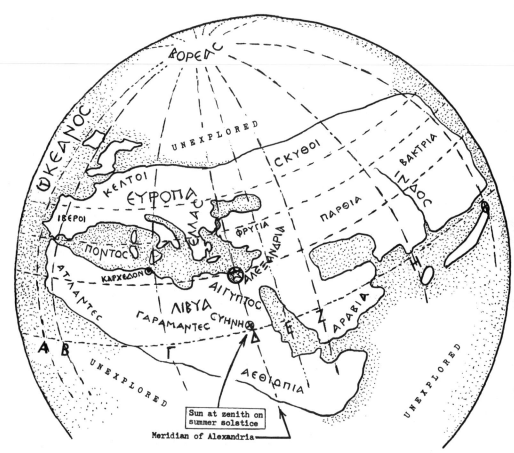

Sun at zenith on summer solstice

Meridian of Alexandria

Eratosthenes could now represent the known world of his day as a segment of a globe, on which he placed a selected number of lines of latitude and longitude. Maps of this type (here inferred, as no actual example has survived) would certainly be carried on all oceangoing ships.

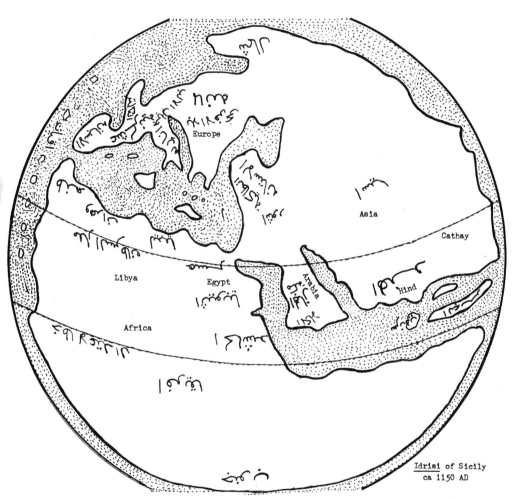

Idrisi of Sicily
ca 1150 AD

After the passage of 1,500 years, the Old World geographers, of which
the Arabs were the leaders at the time, recalled only this imperfect
version of the chart of Eratosthenes and, because of the decline of
navigation and science in Iberia (of which Ibn Khaldun, the great Arab
historian, complained) the old sailing route to America was forgotten
in the decadent universities. Ignorance reigned in most of Europe.

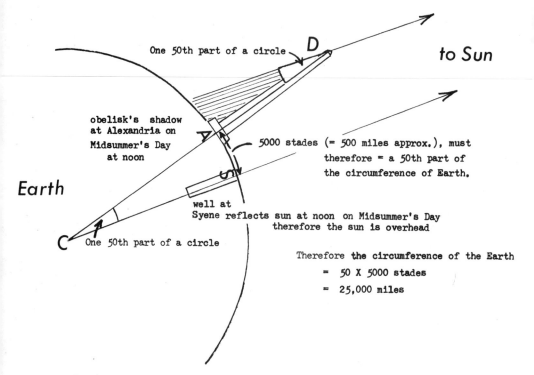

One 50th part of a circle

D

to Sun

obelisk's shadow
at Alexandria on
Midsummer's Day
at noon

5000 stades (= 500 miles approx.), must
therefore = a 50th part of
the circumference of Earth.

Earth

well at
Syene reflects sun at noon on Midsummer's Day
therefore the sun is overhead

C

One 50th part of a circle

Therefore **the circumference of the Earth**

= 50 X 5000 stades

= 25,000 miles

Our voyagers also had charts, though only a few traces of them survive
as inaccurate parchment copies in the Mediterranean, and as petroglyphs in America. The famous observation by Eratosthenes, around
239 B.C., enabled the size of the globe of the earth to be determined,
and hence lines of latitude and longitude could be applied. The observation is explained in this diagram. The sun, being at a great distance
from the earth (as the Greeks then understood) must send effectively
parallel rays of light to the earth. Hence the angle C at the center of the
earth must equal the measurable angle D. Eratosthenes measured D,
and accepted the Egyptian Post Office's official estimate of the distance
from Alexandria to Syene as being 5,000 stades (500 miles). He believed
that Syene lay due south of Alexandria (both estimates nearly correct).
Hence the circumference of the earth has to be 50 times 500 miles, or
25,000 miles.

cator's Projection." Gerhardus Mercator was a professor at the University of Louvain who, in 1568, devised a method of mapping that continues in use today. In the same way, we should think of Maui as a pathfinder who devised certain maps of the hidden face of the globe; so famous that for centuries after, his charts were copied and recopied by American scholars who alone knew of his work. The engraved charts we now have are obviously copies made by Nevada geographers during the middle of the first millennium after Christ. The chart engraved wholly in Libyan is probably older than 650 A.D. The one that is written partly in Libyan and partly in Kufic Arabic must have had the latter text (at least) engraved after 650 A.D. None of the charts can be younger than ca. 1250 A.D., for the Nevada scientists had already departed by that date, to escape the invading hordes as the Age of Barbarism came to North America to usher in a belated Dark Age such as Europe had experienced when the Roman Empire collapsed under the attacks of our northern ancestors.

Maui's original charts would be drawn in all probability on stretched animal skins, the material called parchment. Perhaps ancient parchments still exist somewhere in the arid Southwest, buried in the sand and dust that has covered the cities of the Hohokam.

In the third century B.C., Alexandria, where Eratosthenes had carried out and published his famous calculation, was the world metropolis. Therefore, when Eratosthenes drew his first world map, based on the information as to distances given by the traveler Hecataeus (ca. 500 B.C.), whose *Geography* was in the Library of Alexandria, he drew a primary meridian through Alexandria. Four centuries later, the Greco-Roman geographer and astronomer Claudius Ptolemaeus transferred the primary meridian to pass through the Canary Islands, the westernmost point of the Old World. After the seventh century A.D., the Arab geographers (who alone kept Western learning alive through the Dark Ages) again transferred the primary meridian, which was now made to pass through Mecca, the religious metropolis of the Arab world.

Thus we can date maps as to the period of their construction by taking note of the position assigned to the primary meridian. (Nowadays it is set to pass through Greenwich, England, by international agreement.) Neither of Maui's maps shows the Old World, so we do not see *directly* where he placed the primary meridian. However, we can deduce its position because he shows the ancient International Date Line.

As soon as Eratosthenes established that the earth is a sphere of measurable magnitude, it became apparent that somewhere on the earth there had to be a meridian where the day officially begins. Since the earth is a rotating sphere lit by the sun, different longitudes experience sunrise and sunset at different times. For convenience, there has to be a place where the day starts, and all places to the west of that line experience daybreak at successively later times, through twenty-four hours; this causes a difference of one day in calendar date on either side of the starting line. To minimize inconvenience, the starting line was set at the maximum distance from the meridian of Alexandria; 12 hours of time and 180 degrees of longitude.

Glance at a globe of the world and follow the meridian that passes through Alexandria right across the North Pole and down the other side in the Pacific Hemisphere. It passes about 10 degrees to the east of Hawaii. This then would be the International Date Line in 231 B.C.

Now examine Maui's map, and you will see a north-south line of dots passing about 10 degrees to the east of Hawaii, labeled in Libyan letters L-W-N Ra, corresponding to Libyan Arabic *Liwan-Ra*, the Curve-of-Ra, or Meridian-of-the-Day. It is clear that Maui placed the 180th degree of Alexandrian longitude here, on the opposite side of the globe, and therefore that he set the date line here.

Two inferences now follow. (1) Evidently the primary meridian of the period when this map was made was still located at Alexandria. Thus the map we have inherited from the ancient cartographers of Nevada still retains the meridian determined by Maui, and is not a later revision to match the Roman mapping system of Claudius Ptolemaeus, or the Arabian system based on Mecca. Accordingly, I date the map to Maui's own period, even though it is a copy made later. And (2) the correct positioning of the meridian antipodal to Alexandria shows that Maui had a means of measuring longitude, either by dead reckoning or by using the newly invented hourglass, or both. It also shows that he was a very careful navigator, since no serious error of longitude resulted from his rather elementary equipment.

Another interesting inference follows, too. Maui would be warned by Eratosthenes to observe the same day twice over when

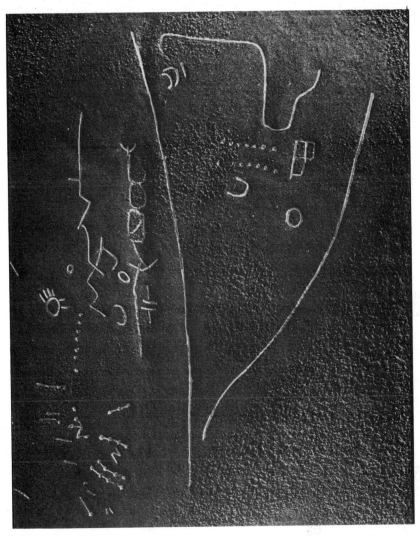

Meanwhile the art of navigation and cartography was kept alive in western America by the mariners of the arid states. They produced their own maps of the "Hidden side of the World," now known to them, of course. The original maps, no doubt drawn in detail on hides or parchment, are lost, but petroglyphs more or less simplified for schoolroom instruction of the young, have survived. This easily recognizable outline of North America from Hudson Bay to Panama, but omitting Florida and Baja California, is one such petroglyph yet extant. It seems to date from about 200 B.C., to judge by the Libyan lettering, but the Kufic Arabic annotations show that it was still in use as late as about 750 A.D. or later. Its location is not stated here, pending official action to protect this relic from vandalism. *Replica, photo Peter J. Garfall.*

A finely executed cliff petroglyph of a horse, discovered by Gloria Farley in the Cimarron region, is unusual in having a Libyan brandmark shown, H-N, "Fleet-of-foot." In ancient Libya statues were erected to successful racehorses, and perhaps this commemorates one such, though not an American cup winner. *Replica, after photo by Gloria Farley.*

Opposite page: Either American mariners who visited China, or Chinese traders who visited western America, must have brought this ceramic Buddhist piece. It was found, together with crude American copies in stone, in a burial mound at Teocalli, Mexico, by Dr. H. A. Monday. *Replica by Dr. Clyde Keeler, photo Peter J. Garfall.*

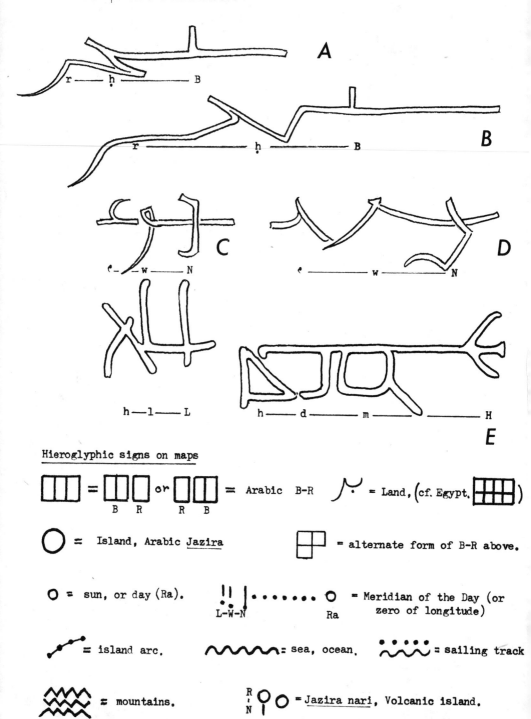

Hieroglyphic signs on maps

⊞⊞⊞ = ⊞⊞⊡ or ⊡⊞⊞ = Arabic B-R   ⌣ = Land, (cf. Egypt. ⊞⊞)
         B R   R B

◯ = Island, Arabic Jazira   ⊞ = alternate form of B-R above.

◯ = sun, or day (Ra).   ‖ | ······ ◯ = Meridian of the Day (or
                         L-W-N   Ra   zero of longitude)

•—•—• = island arc.   ∿∿∿ = sea, ocean.   ∿∿∿ = sailing track

XXXX = mountains.   R|N ◯ ◯ = Jazira nari, Volcanic island.

•••••• ⊞ = Land boundary.

ANCIENT LIBYAN MAP OF NORTH AMERICA AND THE PACIFIC OCEAN

Professor Ali Khushaim of the Libyan Studies Center, University of Tripoli with Fell, in discussion by a reduced copy of the chart of North America and the Pacific. *Photo Peter J. Garfall.*

Opposite page: Explanation of the Libyan lettering and the annotations added in Kufic Arabic to Maui's chart of North America. The two vertical lines of Kufic placed beside the Pacific coast are here given horizontally, and read from right to left, taking them in the sequence B, D, E. The consonants are shown with identification, and the phonetic rendering intended is *Bahr Naw'i, Hamid-hu 'Llah* (Stormy Ocean, May God calm it). For comparison are also shown A, the word *bahr* (Ocean) rendered in Maghrib Kufic in the style of Ain Lahag, Morocco, ca. eighth century A.D., and C, the word *naw'i* (stormy) similarly rendered. Since the chart is attributed to M-w (Maui) in the Libyan lettering on the chart, it is asumed that the Kufic words are later additions, and that the rest of the lettering (in Libyan script) is much older, presumably copied from a lost original made by Maui himself, ca. 231 B.C. Note that of the two letters ẖ and h, the former is pronounced like German *ch*. Note also that certain consonants, when at the beginning of a word, are written differently from their form when in the middle, or at the end of a word. All the letters are written differently in the modern Arabic script, called Naskhi. The beaded lines on the lower parts of the map appear to be much later additions, perhaps by Shoshone tribesmen, imitating the Naskhi modulus.

Replica of petroglyph apparently depicting the Hawaiian Islands and adjacent region. The grid-like markings and other irrelevant lines on the lower part of the map are believed to be later additions, not related to the original map. *Photo Peter J. Garfall.*

Explanation of markings on the foregoing chart.

Chart # 1, Northeast Pacific (words read right-to-left)

= G-A-W-Y, Modern Kauai.

Y— W–A–G

= U-W-H, Modern Oahu

H ——— W — U

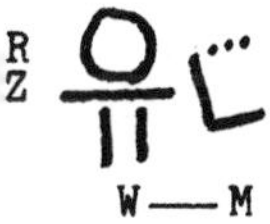

= M-W Z-R, "Maui's Plantation", Modern Maui.

W —— M

= J-F-Y Land = Sierra Madre Occidental, Mexico
(literally, "Mountain Land")

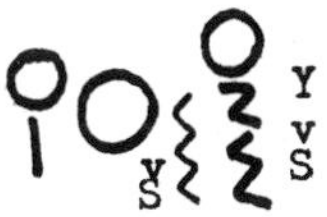

Y   J   Land

= S-S-Y (Island) N-R = "Great Volcanic Island" = Modern Hawaii
(called H-W on Chart # 2).

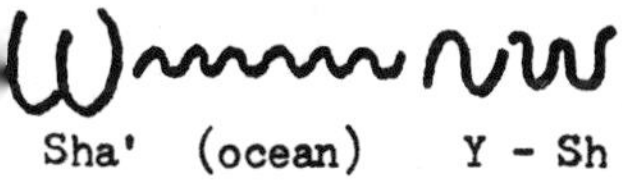

= "Announcement of new discoveries in the Ocean."

Sha'   (ocean)   Y - Sh

Chart # 2, North America (words read left-to-right)

(Note: Annotations in Kufic Arabic shown separately on page   ).

= Arabic mamanu "Passage obstructed" (i.e., Northwest Passage)

-M—N

= H-W (Island) = Modern Hawaii.    = D-F R-N, "Coasts sighted."

—W

= M-H-W = "Compressed" (i.e., portion of west Pacific omitted).

-H—W

= M-R Egyptian, "Land Across the Sea."    = R-S-M, "Chart."

M—R   R S M

= M-W, Maui.    Lower part of Monogram, perhaps = S-S, in
                    which case entire monogram is to be read as
M—W   "CHART BY MAUI THE NAVIGATOR"

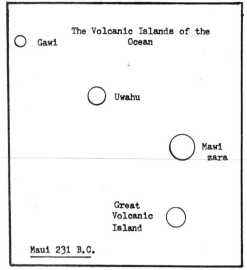

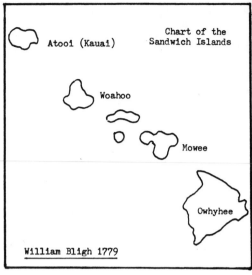

Two charts of the Hawaiian Islands, separated by 2,000 years. Maui's version (left) correctly names Kauai (as *Gawi,* within the limitations of Libyan orthography), whereas Bligh's map, dating from Cook's discovery of the Islands in 1779, renders the name as *"Atooi."* Both explorers spell the name of Oahu with an initial W sound. Maui appears to have settled on the island called Maui, as it is labeled on his chart *Maui zara* (Maui's estate). He apparently recorded the large island of Hawaii from a distant sighting, as its relative size is much too small. Maui names the group on his chart as *The Islands of Fire,* a term which in Libyan also means Volcanic Islands. Lanai and Molokai are omitted in Maui's chart. On Maui's chart of North America and the North Pacific Ocean, the Hawaiian Islands are marked *Hawa.*

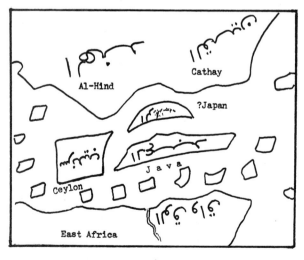

The superiority of the North American geographers over their contemporaries in the Old World is clear from this chart by Idrisi of Sicily (fl 1150 A.D.). The Arabic is inverted as Idrisi set south at the top. Sarandib (Ceylon) and Jabadin (Java) are grotesquely shaped and misplaced, East Africa occupies the Indian Ocean, and the chart would ill serve a mariner. Serendipity, the chance discovery of the unexpected, is a modern word derived (with singular propriety) from the Arabic name of Ceylon.

Professor Raymond A. Dart, the distinguished South African anthropologist, examining Polynesian skulls with Fell during a recent visit to the Epigraphic Society. The inscriptions reported in this chapter, and in earlier publications of the Society, imply considerable Libyan connections with Polynesia. These inferences are now supported by studies of skull measurements, and a group of anatomists at the University of Alabama, led by Professor Albert E. Casey, find that the cranial structure links the ancient Maori of New Zealand with North African, Iberian and Zuni peoples, as well as with some tribes of New England and northeastern Canada. The skull in Professor Dart's hands was excavated from a New Zealand mound by Fell in 1937 and shows unusually strong bone structure. *Photo Peter J. Garfall and Stephen A. Sylvester.*

crossing the date line from west to east, as otherwise he would arrive in America and find his calendar one day ahead of the Libyan colonists who had crossed the Atlantic. Magellan, who sailed in the opposite direction ought, by the same reasoning, to have jumped a day when crossing the date line. But no astronomer warned Magellan of this, so he did not do so. And although every man on board his ship had kept a careful record of every day spent on the voyage, when the ship returned to Portugal, the entire crew and officers were astounded to discover that every man jack of them had somehow lost a day, for everyone in Portugal was using a calendar one day ahead of their ship reckoning. Within a few hours, the cause of the mystery was solved by Pigafetta, the learned chaplain on board.

Throughout the length and breadth of Polynesia, Maui's historic voyage of discovery is remembered as a legend, which now can be identified as real history. The legend says that Maui fished up new land from the sea—a poetic way of recording his discovery of lands hidden beneath the horizon. The legend also says that Maui captured the sun and slowed him down so that he took two days to cover the distance across the sky usually covered in one day.

The origin of this second Maui legend is now also to be seen as a historical fact. Unaware of the scientific reason for living the same day twice over as they crossed the newly identified Curve-of-Ra, Maui's sailors would suppose that their calendar would have to be one day behind that of everyone else. So, on landing at Panama, or wherever the historic landing was made, Maui's sailors would be astonished to find that the calendar of the Libyan colonists who had reached America by crossing the Atlantic, was in perfect agreement with their own, even though they had lived an extra day and their Panama compatriots had not. I have little doubt that this circumstance is responsible for the legend that Maui slowed the sun in his course. It also tells us that the men who crossed the date line with Maui on the way to America also entered Polynesia, for the legend of Maui and the sun is a Polynesian heritage.

Soon I had translated enough of the writing on the engraved charts to satisfy myself as to their real nature and authenticity (their existence had been known for at least twenty years, and teams of investigators had certified them as ancient Indian petroglyphs, and registered them in the photographic file at the University of California, Berkeley). I called my wife Renee to see the finds, and before long, Peter Garfall saw them, too. We discussed what should be done next.

Happy Gladwin wrote: "Since you telephoned to me, I have been in a sort of trance . . . you will understand the importance of dates from inscriptions which tend to support my chronology of the Southwest." From the United Nations Educational and Scientific Organization came Professor Ali Khushaim, who wasted no time in checking my readings of the Kufic texts. Like us he was enthusiastic, and took back photographs to discuss with colleagues in Libya and Paris. We decided to make no public announcement for the time being.

It was one thing to see and analyze the charts, as reproduced in the line drawings traced from the original photographs, and published in the existing literature on the petroglyphs of the western deserts. Alas, it proved quite a different matter to visit and examine the petroglyphs in person. Through an unhappy chapter of events, serious illness overtook Dr. Robert Heizer, senior author of the primary reports on these inscriptions just at the time when I began to plan to visit the sites. Meantime, on the basis of published information, I asked colleagues in the West to undertake the rediscovery of the localities where the maps were said to be, but their efforts were fruitless. (Eventually we learned that one reported location was in error by a distance of eight miles.) When, at length, it was possible to seek the advice of leading authorities, we learned that the original reports had been based on photographs submitted by yet another collaborator sixteen years earlier. To him we now took our inquiry, only to learn that his photographs had been deposited in another place where they have not yet been located. So there was nothing for it but to begin the search all over again. As of now, the major map site has not yet been rediscovered, though associated petroglyphs that were reported on the same occasion have been found, and the secondary site has also been visited. Work is, therefore, still underway, and, until completed, we have to depend wholly upon the accuracy of the line drawings traced from original photographs presently inaccessible. Of one thing at least we can be sure (from personal experience), the area in which the inferred maps occur is so remote, so wild, and so inaccessible that vandals, at least, are unlikely to destroy the sites before we have found them again.

Going to School in Ancient America

If the great festivals were joyous occasions in ancient America, as they were in the homelands of the Mediterranean, life in a New World was a serious business for the colonists. Nor would they forget that the original purpose of the seasonal festivities was to render homage to the gods of nature whose favors they sought for the sprouting seed, and to whom they rendered thanks for the maturing harvest.

When colonists first come to a wilderness, their immediate concern is to learn how to survive. After that, if we may judge by the Pilgrims in Massachusetts, their next anxiety is to ensure the survival of their traditions of religion and learning by establishing schools for the young.

In the eastern states, where modern colonial activities resulted in a chaotic destruction of the Amerindian antiquities, grossly disturbed both by farming and by the havoc wrought by souvenir hunters and grave robbers, the fragile relics left by the winter frosts have bequeathed little enough to us of any ancient writings cut on rocks. Writing on less durable substances, such as birchbark and wood, suffered even more severe deterioration through the effects of time and weather. Therefore, so far no evidence of ancient schools has been recognized in these regions.

But in the less densely settled regions of the West, where modern colonists arrived late, and where the dry climate aids the survival of ancient engravings on rocks, the situation is different. Here we may expect better luck in recovering the history that the eastern states have all but lost.

In the ancient countries of North Africa, where the weather is warm, schools have been held in the open air for countless centuries. The teacher stands or sits in the center of a ring of pupils, and either dispenses his lessons already engraved or painted on wooden plates, of which each student receives an example to learn by rote; or else he chalks his lesson on a larger board, or on a convenient rock face. The pupils may transcribe the lesson onto bark or leaf or other temporary material, soon to be discarded, but the teacher tends to conserve his own efforts by using wooden plaques which last from year to year (though not from century to century). Schools of this kind still survive among some of the Bedouins and in Ethiopia and the Sudan and Somalia, in country or desert areas far from towns.

I believe that most of the texts, diagrams, and charts that we are now identifying in the arid western states, engraved on rock, represent the last surviving fragments of what was once a system of schools at both elementary and higher levels of learning.

Years of devoted field work by Californian archeologists who have collected and recorded thousands of the petroglyphs of the arid West, in particular the researches of Professors Robert Heizer and Martin Baumhoff, led them to suspect a relationship between the sites of the petroglyphs and the game animals depicted in them. After conferring with zoologists, they proposed that many of the sites were temporary camping places where hunters seasonally stayed during the weeks when game animals are migrating to and from the summer and winter grazing areas. Thus, according to Heizer and Baumhoff, the sites would be occupied only during certain months of each year. My opinion coincides with theirs.

During the winter months, many of the sites would be buried under snow and, lacking game, in a territory too arid to support agriculture, the hunters would certainly not remain in so inhospitable a place. They must have retreated to lower altitudes at these seasons of adversity.

If we read the writings of ancient mariners of the Mediterranean, or, more precisely, the writings of literate people who associated with ancient mariners, such as the Greek poet Hesiod in the eighth century B.C., we learn that the Greeks of the archipelago in the Aegean led a double life. In winter they beached their vessels and retired to subsist upon the previous summer's produce. In spring they sowed their crops. In summer they departed on piratical expeditions to foreign coasts. In the fall they came home with their ill-gotten gains and harvested their crops.

Study of the inscriptions in Nevada and eastern California discloses that the vanished scribes were familiar with a similar lifestyle. Their charts and their nautical diagrams and advice to mariners show that they were a maritime people. The ferocious aspect of their dragon-ships, as depicted by contemporary artists in both North and South America, suggest a race with Viking inclinations. I suspect that the ancient dwellers in the northern arid states in western America practiced the ungentle art of the Vikings during the summer, returned to their tent villages in the lower Colorado valley during winter, and went hunting in the spring and the fall when the game herds were on the move. Farther south, in Arizona and New Mexico, their cousins led a settled life. They had introduced irrigation on the North African plan, and so brought the arid lands under cultivation.

Most American men in their youth have sat around campfires to hear the tales of more experienced elders: it is a kind of education at the hands of older masters in the art of living in the woods and mountains. To my mind, such modern activities owe much of their hold over the young because they evoke, in a very personal way, the tradition of times gone by.

I believe that one thousand and two thousand years ago American youth was instructed around the campfire, during the hunting seasons, by those more cunning old-timers whose expositions of the nature of the world, and the art of navigation, found eager listeners among the young. When the hunting was over for the year, they returned to the rivers, sailed their ships back to the coast, and prepared for their seasonal forays across the great waters. In the case of the longer voyages, the summer would be spent at sea. The following winter they would go ashore in the foreign land, to return home to their lairs in western America the following summer.

To undertake such long voyages as those from California to China and back again, far exceeding the forays of the European Vikings, these sailors required skilled navigators and learned astronomers and mathematicians. Hence there arose this remarkable civilization of Nevada and California; a mobile community of nomads and sailors, playing a dual role under the cunning leadership of men well versed in the science of the seas.

Thus it happens that the rocks of these western states carry many a diagram, with or without lettering, that is familiar at first glance to those of us who have been trained as oceanographers or marine scientists or mariners, while they apparently lack significance for the general archeologist or anthropologist and have therefore been recorded as "primitive pictographs" of unknown significance.

In this present chapter, however, I deal with a more homely theme: learning to write, the fundamentals of a grade-school system that probably could equal that of any other in the world two thousand—or one thousand—years ago.

As can be seen from the illustrations on pages 302–303, we are confronted at many sites in the western states, especially Nevada and eastern California, with simple formulas in which a letter of the Libyan alphabet is associated with a picture of a familiar object whose name, in Arabic, begins with that letter. In some cases, the letter or letters spelling the entire name are made into a rebus, as in the case of *rajul* (man), where the consonants R-J-L are shaped to suggest the figure of a man (vowels are omitted in ancient written Arabic).

Similarly, what appear to be school lessons in Ogam script, illustrated by the animal or subject named, occur at various sites discovered in British Columbia by John Corner in 1968, though the Ogam was not at that time recognized. Especially common are these Ogam texts in Fraser River lakes region, near areas where the Gaelic-related Takhelne tongue is or recently was spoken, and where occur also stone chambers of uncertain origin. These latter are presently under investigation by Bruce Macdonald.

Simple arithmetic was doubtless also taught at the same grade schools but, for convenience, I have grouped the corresponding numerical inscriptions with more sophisticated mathematical expressions.

Last, although we have no direct evidence as yet in written form, it now seems virtually certain that the traditional Pima chants of the Southwest, which (in *America B.C.*) I have shown to be recited in corrupt Arabic, must originally have been brought to America by Arabic-speaking colonists. Some of these chants are very simple and shortened versions of Aesop's *Fables,* a Greek classic that would be well known to ancient Cyrenian schoolteachers in Libya. It is likely that the grade-school children of the Hohokam people of the arid West would be instructed through that medium. I therefore include here two new translations from the Pima chants recorded by Russell (1908), and hitherto regarded as untranslatable, or rendered in the ludicrous alleged translations of

The ancient Alphabet Stone of Kilmalkedar, near Dingle, County Kerry, Ireland, is engraved in Celtic script like that used by the scribes of the Book of Kells around 750 A.D. This, and the cross engraved on the face of the stone, imply that Christian monks probably taught the alphabet to young children. In the open air, in fine weather, the children gathered in a circle around the teacher and his stone "blackboard," in much the same way as ancient North African children were taught. The Allen Springs Alphabet Stone of Nevada is a thousand years older than the Irish stone, and uses an alphabet that preceded the Tifinag script of Christian times and was in vogue as a literary script during the reigns of the Libyan monarchs of the second century before Christ. The script of the Allen Springs stone also matches that of the oldest maps of North America and of Polynesia, signed by Maui, the Libyan navigator who discovered the west coast of North America.

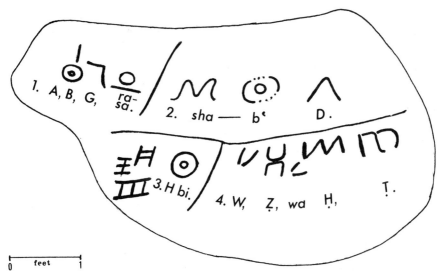

1. A, B, G, ra-sa.
2. sha — bʻ   D.
3. H bi.
4. W, Ẓ, wa   Ḥ,   Ṭ.

feet
0   1

The ancient Alphabet Stone of Allen Springs, Nevada, gives the sequence of letters in the pre-Islamic Libyan alphabet. Long suspected, but never before demonstrated, the ancient North African alphabet follows the same sequence as the ancient Semitic letters, and Greek, unlike the modern Arabic alphabet which supplanted it both in America and North Africa. If we give the letters the names by which they would be known to the Cyrenean Libyans, then the inscription reads:

1. Alpha, Beta, Gamma come first.
2. Add to them Delta.
3. Hepsilon next.
4. Digamma (W), Zeta and Heta, Theta.

(the alphabet evidently continues on some other stone not yet discovered). If we give the letters the names by which they were probably known to the Libyan Arabs, the inscription would sound:

1. Alif, Ba, Gim come first.
2. Add to these Dal.
3. Soft Ha next (written in any of the three ways shown).
4. Waw, Zav, and then guttural Ha, Theta.

This Libyan alphabet stone, the first ever found, may be compared with the similar Gaelic Alphabet Stone of County Kerry, Ireland, shown on page 300. That such a stone should be found in North America gives clear testimony that the ancient Libyans came here, not as visitors, but as permanent settlers who established schools and reared their children as Americans. The following pages illustrate the grade-school lessons that these early American children received. The script style shows that the period is that of King Masinissa, approximately the second century before Christ. The Allen Springs stone was discovered by Professors Robert Heizer and Martin Baumhoff (1962) and reported as "curvilinear Indian petroglyphs," of no known significance, but they recognized the antiquity of the site.

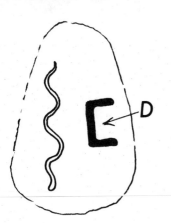

D stands for <u>Dud</u>
(which is Arabic
and means <u>Worm</u>)

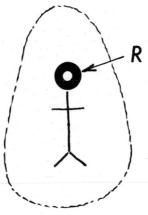

R stands for <u>Rajul</u>
(which means <u>Man</u>)

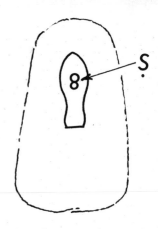

Ṣ stands for <u>Sandal</u>
(a Greek word bor-
rowed by others)

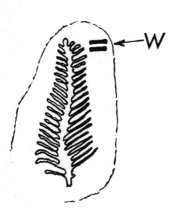

W stands for <u>Waraq</u>
(which means <u>leaf</u>).

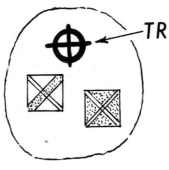

TR stands for <u>Turs</u>
(which means warshield).

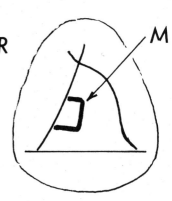

M stands for <u>Ma'war</u>
which means <u>tipi</u>.

S stands for <u>Sidra</u>
(which means chest).

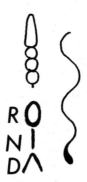

DNR stands for <u>Danar</u>
(which means <u>rattle</u>).
Note that some letters
change if written
vertically.

RJL spells <u>Rajul</u>,
a man.

Opposite page: Typical Libyan alphabet stones from Nevada and Inyo, California sites, as recorded without decipherment by Heizer and Baumhoff (University of California Press, 1962).

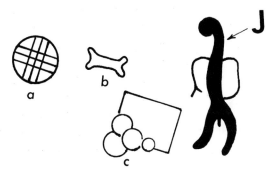

A Libyan alphabet stone giving J (is for *Jaza,* which is *money*), and illustrating the word by petroglyphs of Iberian coinage a, an ingot b, and a money box c. The teacher has made the Libyan letter J resemble a man. The site is in Inyo County, California, number 48 in Professor Julian Steward's numbering.

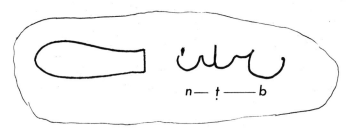

Another Libyan example, B-T-N spells *sole* or *footprint* in Arabic, from the Lagomarsino site in Nevada.

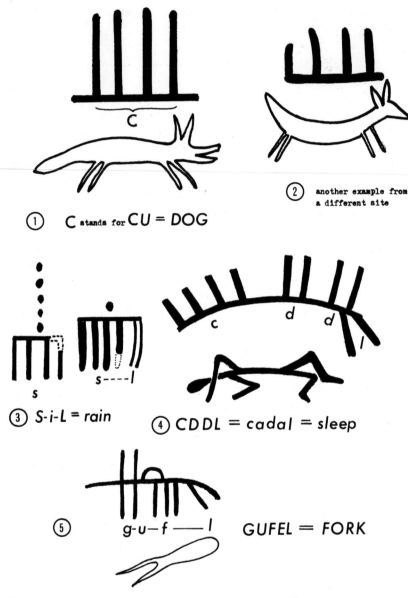

① C stands for CU = DOG

② another example from a different site

③ S-i-L = rain

④ CDDL = cadal = sleep

⑤ g-u—f——l GUFEL = FORK

Similar teaching methods were used by the British Columbia Gaelic-speaking Celts, evidently the forebears of the Takhelne people of the Fraser River lakes, as reported by Fell (1976, Hammond Museum Lecture). These examples were located by John Corner (*Pictographs in the Interior of British Columbia,* 1968) who, however, did not recognize their Ogam content or significance as writing.

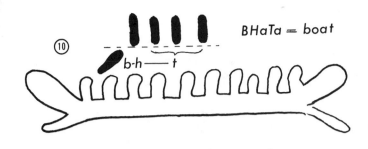

BHaTa = boat

b-h —— t

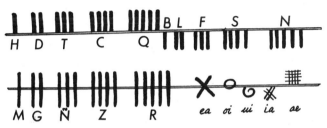

| H | D | T | C | Q | BL | F | S | N |

| M | G | Ň | Z | R | | | | |

ea oi ui ia ae

Boat pictograph with Gaelic Ogam word BH-T (*bhata*, boat); and below the Ogam
alphabet as used in New England and British Columbia, vowels usually omitted.
Principal sites in British Columbia where Ogam may be seen are Corner's
sites 5, 6, 7, 51, 65, 81, 94. Ogam also occurs widely in Oregon and Washington
and parts of Nevada.

Gaelic school lesson, British Columbia. The Ogam spells F-R (*Fir*, men or people).
Ogam without vowels was originally reported from very early Irish inscriptions
by Eoghan Ruadh ua Suilleabhain, and recorded under the name *ogam consainne*
(consonantal Ogam) by the Irish Lexicographer Padraig Dineen in 1901. When
rediscovered in America, and reported in *America B.C.*, the idea was ridiculed;
but hundreds of pictographs, accompanied by appropriately lettered Gaelic
words in *ogam consainne* have now been discovered and their evidence is
conclusive that ancient Celts, speaking a language very similar to Irish Gaelic,
once occupied the American sites where the inscriptions are found. This example
was originally recorded by John Corner in 1968, seven years before the first
ogam consainne was recognized in America. *Photo Peter J. Garfall and
Stephen A. Sylvester.*

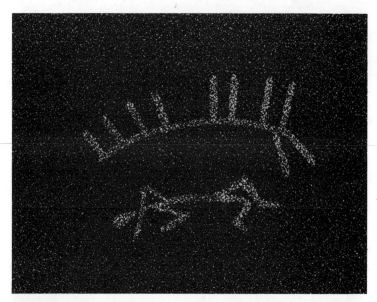

Gaelic school lesson, British Columbia, originally discovered by John Corner. The letters spell C-D-D-L (*cadal,* sleep) and a matchstick figure beside them shows a sleeping man. *Photo Peter J. Garfall and Stephen A. Sylvester.*

The horned Celtic hunting god Cernunos holds a trident in this Nevada petroglyph at the Lost City site. *Photo Peter J. Garfall and Stephen A. Sylvester.*

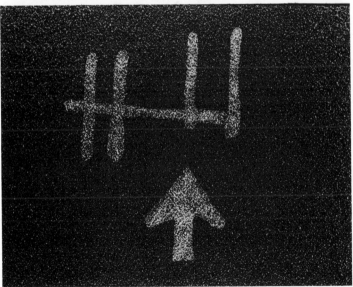

Gaelic school lesson engraved at a Valley of Fire site in Nevada, recorded by Heizer and Baumhoff (1962). The Ogam letters G-L beside the pictograph of a child stand for Gaelic *Gille*, a boy. *Photo Peter J. Garfall and Stephen A. Sylvester.*

Gaelic school lesson at another of John Corner's sites in British Columbia. The letters G-D in this case spell *Gad*, a gaff or spearhead. *Photo Peter J. Garfall and Stephen A. Sylvester.*

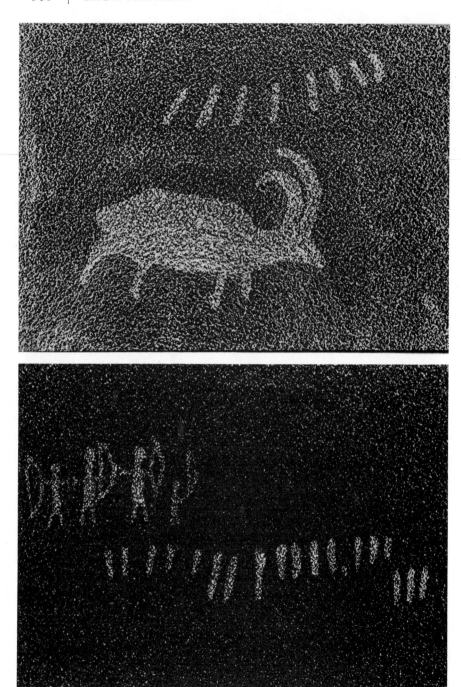

Gaelic school lesson employing the same Ogam letters G-D, but as the pictographs show, here they stand for another Irish word, *Gad*, a twisted spiral coil, as used in beginning a basket made from twigs or grass; and the goats to the left show that the alternative reading *Ged*, a goat, was also intended. *Ged*, like many other Gaelic words, is a borrowing from Norse. The pictograph was first recorded by Heizer and Baumhoff (1962) from a site in California. *Photo Peter J. Garfall and Stephen A. Sylvester.*

Opposite page above: Gaelic school lesson, Atlatl Rock, Valley of Fire, Nevada. The letters R-T stand for Old Irish *Rete*, a ram, and the species depicted is the Rocky Mountain Bighorn Sheep. Originally reported by Heizer and Baumhoff (1962). *Photo Peter J. Garfall and Stephen A. Sylvester.*

Opposite page below: Gaelic school lesson, Columbia Lake, British Columbia, originally recorded by John Corner in 1968. The ogam letters read D-D H-G M-C T-F, to be understood as Gaelic *Daidi (h)og maca, tafa(n)*, Old Irish dialect for "Fathers and sons hunting." *Photo Peter J. Garfall and Stephen A. Sylvester.* Details of the decipherment of all the above Ogam inscriptions, and many others, can be found in Fell (1978) *Inscriptiones Gadelicae Americanae.*

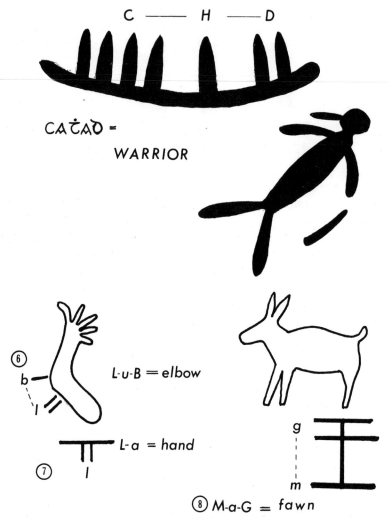

C — H — D

CAṪAꝊ =

WARRIOR

⑥
b —

l

L-u-B = elbow

L-a = hand

⑦ l

g

m

⑧ M-a-G = fawn

Further examples of teaching sites in British Columbia Ogam Gaelic. Like the New England Ogam, the vowels are usually omitted, a practice in conformity also with the Libyan manner of writing in Nevada and states between British Columbia and Nevada.

the Papago interpreter of the Smithsonian party led by Russell, so absurd as to be devoid of meaning.

Aesop's fable *The Fox and the Crow* was among the contributions that Cyrenian Greeks evidently made to ancient Libyan literature, for it is to be found in the Hohokam relics that we can now recognize in the Pima Chants collected by the Smithsonian ethnological expedition led by Frank Russell in 1901–02. As published in 1908 (*26th Ann. Rpt., U.S. Bur. Ethnol.,* pp. 316–17) an alleged "translation" was provided by a Papago interpreter. It reads as follows:

COYOTE SONG

Coyote stands, songs commence. (*Repeated*)
Girl at puberty woman hurry came, coyote songs stretching. (*Repeated*)
Eagle feathers, Eagle feathers, you that that my hat made,
You that that my hat made, more looks, me heart, more looks.
Around water, around water; there in coyote blue dyed, I in toward run.

(Sotto voce, one wonders that Dadaism is not more appropriately traced to Washington D.C., rather than to Austria of a decade later.) It is interesting that, as usual, the one correct key idea, given in the title, is reflected in the supposed translations—in this case *coyote* (for fox). I propose the following corrected version, reading the Smithsonian transcription as Arabic, corrupted by seven centuries of memorizing following the loss of the written alphabet during the barbarian invasion.

1. original Pima text as written phonetically by Russell.
2. equivalent Arabic roots, in dictionary form. 3. translation.

Aesop's Fable of the Fox and the Crow

Pima	1.	Panai	kuki waka.	Nyunyui rsarsan	ut cona.	
Arabic	2.	Bunni *	qa'qa' wakd.	Na'yna'iy rasm	'tuqub.	
English	3.	A brown-fox a crow desired. This fable tells of his cunning.				
		(*repeat*)				

Pima	1.	Tco	vanga	mohofi.	Yaikapi worsan	yimu panai.
Arabic	2.	Taqqa	waniya	ma'ihuha.	Yakaza waswasa	'ima bunni.
English	3.	He feigned illness and fell over. With furtive glances played-his-act the fox.				

Pima	1.	Nyunyui valuna	himu	pahangu	yahanu.	Komus huku,
Arabic	2.	Na'na'a wahla	himaj	bahha	yauhunu.	Kama hukkum,
English	3.	Cawing, fearing his appetite, the-croaker kept-his-distance. At last he-flew-down				

Pima	1.	Vany—vanam	hat	conaa	va hama	tco.
Arabic	2.	Wany—wanan	hatta	kana	wahm	taqqa.
English	3.	relaxing-his-vigilance and-stayed-on the-ground deceived by the fraud.				

Pima	1.	Ikamanyi	imoi	taku	vahama	tco inga sikali rsonu.
Arabic	2.	Kumana	'ima	taqqa	wahm	tuquls sakira rasuna.
English	3.	Lying-in-wait the-trick acted-out the-deceiver, wily, feigning to be lifeless.				

Pima	1.	Kama	ku-ta	Ngu	Panai	sitcu	na-kimu mam
Arabic	2.	Kama	kata	Naga	Bunni	sata	naqima mimma
English	3.	At-length hopped-nearer the-croaker. The-fox pounced and attacked by means of					

Pima	1.	a-sina	kon yu	nga	wuwui	Va Pai'muna.
Arabic	2.	asinna	kunya	nagba	wa'wa'a	Fa Bun'munya
English	3.	his teeth, then gobbled it down with-a-yelp. Thus Fox had-his-wish.				

---

* The Libyo-Iberic root *bunni,* meaning a brown animal, is evidently the word *bunny* of Old English nursery language. In America its expanded use includes the derivative *panai,* desert-fox or coyote of classical Pima (Hohokam), as well as other applications. The Oxford English Dictionary is silent on Iberic roots.

The Fox and the Seashells
(Another Fable by Aesop)

Pima	1.	Kaka	mangai	kaka	itcovu	kaka	wota	miyanna
Arabic	2.	Konka	mauwajan	kaika	jawazal	kaika	watr	muyun
English	3.	Shells	marine	and	eggs	of	quail,	each	with	the	other	confused,

Pima	1.	lumun	gali	muliva	tatai	pan
Arabic	2.	lamma	galat	malawan	tazaj	bunni
English	3.	were collected in error day by day freshly by a brown fox.
		(repeat)

Pima	1.	Yuina	himu	tcutcu	nangi	kaka	itcova
Arabic	2.	Yauma	himaj	taqqtaqq	nagba	kaika	jawazal
English	3.	One day he was hungry so he cracked open and gobbled up the eggs of quail.

Pima	1.	Kaka	wotu	vai	lukai	lumun	gali
Arabic	2.	Konka	watr	wa'y	luqyan	lamma	galat
English	3.	The seashells one by one he carefully laid aside as collected in error.

Pima	1.	Nyui	naku	kaka	van	yuina	himu.
Arabic	2.	Niya	naqd	konka	bunni	yauma	himaj.
English	3.	Decided to store up the seashells the brown-fox for a day of famine.

The English proverb answering to this Greek and Pima fable, transmitted through the Arabic of the Hohokam, is "Chicken today, feathers tomorrow," and the sentiment is basically "Live for today, let tomorrow take care of itself."

The "translation" of the above fable given to Russell by his Papago informant runs as follows (*Ann. Rpt. Bur. Ethnol.* 1908, p. 312):

Quail Song

Gray quail bunched grouping, coyote came running looking.
  (*Repeated*)
Blue quails bunched ran together, coyote saw, sideways looking.
  (*Repeated*)

Once again, although the meaning of the chant is lost, the subject matter, in this case the quail (rather than its eggs) has been remembered, and the brown desert fox of Africa is appropriately replaced by the coyote, its American desert equivalent. In Russell's orthography, the letters *tc* stand for the sound *ch,* which is the unvoiced equivalent of *j;* hence I equate *itcova* (ichova) with the original Arabic *jawazal,* of which the modern sense in Arabic is *pigeon.* The letter *v* is usually the Pima equivalent of Arabic *w.*

Ancient American Mathematicians

Many rocks in Nevada carry strange engravings that clearly express some kind of mathematical operations. The exact nature of the signs varies, and we can distinguish two major categories; one which is older, and lacks a zero sign, and in which the ciphers have values not dependent upon their position; and a second, later, system in which numbers are written in much the same way as we do today. Until recently all these signs were a mystery, and they were not recognized as numerals, but called "Great Basin Curvilinear." Ancient Portugal yields the clues to solve the mystery.

Monetary Value	*Written Symbol*
5 testoons (= half-escudo)	—
10 " (= one escudo)	|

Monetary Value	Written Symbol
15 "	| —
20 "	|
25 "	|
30 "	||
35 "	|| —
36 "	|| — ·
100 " (= ten escudos)	ⓘ

The ancient Portuguese manner of expressing monetary values (according to dos Santos, 1963). This old Iberian system, apparently brought to Portugal by the Moors from North Africa, can be recognized as the ancient Nevada system of numerals, used before the introduction from India of the Sanskrit decimal system.

The numerous square grids encountered on the Nevada petroglyph sites are practical demonstrations of multiplication. Thus, for example, at University of California site Mi-5 (at Whisky Flat, Mineral County, Nevada) Professors Heizer and Baumhoff found this petroglyph.

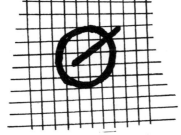

They could find no explanation for it but, as is now obvious, it shows the ancient Iberian numeral 100 superimposed on a grid containing exactly one hundred small squares. At many sites we find squares or rectangles that illustrate such arithmetical rules as 7 times 7 equal 49, or 7 times 8 equal 56, and so on. I have no doubt that these are located at sites where the ancient schoolmasters taught the young Hohokam boys basic arithmetic at times when the hunting permitted a change of activity.

University of California petroglyph site C1-123 is located at Keyhole Canyon in Clark County, Nevada. Here we find illustrations of gaming counters, or jettons, each carrying its designated value in Iberian numerals. And beneath the engraved pictures of the jettons we find the ancient Libyan letters S-R-D, written in accordance with the older manner of reading from right-to-left, and spelling the Classical Arabic word *Sard,* which means in modern Arabic "enumeration." Evidently its ancient meaning was "counting" or "arithmetic."

Even though we have only these fragmentary petroglyph records to judge by, it is obvious that the Hohokam people were equipped to carry out all the fundamental operations with numbers that would be required by their trading activities, and that they could keep written records of them. Obviously such records would be made on birchbark or similar writing materials, of temporary value only, and long since decayed and vanished from the ruins of their dwellings and camp sites. Only these permanent rock glyphs remain, as mute testimony to places where the ancient schoolmasters gave their lessons.

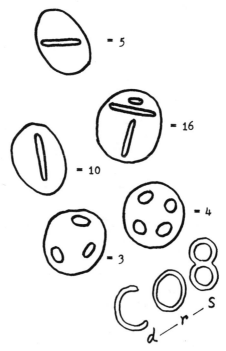

Petroglyph at Keyhole Canyon, Nevada, showing numerical values of jettons in accordance with the ancient Iberian system of numerals, and identified by the engraved Libyan word S-R-D ("enumeration"). After Heizer and Baumhoff (1962).

Here are some examples of how ancient Americans carried out arithmetical operations before the invention of decimal numbers:

1. Add four to three, how many do we have?

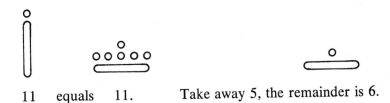

2. Take five from eleven, how many remain?

11   equals   11.   Take away 5, the remainder is 6.

3. Multiply six by two.

Take 6 two times, rearrange the signs, to obtain 12

or, we can make a grid, one side of 6 units, the other of 2 units and then count how many units we have

which is the same as   2 + 5 + 5

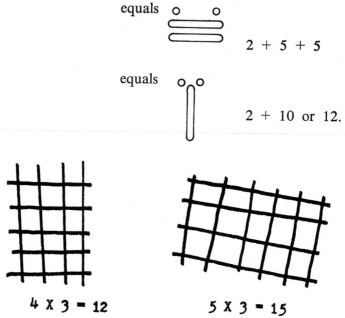

equals 2 + 5 + 5

equals 2 + 10 or 12.

4 X 3 = 12   5 X 3 = 15

Other examples of multiplication grids at the Whisky Flat site where ancient Nevada schoolmasters once taught arithmetic to Hohokam youth.

In modern North Africa, almost identical teaching procedures are still in use for giving instruction in arithmetic. Below is shown a portion of such a multiplication grid printed in exercise books sold for school use in Tripoli today. I brought back examples for comparison with the ancient Nevada arithmetical petroglyphs. I reproduce only the lower values of the grid, which actually extends to factors of ten along both the vertical and horizontal axes. The numerals are in this case given by their modern Arabic signs, ultimately derived from the same Sanskrit decimal ciphers that we find in Nevada at sites of lesser antiquity, dating from after the third century A.D.

Opposite page above: Portion of a modern multiplication grid as used in schools in Libya today. The numerals in the top row, reading from right to left, are 1 to 5. The rest can be deduced by inspection. A similar system is used on road maps in America to give the distances between towns.

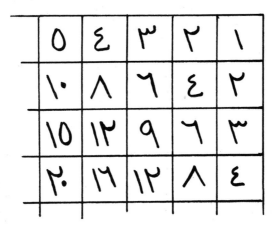

On the basis of the observed numeral signs on the Nevada school sites, and the multiplication grids there, and still in use in North Africa, we can now deduce what a Nevada schoolboy would actually write on his birchbark, or wooden palette, to record his lesson in those early days before the decimal system of numerals was introduced from India. It would look something like this:

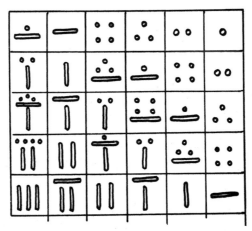

Inferred multiplication grid of the ancient Nevada schools, with the numerals inserted in the squares. The values of the signs can readily be determined by inspection.

The system of numerals in use in ancient Nevada (and doubt-less throughout the Hohokam territory, in Colorado, eastern California, New Mexico, Utah, and Arizona) shows a considerable resemblance to that adopted in Mexico after the first century A.D. It would seem likely that the two systems are in fact related, and that both derive from the ancient numerals of the pre-Islamic peoples of North Africa and the Iberian peninsula.

Ancient American Arithmetic

After the third century A.D., the ancient Hindu numerals were brought to America by the Nevada mariners.

They are:

	0	1	2	3	4	5	6	7	8	9
Hindu (Sanskrit) style	o	ꞁ	꠲	꠱	꠱	Ɋ	꠵	꠳	Ꮓ	꠯
Ancient Nevada style	O	Ꝗ	ꝺ	꠱	꠱	ꝺ	6	꠵	ꝺ	꠯

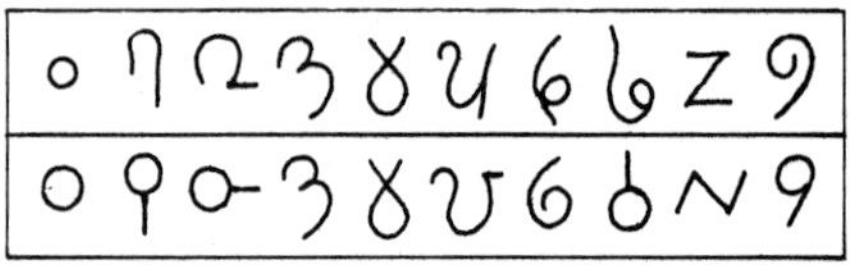

The signs for the operators are: plus   equals   minus

o   oo   /

These are the initial letters of the Tifinag (Libyan) alphabet for Arabic words meaning *add, give,* and *take away.*

To answer the question "What is given by adding 88 to 194" we use the abacus, as depicted on the Indiana calculus stone, and pebbles to represent the numerals. As the Nevada notation is decimal, we write numbers the same way as in modern arithmetic.

Thus 88 plus 194 is written:

NN ∘ ꝺꝺꝺ

The first column on the right of the abacus is for units, the next is for tens, next for hundreds, and the one on the extreme left is for thousands.

To carry out the sum, place the number 88 on the abacus by putting one pebble on each of the first 8 units of column one, and 8 pebbles similarly on column two. In the diagram I show these as black pebbles.

Now we add 194 in the following way. Place 4 more pebbles on the units column, then, since there are too many now, take away ten of them and replace them by one extra pebble in the tens column. There are now only two units left. Do the same to the tens column, adding 9, and then giving a pebble to the hundreds column, leaving eight pebbles in the tens column. The answer to the problem is therefore 2 hundreds, 8 tens, and 2 units. Therefore

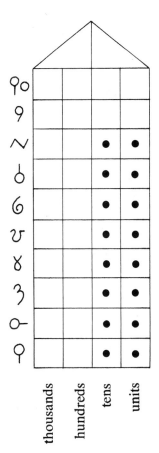

Subtraction is performed by taking pebbles off the board. Multiplication and division require two abacus boards, but we do not yet know if the Nevada people used that method.

We are tempted to inquire: "What use did the Nevada colonists have for a calculator capable of dealing with quantities measured in thousands?" And, since the pictograph from which the abacus was constructed came originally from Indiana, what use would the ancient people of Indiana have for the device?

Answers are ready to hand. The Nevada people were traders as well as hunters and mariners. Evidently they hunted seasonally in the uplands not only for meat, but also for the furs and hides that the game animals yielded. Their Libyan ancestors were well versed

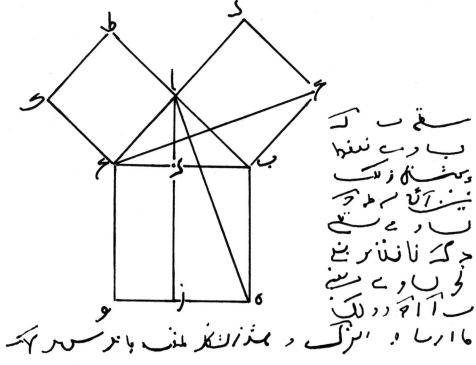

While American scholars preferred the empirical method of solutions and approximations by scale drawings, Arab scholars in the Old World kept alive Euclid's more sophisticated but laborious treatment of geometry. Above is a portion of Tabit Ibn-Qorra's exposition of the theorem of Pythagoras in 890 A.D., when Europe was only beginning to emerge from the Dark Ages following the destruction of libraries and universities by the barbarians. For contrast, see page 326 for the ancient Nevada scholar's demonstration of the area of a triangle.

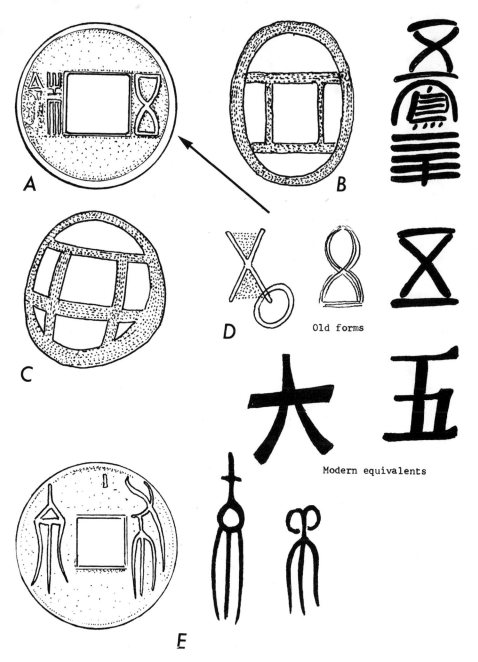

Some foreign languages were apparently studied by young mariners while in training for their future experiences overseas. These petroglyphs, B, D, E, depict salient features of the coins of the Han dynasty of China (third century B.C. to third century A.D.) A, and the later Sung dynasty, E.

Old forms

Modern equivalents

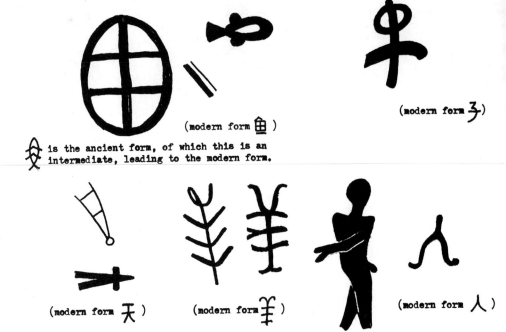

(modern form 田)

(modern form 孑)

⊕ is the ancient form, of which this is an intermediate, leading to the modern form.

(modern form 天)

(modern form 羊)

(modern form 人)

Examples of Chinese ideograms in the old style, with modern forms for comparison, found at Atlatl Rock in the Valley of Fire, Nevada, where it would appear an ancient scholar once lived or taught—or an American who had visited China. The ideograms signify fish, boy, comet, mountain sheep, and man.

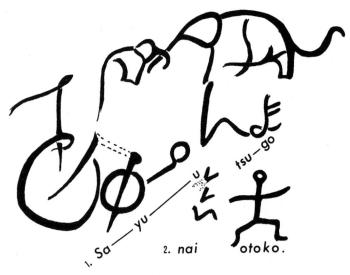

1. sa—yu   2. nai   ̃otoko.   u̇—tsu—go

Hiragana Japanese letters, not older than the ninth century A.D., spell out a Japanese proverb on a boulder near the confluence of Ada and Smoke Rivers in Idaho, found and photographed by Douglas Blizzard, president of the Early Sites Research Society, in 1946. "Mighty is the Elephant, Not so Man." Drawn from photo supplied by Gertrude Johnson.

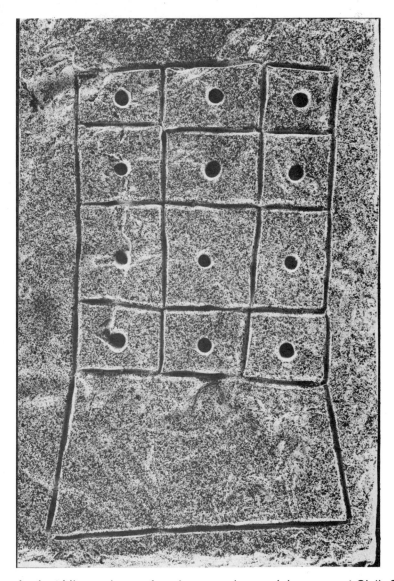

Ancient Libyan abacus, found engraved on rock in a cave at Gleib Qetba, Morocco. It is capable of counting to 124. The column on the right takes small pegs, to be inserted one by one in the holes, each representing a unit, thus the column counts to 4. When 5 is reached the four pegs are removed from column one, and replaced by a single peg in column two, which counts to 20. When 20 is reached, all four pegs in column one are used to yield 24. When 25 is reached, all pegs are removed from columns one and two, and replaced by a single peg in column three. When column three is filled, the abacus registers 100. When every peg is in place, the number registered is 124. This type of abacus was derived from finger-counting, with 5 as the base. In registering the numbers in writing, dots were used for units up to 4, and bars for 5s. Variations of the system are found in ancient Portuguese reckoning, in the Nevada petroglyphs, and in the Mayan system of numerals in Mexico. All appear to date from about the second century A.D. *Universidad de la Laguna, Epigraphic Museum replica, photo Peter J. Garfall.*

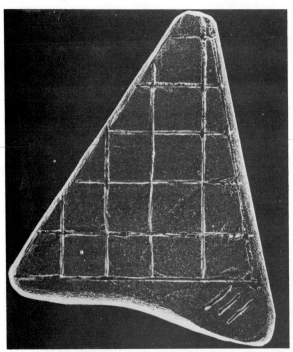

Basic geometry was taught in the ancient Nevada schools by empirical methods. In this petroglyph, also from the Lagomarsino site (which seems to have been the location of a mathematical center) a triangle is shown of height 6 units, and base 5 units. The area can be estimated by counting the complete squares plus the partial squares that are equal or greater than a half, yielding the result 15, shown by the three bars at the bottom right (each bar representing 5). This construction is an elementary demonstration of Euclid's theorem "The area of a triangle is equal to half the base multiplied by the height." *Epigraphic Museum replica, photo Peter J. Garfall.*

Ancient American mathematics lives again for students in a course on ancient patterns of thought offered at Mount Holyoke College. To the left, Professors Steven H. Davol, Martha L. Hadzi, with Fell and students working at a large wooden replica of an abacus engraved on copper, excavated in Ecuador. This type of abacus, not yet known from North America, had a memory bank for numbers, represented by marbles set in cups along the margins, while the operations are carried out on the squared surface, on columns whose values correspond to the bases used in the Mayan numerical system. January 1977. *Photo Peter J. Garfall.*

Mathematical notation in North America was revolutionized in the fifth century A.D., when the Nevada voyagers brought the newly invented Sanskrit system of decimal notation back from India. In this replica of a mathematical petroglyph from Massacre Lake, northwest Nevada, the annual crop report on maize (apparently grown at some lower-altitude location) is given in ancient Libyan script (Arabic language) with the numerals expressed in Sanskrit ciphers. This shows that the ciphers were brought directly from India, for their shapes match the original signs of the first Sanskrit notation, and they differ considerably from the form adopted by the Arabs of the Old World, from whom much later the first European decimal ciphers were obtained in the eleventh century A.D. Thus American mathematicians were far ahead of their Mediterranean contemporaries by this time.

The decipherment is as follows: to the left are Plains (Dakota) hieroglyphs for corn, with the vertically reading Libyan letters spelling S-N (production). To the right, above, the Libyan letters read Ashba zara (plants sown), followed by the Sanskrit numeral 9,074. The next line reads Yana (Harvested) followed by the numeral 9,011. Below is written in cursive Libyan, H-R-M SH-T T-Y M-R-R R-Z-Q, to be read as preclassical Arabic meaning: "Set aside for storage for winter, wholesome food of the Maintainer." The Maintainer (razaq) is one of the 99 attributes of God in the Islamic faith, implying that the inscription postdates the seventh century A.D. *Epigraphic Museum, photo Peter J. Garfall.*

The decimal system of notation required a new type of abacus, to the base 10. This calculus pebble was found in Tippecanoe County, Indiana, by Mrs. Catherine Kramer. One side gives in Iberian script the letters H-S-N (Arabic *hasun,* calculus pebble) and on the other face is illustrated an abacus to the base 10, capable of counting to 19,999 when all squares are filled. The pebble is local Indiana slate. In the presnt-day Algonquian languages, the word *hasun* means stone or pebble —just one example of hundreds of Arabic loan-words in Amerindian tongues. *Epigraphic Museum, photo Peter J. Garfall.*

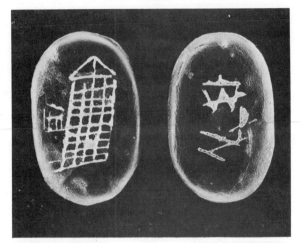

A reproduction of an abacus to the base 10, capacity 19,999, copied directly from the engraving on the calculus pebble shown beside it. *Epigraphic Museum, photo Peter J. Garfall.*

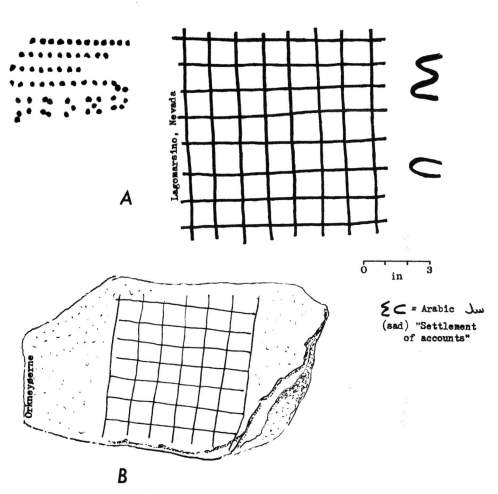

A

Lagomarsino, Nevada

ع ح = Arabic صاد
(sad) "Settlement
of accounts"

0   in   3

B

Orkneyøerne

Abaci are sometimes mistaken for gaming boards. In A, a grid from the Lagomarsino site in Nevada, the two Libyan letters to the side spell the Arabic word S-D (*sad*, settlement of accounts), and thus show clearly the purpose of the grid to have been an abacus. Apparently totals were noted by the dots to the left. In the Orkney Islands, a similar grid engraved on stone and from a Norse site has been reported as a "Viking gaming board"; this is possible, since checkers occur in Norse occupation sites and even influenced Algonquian and Iroquois bead designs (see next chapter), but it is also possible that the board was an abacus of the Nevada type.

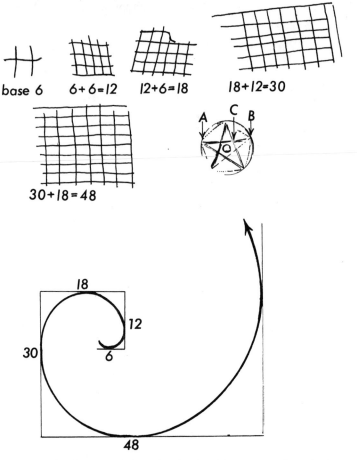

base 6   6+6=12   12+6=18   18+12=30

30+18=48

By far the most sophisticated of the checkerboard patterns found at Nevada petroglyph sites are the grouping at the Whisky Flat site, Mi-5 of the University of California classification, recorded by Heizer and Baumhoff. The contained squares of each of the five associated grids yield a sequence of numbers as shown above, called by mathematicians the Fibonacci series. Among their properties, they yield, when plotted geometrically as shown below, a figure called a *logarithmic spiral*. This figure was known to Pythagoras, who related it to the properties of a regular pentagon (also found inscribed near the Fibonacci series in Nevada), and it was also used in shaping the curve of the capital of the Ionic column. The series also yield the expansion of a reproducing population. Fibonacci was an Italian monk who in the late 1100's disguised himself as a Moslem, with the approval of Pope Innocent III, in order to enroll as a student at one of the Arab universities. Among the mathematical materials that he brought back with him was the series named for him. The Nevada petroglyphs show that the Arabic-speaking Nevada people were well acquainted with the mathematics as taught in Mediterranean Arab universities.

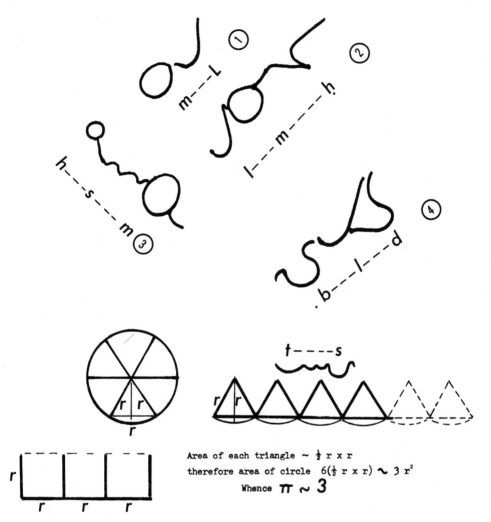

Area of each triangle ~ ½ r x r
therefore area of circle 6(½ r x r) ~ 3 r²
Whence π ~ 3

Of less theoretical interest, but greater practical usefulness in a country that lacked traction animals, and therefore had no sophisticated use for the wheel, is this petroglyph at Steward's site 202, the so-called Court of Antiquity in Washoe County, Nevada. It yields in Arabic Kufi script an instruction on how to find the area of a circle. Divide it into six equal sectors, and then rearrange them as shown. The text reads in Arabic *Lamma Hamala Misaha dulab* (Reunite to obtain the area of a circle). The area is then given by the previous theorem for the area of a triangle (page 326), as set out above. It yields an approximation for π of 3, as against the more correct value of 3.142. Until recently one of the southern states of the Union recognized the legal value of π as being 3, which is also the value assigned to this constant in the Old Testament.

a

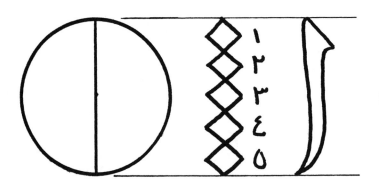

b

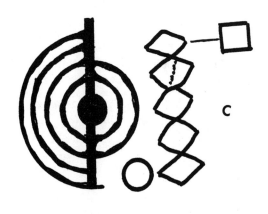

c

d

The western desert states of North America have thousands of fantastic "humanoid" rock-cut engravings of the general character shown in a above. For decades their meaning has been obscure. Some of them resemble slim human figures with beaded expansions, others have concentric rings superimposed on matchstick figures. Most distort the human body in an inexplicable manner, omitting limbs, or having too many limbs, or the limbs twisted, and nearly all have bead-like or diamond-shaped thickenings of the central vertical axis. The series shown in a are from a much larger assemblage collected by Professors Heizer and Baumhoff from various locations in Nevada and California. An explanation of their origin may be offered as follows:

When calligraphy, the art of fine writing, developed in the Arab world, after the dawn of Islam and it became a religious requirement to render the letters of the Koran in the finest style, Arab schoolmasters taught their pupils the correct proportions of letters by making use of the diagram shown at b. It depicts the letter Alif (A), rendered in Naskhi Arabic script as a stroke, as shown to the right. Five diamond accent-points are to equal in height one alif; also, every letter of the Naskhi alphabet must fall within the confines of a circle whose diameter equals one alif. This standard of proportion is called the *Naskhi module.*

In c, a petroglyph discovered by Professors Heizer and Baumhoff at University of California site Wa-35, in Nevada, we see an ancient Nevada schoolmaster's version of the Naskhi module, engraved on bedrock at what was evidently a teaching site. It repeats the formula "Five diamond points equal one Alif," and also requires square and round points to conform. The concentric circles pass through the center-points of the 5 points if they are superimposed on the circle, whose diameter equals one Alif. In d, to the right, is a simplified lesson, near Massacre Lake, Nevada. It too relates the five points to one Alif, but the exactness of the subdivisions is now less marked, as the diamonds do not touch.

Various intermediate forms show that when the Arabic-speaking population of the western desert states was driven south (or fled abroad) around the twelfth century A.D., as the invading barbarian hordes of Athapascan peoples (Apache, Navajo) took possession of their territory, the old school sites now became objects of curiosity and religious veneration of the non-literate invaders. Before long the Athapascan and also Shoshone and other invaders began to imitate the school lessons, and converted the diagrams into the peculiar mythical monsters and humanoid figures that are so commonly found today.

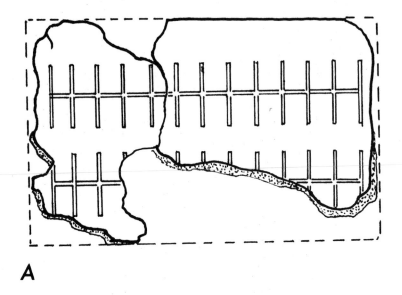

A

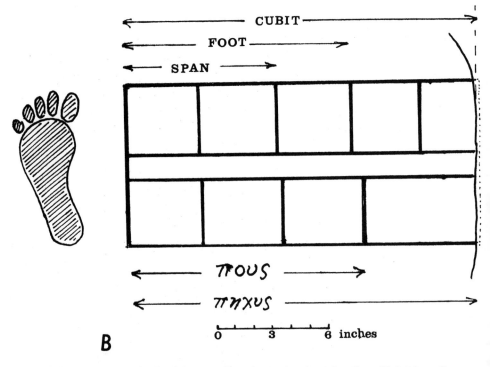

B

A Nevada petroglyph yields an American standard for the official length of a foot, a span and a cubit, apparently to the North African standards. It is designated hieroglyphically by the engraved figure of a foot beside the measured standards. For comparison, A above, one of the engraved stone standards of measure in the paving of the marketplace in Leptis Magna.

Table of Arabic letters.

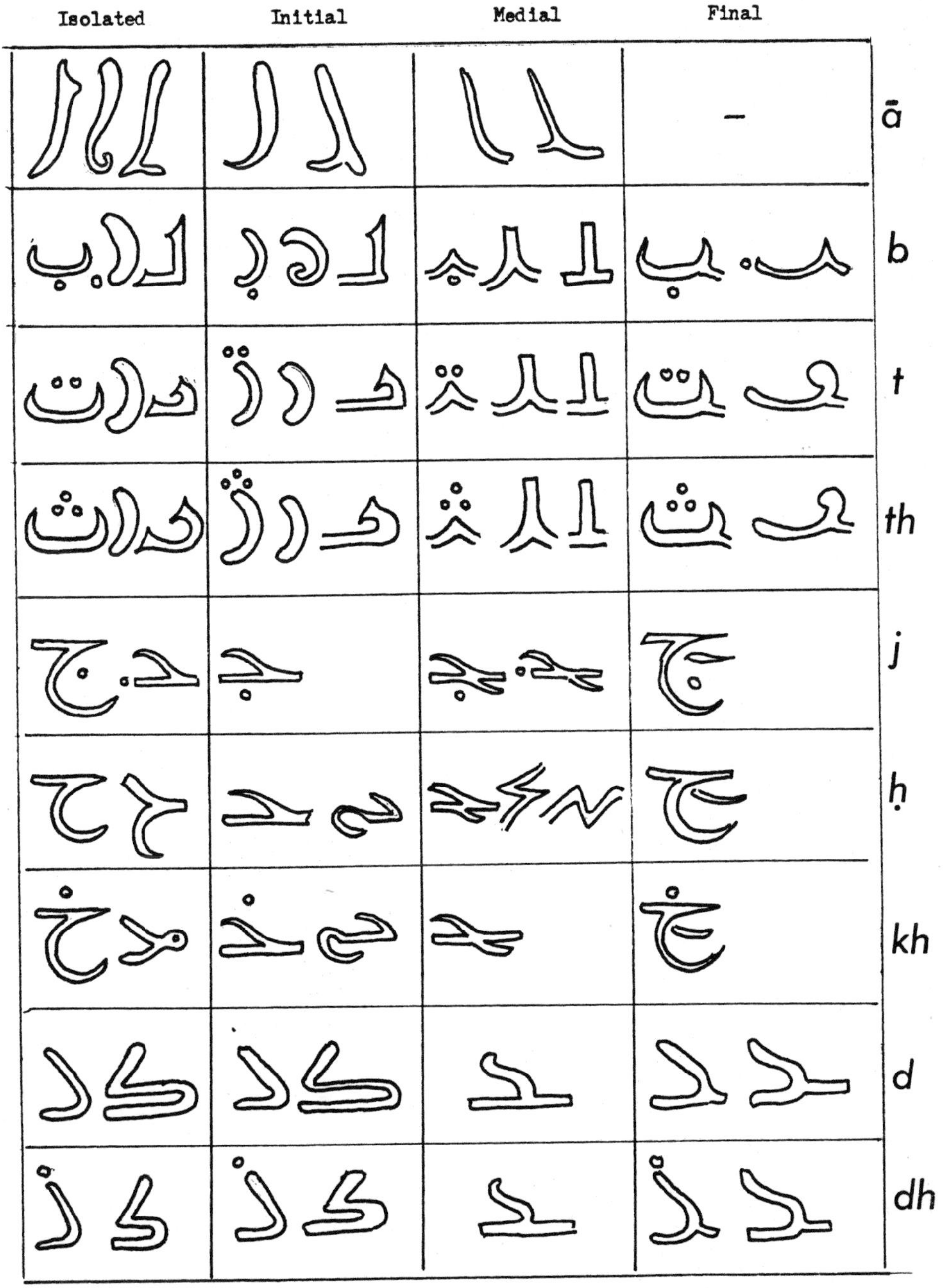
Isolated
Initial
Medial
Final
ā
b
t
th
j
ḥ
kh
d
dh

Table giving Arabic letters

Isolated	Initial	Medial	Final	
ر د ر	ر -	ر ر	ر	r
ز ز ز	ز -	-	ز ز ز	z
س س س س س	س س س	س س س	س س س	s
ش ش ش	ش ش	ش ش	ش ش	sh
ص ص	ص ص	ص ص	ص ص	ṣ
ض ض	ض ض	ض ض	ض	ḍ
ط ط	ط ط	ط ط	ط ط	ṭ
ظ ظ	ظ ظ	ظ ظ	ظ	ẓ
ع ع	ع	ع ع	ع	ʿ, ʿ

Arabic letters (continued)

Table of Arabic letters.

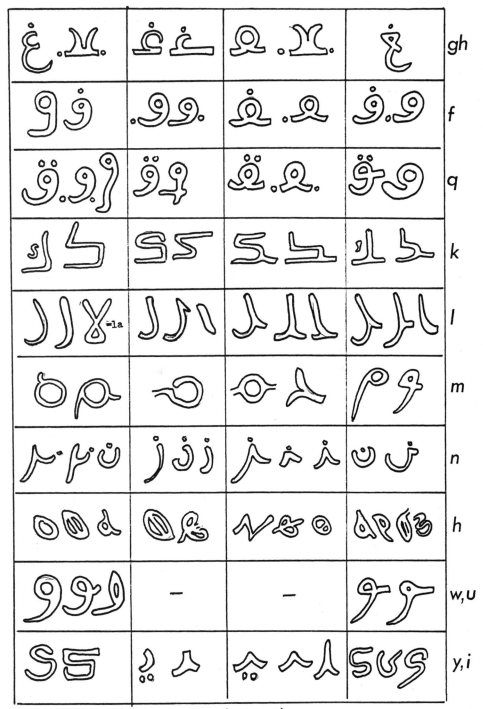

Arabic letters (continued)

Table of Arabic letters.

in tanning leather by using bark. Thus the Nevada mariners had a marketable commodity, which Roman writers tell us was eagerly sought on the wharves of India and China. But the Chinese had wares to sell in return—exceedingly costly wares, such as silk, porcelain statuettes, and such wonders (after the ninth century) as spectacles and magnifying glasses. To compute the value of such sophisticated products in terms of rabbit skins or buffalo hides would be a complex operation if fingers alone are available. The abacus would be the answer, and, once the Hindu place method of notation was invented, traders would seize upon it and carry the new mathematics far and wide.

The Indiana evidence comes from an engraving on a flat pebble which also carries the word "calculus pebble" engraved in Iberic characters, spelling the Arabic (and Algonquian) word that has that meaning. Clearly the Algonquians of Indiana were trading with visitors who sailed the Mississippi and its tributaries, bringing wondrous wares from Europe. What wares? Phoenician urns, such as the one found recently by Salvatore Trento's group in New York (page 78), or the ceramic elephant statuette shown on page 287. And also, in all probability, perishable wares that have not survived, such as silk from China and purple cloth from Phoenicia.

Prior to the invention of the decimal place system in India, a calculator such as the abacus was essential, for neither the Roman nor Greek systems of numerical notation provided any method of calculating, save only by use of the abacus. If the Phoenicians— or their African cousins, the Carthaginians—traded in expensive wares with Americans, then the small abaci to the base 5, apparently designed to use the Iberian AL-K-H-N system of notation must have served (see page 325 for explanation).

As can be seen from the blackboard entries visible in the photograph on page 326, mathematical operations with the Iberian system are similar to those of the Mayan system of arithmetic. Both the Mayan and the Iberic systems use up to 4 dots for units, followed by bars for fives. The word *al-kahan* spelled by taking the alphabetic values of the signs also used as numerals in the Iberian system is preclassical Arabic (hence of Old World origin). So far as

I know, it is not a Mayan word. Both the Mayan and the Iberian systems seem first to appear in the second century of our era. I therefore suspect a common origin and that Arabic speakers invented the system; but this does not necessarily mean that it was acquired by Mayans from Iberia. It might have been the work of Iberian settlers in America, influenced by Mayans. If the latter proves to be the case, then we would have to acknowledge the Iberian notation system as something transferred from America to the Old World; the evidence cited above precludes any notion of the system having been invented independently in Mexico and Europe.

And just as the mathematical notation of ancient North America implies a common origin with that of Iberia and North Africa, so also do the conventions of the written alphabets. As shown in the tables on pages 335–337, the ancient Arabic scribes of North America followed precisely the same rules as those of their colleagues in the western Mediterranean. Not only are the letters of the alphabets identical, but more than that, the form of each letter varies in the same way, according to whether it stands alone, or stands at the beginning of a word, or in the middle of a word, or at the end of a word. The American scribes used letter-forms, and followed writing rules, matching those of the eighth century A.D. in the western Mediterranean. And since we know that Arabs were already present in those regions a thousand years before the coming of Islam it follows that the North American Arab scribes must have come here from the lands of the Mediterranean. Under no circumstances could the North American writing system have been independently invented.

In May 1979 Dr. Jon Polansky, at my request, submitted the evidence to Professor Robert F. Heizer, the eminent archeologist of the University of California whose explorations had brought to light so many of these inscriptions. As might be anticipated, Dr. Heizer immediately perceived the reality of the foregoing arguments. Thus, as this book goes to press, it is with the heartening news that, in California at least, my results are now being viewed as a logical continuation of the groundwork laid these past fifty years by the archeologists of that part of North America most richly endowed with ancient records of our past. To Robert Heizer, as also Harold Gladwin, and to their former colleagues in the field, Professors Julian Steward, E. Renaud, and Martin Baumhoff, let us acknowledge a debt of gratitude for arduous explorations and faithful recording of inscriptions, whose key now lies within our grasp.

Norse Visitors and Settlers

Until Thormod Torfason wrote his *Historia Vinlandae Antiquae* in 1705, few scholars outside of Scandinavia had ever heard of Norse voyages to America, and even then skepticism reigned for nearly two centuries. So in 1930, when word reached Dr. C. T. Currelly, director of the Royal Ontario Museum, that an unusual sword and battle-axe had been discovered on May 24 at Beardmore, Ontario, he wasted no time in dispatching a member of the museum staff to investigate. The find was made by James Edward Dodd, a prospector whose dynamite brought the objects to light under a big clump of birches. A Professor McIlwraith visited the site with Mr. Dodd and was shown the imprint in rust on the rock where the sword had been lying, and also found a piece of iron in the soil that had covered the weapons. A shield that was part of the cache had fallen to pieces, though its boss remained. The artifacts were taken to the museum and in due course identified as Norse by experts, and dated to the first quarter of the eleventh century, about 1025 A.D. This is the period of the first voyages to Vinland by Leif Eriksson, beginning in 1000 A.D., the year of Iceland's conversion to Christianity.

Belief in Norse voyages to America waxes and wanes as capriciously as the rise and fall of women's skirts. By the late 1930's it was widely accepted as true that the Vikings came here and that their relics had been found. Then, in 1940, from his Harvard chair, Admiral Samuel Eliot Morison maintained that Columbus had no predecessor—and woe betide any who disagreed with this pronouncement. By 1961 the Royal Ontario Museum had issued the statement: "It has not been possible to authenticate the story of the alleged discovery [of the Beardmore objects] nor to prove that the objects are of undoubted Viking origin." The Museum now attributed the date of discovery to 1931 or 1932, as opposed to the precise date given by its former director.

Few scientists would now dispute the reality of the Norse presence in America, and current research is directed more to the unraveling of the confused and incomplete record of their visits and settlements.

The Icelandic sagas tell us that Greenland was settled by Icelanders in 985 A.D., and that the founder's son, Leif Eriksson, departed on a voyage fifteen years later that took him to a new land lying to the southwest that he called Vinland. A settlement was begun, but hostile relations with the natives forced its abandonment after a season or two.

How would the Norse visitors be viewed by the Algonquians whom they encountered during these incursions? Scarcely as bringers of civilization! It would be hard to find a more civilized or peaceful country today than Denmark, or more gracious hosts than the kind people of Scandinavia among whom my wife spent a year in 1953. But these same Norsemen descend from singularly unruly ancestors.

While I lived in Copenhagen, I was able to examine an abstract of Norse ecclesiastical records prepared by Andreas Nissen for the cathedral church of St. Ansgar; a document most enlightening on the spread of Christianity through the north during the ninth to eleventh centuries. But later, when I came to compare these Danish records with those of the English churches and cathedrals, some strange anomalies became evident. One thing was clear: the conversion of the Norsemen to Christianity had nothing whatever to do with moderating their ferocity. Let me illustrate the dichotomy by some comparisons of the two sets of records.

The English records tell of ferocious raids by Danes upon English churches and towns from 783 A.D. onward for the next 300 years. The Danish records tell of steady Christianization of Denmark from 822 onward—the year when Pope Paschal sent Archbishop Ebo to Denmark. By 830 A.D. Archbishop Ansgar established his archdiocese from Lund, in southern Sweden. By 946 so many Danes had adopted Christianity that Pope Agapitus II found it necessary to establish new bishoprics at Aarhus, Ribe, and Schlesvig. By the same date, the Danes had carried out a successful series of seventeen attacks and massacres on the English towns. By vote of the Althing (House of Representatives) of Iceland in 1000 A.D.—the same year that Leif Eriksson landed in Vinland to begin temporary American settlements—the whole island became Christian. Eleven years later, in 1011, the Danes destroyed the cathedral town of Canterbury in England, and murdered Alphege, the Archbishop of Canterbury. In 1054 Iceland was accorded its own first bishopric, at Skalholt, and in 1060 three more bishoprics were set up in Denmark by Pope Nikolaus II. Nine years later, the Danes burned York in northern England, and left 3,000 Normans dead. Eleven years later, in 1080, Pope (Saint) Gregory VII established the first bishopric of the Faeroes.

One is left with the impression that the rapid headway in the spread of the gospel of peace in Scandinavia was in no way related to any improvement in the neighborly manners of the Norsemen themselves. It seems that manslaughter from Monday to Saturday could be confessed and absolved each Sunday following. This gave adequate employment to the pastors and accounts for the extraordinary number of churches that the Norsemen built for themselves: the more they burned in England, the more they raised to the glory of the Lord back home, frequently decorating them with booty snatched from Celtic and Saxon ecclesiastics.

Take now the record of the Greenland settlements, painstakingly being reconstructed by Danish and Norwegian historians since the polar ice began its retreat in the 1920s, to disclose the long-forgotten western settlements on the American side of Greenland.

Greenland itself was discovered by Erik the Red, in exile from Norway for killing friends of the king. He made a so-called eastern settlement at the southern tip of Greenland, and a so-called western settlement on the west coast near where modern Godthaab stands. Within a few generations, the settlements had so prospered (the climate was milder then) that no fewer than sixteen well-constructed stone churches arose, followed by a fine cathedral built at Gardar in the south. Pope Paschal II appointed Erik Gnupsson the first *bishop of Greenland and Vinland* in the year 1112, implying that by then there must have been additional congregations and churches on the American mainland. Gardar was made the permanent seat of a bishopric by Pope Callixtus II in 1124. Meanwhile, Iceland had acquired a second bishopric in 1106, again by the action of Pope Paschal II. For at least the first century after the Greenland settlements were begun, the Danes and Norwegians in Europe were bringing annual dread, death, and disaster upon the hapless peoples of England, Scotland, and Ireland. Hence it seems improbable that Leif and his fellow rovers would play the part of gentle servants of God in their descents upon the American coast. That the *skraelings* (American Indians) were so unfriendly as to fire arrows at them, from one of which a relative of Leif met his death, would seem therefore to be no reflection upon the hospitality of the Algonquians. No doubt they were following an old law, well understood among the Norsemen: an eye for an eye, a life for a life, as the Islamic version still renders it.

Thus it would appear likely that the initial relations between the Greenland Norsemen and their American Indian hosts were decidedly unfriendly. Three centuries later, however, the situation had reversed. The Danes and Norwegians in the homelands became neglectful of sending annual supply ships to the Greenland colonies. During this period of deprivation, English mariners from Bristol made occasional visits to Greenland, bringing, among other things, the latest fashions of the 1300's, for we find the bodies in the Greenland burial grounds wearing garments that would have passed muster at the courts of medieval Europe. Probably from these English visitors word spread, eventually reaching Rome, that the Greenlanders had become altogether too friendly with the *infidels,* whose heathen practices, it was said, were being adopted by the Greenlanders. But before inquiring further on those lines, there are matters related to the earlier period which engage our attention. What, if anything, followed from Leif Eriksson's first visits to Vinland? Were these initial contacts of the eleventh century maintained?

Recent discoveries in America and in Europe support the view that Leif's voyage must have been followed by a succession of other voyages, ranging southward beyond the Canadian Maritimes, along the New England coast, then farther southward around Florida to the mouth of the Mississippi, and then up the Missis-

Godthåb
Gardar

ice pack

L'Anse au Meadow

Lockport

Beardmore

Rocky Nook Cole Harbor

Brandon

Newport

Tulsa

International blackmail on a major scale is represented by these coins
(A, B). *Danegeld*—money paid to the Danes to stay away from
England—amounted to 55 million pieces. Wherever the Norsemen and
Danes voyaged, they carried large numbers of the English silver
pennies (A) obtained by annual levies on Aethelred II, king of England.
Between 991 and 1012 A.D., English records disclose that no fewer
than 37,200,000 pennies were paid as *Danegeld* to Sven, king of
Denmark, and Olaf, king of Norway. In 1014 a further 17,280,000 were
paid to Sven's son Cnut (B). By the time the Viking settlements in
Greenland and Vinland were undertaken, these silver "Long-cross"
pennies were the principal coinage of the Norsemen. Algonquian and
Iroquois *runti* shell beads appear to be a northeastern American
imitation of the Long-cross coins (C). Buried hoards of Aethelred's
pennies are still discovered in Denmark today and are resold to England
for coin collectors. With the advance in metal detection, American
examples ought soon to be discovered. D, E, Two Norse gaming jettons
found in Dublin, believed to date from the 1100's. (*D, E, courtesy of
Bord Failte, Irish Government.*)

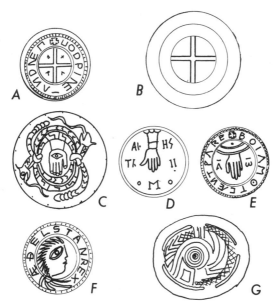

Engraved shell disks found in burial mounds in the eastern United
States, resembling the Viking coinages current at the time of Leif's
voyage to Vinland, 1000 A.D. A, penny of Sven Forkbeard 990–1012, and
B, engraved shell disk from burial at Nashville, Tennessee. C, hand
enclosed in coiled rattlesnakes, similar to serpent-enclosed Norse
epigraphs. D, penny of Edward the Elder, and E, of Aethelred II,
minted as *Danegeld*, in 999 A.D., the hand of God signifiyng the
approaching millennium of 1000 A.D. C is an engraved shell disk from
Carthage, Alabama, in a mound burial, and a similar example is known
from Lake Washington, Mississippi. F, penny of Aethelstan,
representative of many crude Saxon and Norse pieces whose design
appears to be reflected in the Nashville Mound disks, example G.

Gloria Farley of Oklahoma beside the inscription on the giant
Heavener runestone in the State Park on Poteau Mountain.
Photo courtesy Gloria Farley.

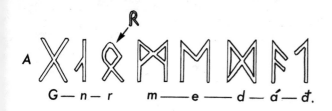

A G — n — r   m — e — d — á — đ.

B G — n —ng   i,   e — á— j — th.

C M — æ — d — o — k.

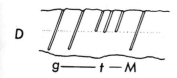

D g —— t — M

A. Heavener inscription, Norse, but meaning uncertain. B, Poteau inscription, Norse, but meaning uncertain. C, Shawnee inscription believed to be a headstone reading *Madok*. D, Ogam inscription on a Welsh stone reading, in retrograde direction, M-T-G or *Madog*. The Oklahoma runestones are in an alphabet not exactly matched elsewhere, and consequently have been the subject of varied decipherment. They still remain problematic.

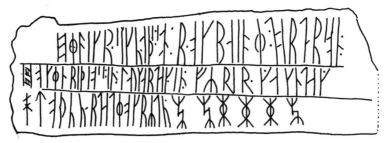

1. ¶ELIKR·SIKUATⱢS·SONR·OK BAINE·TORᵭRSON
2. ¶OK·ENRITⱢ·IONSSON LAⱤKARTAKIN·FYRIR·GAKNTAG
3. HLOPU·UⱤDA·TE·OK·RYDU· ⅄⅄⅄⅄⅄⅄⅄

Above, inscribed stone and, below, its transliteration, found on the top of a cairn of stones erected at Kingiktorsoak, near Disko Island, Baffin Bay, and believed to record a Norse voyage of the fourteenth century. The translation reads: (1) Erling Sigvatsson and Bjarni Thordarson (2) and Eindridi Jonsson on the Saturday before Rogation Day (April 25) (3) raised these cairns and wrote this. DDCCCL." The stone is now in the Copenhagen National Historic Museum.

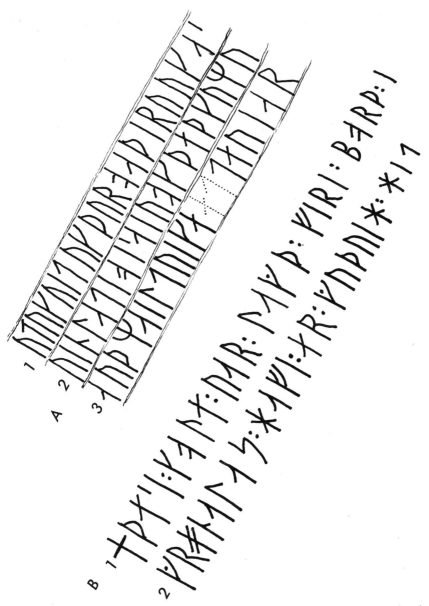

Two Old Norse inscriptions that refer to North America and Greenland. A, from Hönen, Ringerike, Norway, is believed by Scandinavian scholars to date from early in the eleventh century. It reads in translation (1) "Far and wide they sailed, in want of dry clothing and food (2) They came upon ice in the unsettled region of Vinland. (3) Those who are dogged by bad luck die young." B, carved on a wooden slat found in an empty coffin excavated at Herjulfsnes, southern Greenland, reports that the coffin's rightful owner had to be buried at sea: (1) "This woman was cast overboard into (2) the Greenland Sea. She was named Guthwih (Gudvig)." *Sophus Bugge (1902) and Olaf Strandwold (1948).*

Petroglyph depicting the carved
figurehead of a Viking ship recorded
by Professor E. B. Renaud in 1938
from his site N.M.224 on the upper
Rio Grande, New Mexico.

Opposite page above: On the island of Gotland in the Baltic, this
boulder maze, located at Trojaborg, was obviously constructed on the
pattern of the labyrinth of Knossos. Gotland was an important trading
center in Classical times, and thousands of ancient coins have been
recovered from the soil. It is probable that the maze was patterned after
one of the coins of Knossos. The spiral boulder maze near
Lockport, Manitoba, may be a confused recollection of a maze of the
Trojaborg type, constructed by Vikings of Vinland.

Opposite page below: A 2,000-foot serpent coiled to form a spiral 100
feet across. Numerous mazes constructed of boulders occur in Sweden,
Lapland, Finland, and Iceland. Some have been dated to the Bronze
Age, the age of others is unknown. (A similar modern relict is the
line of whitened boulders that marks the Arctic Circle in Sweden.) In
Britain mazes were generally constructed from raised turf, so many of
them have been destroyed by plowing. The purpose of the structures
is unknown. A boulder maze 100 feet across, similar to the one
illustrated, occurs between Beauséjour and Lockport, Manitoba.
(Informant Betty Nickerson, Ottawa.)

West

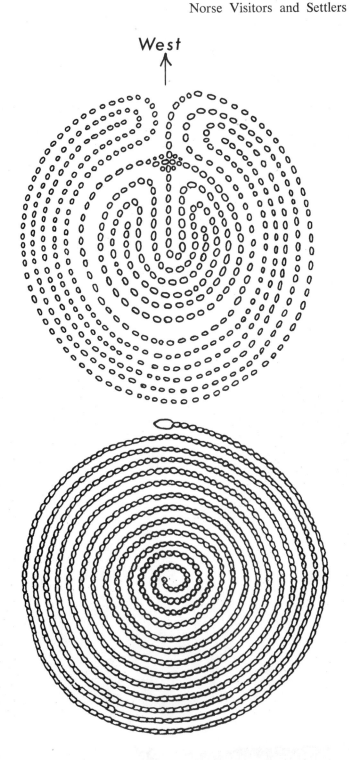

Frederick J. Pohl of New York, eminent historian of the Viking age in America and author of five books dealing with the Viking voyages and settlements, and another on the voyage of Prince Henry Sinclair from the Orkneys in 1398. Over the span of his writings, since 1942, Pohl has seen the attitude of most historians change from the skepticism of the thirties and forties to tacit acceptance.

Iron battle-axe found at Rocky Nook on the Massachusetts coast, near Plymouth, formerly in the ownership of William Goodwin and now in the Wordsworth Athenaeum, Connecticut. The markings are letters of the Tifinag alphabet of Libya, though the axe appears to be Viking. *Photo Malcolm Pearson.*

In 1938 Professor
E. B. Renaud
recorded this petro-
glyph of a warrior
wielding a battle-axe,
apparently a Viking,
at his site N.M.51
in the Rio Grande
valley of New Mexico.
Replica Epigraphic
Museum, *photo
Dr. Julian Fell.*

Another iron battle-axe
apparently of Libyan or
Viking origin found at Cole
Harbor, Nova Scotia, and
later in the William
Goodwin collection, now
in the Wordsworth
Athenaeum, Connecticut.
*Photo Malcolm Pearson of
rubbing made by him.*

A, B, C, petroglyphs in Colorado apparently depicting Vikings and their weapons, observed and recorded by Professors E. B. Renaud and Julian Willard. D, E, F, round battleshields of leather of the Pima tribe, Arizona, Smithsonian Institution. G, H, I, similar Libyan battleshields depicted in mosaics of North Africa, Fell. J, K, battleshields of early Norse warriors depicted in pictographs on the monuments of Gotland, Sweden.

sippi River and its tributary the Arkansas, into Oklahoma. Later still, the contacts extended to Colorado; and on the north coast of Canada, around Labrador, into Hudson Bay, where landings gave access to parts of Manitoba and Ontario.

Early in 1972, the Irish press began to report the extraordinary discovery of hundreds of pewter tokens in a medieval cesspit in Dublin. Eventually, over 2,000 of these coinlike objects came to light. They are tentatively supposed to be small change used in Irish taverns, possibly in the 1200's; as Dublin was largely settled by Norsemen (who promptly came under Celtic influence), the tokens may be regarded as reflecting equally Norse or Celtic taste in art (page 210). Other objects dating from the years 1000 to 1200 also found in Ireland are gaming pieces with characteristic designs (page 212). Further, the enormous amounts of blackmail paid by the English to the Danes to quit harrying the English shores consisted of over 50,000,000 silver pennies (page 346), a currency that became widespread wherever Norsemen went, and hence presumably would be used in Greenland. Now the interesting thing is that we in America have known for long of the designs of these newly discovered Irish-Norse tokens and gaming pieces, but to us they became evident as *beads* or *pendants,* carved by the Algonquian Indians and the Iroquois from shell. I believe these American artifacts can best be explained as locally made copies of pewter and silver tokens and coins introduced originally by Norse visitors of the eleventh century and after.

Nor are these the only objects of like nature. Since the Tennessee mounds were first investigated a century or more ago, a well-known series of shell disks has come into the collections of the museums, having highly distinctive motifs that have never satisfactorily been explained (page 347). I believe these, too, are to be regarded as American imitations of coins introduced originally soon after the year 1000, and hence presumably introduced by Leif and his successors. Ancient coins found in America often have a hole pierced at one side so that the coin can be worn as a pendant, the hole placed so that the design is displayed the right way up. Probably the medieval coins were similarly used, and when the supply failed, the Amerindian artists proceeded to make local copies from mother-of-pearl.

One of the most distinctive designs shows a hand surrounded

by a circular frame, formed from two serpents (rattlesnakes). Norse designs (and grave inscriptions) commonly are enclosed by twined serpent patterns. The hand motif relates to the year 1000. As the year 999 advanced, rumors spread through Europe that it was the last year of the world's existence. It was argued that the approaching millennium would be the year of the establishment of God's kingdom, the dead would arise, and the wicked would be judged and condemned to eternal hellfire.

Some monks endowed with unusual business acumen discovered that wealthy barons and other landowners were willing to seek an accommodation with the Church by making over large tracts of their holdings to local monasteries in return for the needed absolution from past crimes. The English geologist Lyell, for example, when traveling in Sicily in the early 1800's, had been mystified by the large number of monastery foundations that dated from the year 999. Upon inquiry, he was shown the title deeds, which invariably began with the words *appropinquante mundi termino* (the end of the world being near at hand) or *appropinquante die magno judicii* (the great day of judgment being nigh). Added inducement to the pious was achieved by the moneyers (usually bishops) having coins struck that showed the hand of God appearing through the canopy of heaven.

Thus, when we find patterns of the type described engraved on disks in American mounds, or used as necklace elements or pendants by Amerindians of the eastern tribes, my instinct is to relate them to the introduction of coins and tokens struck around the year 1000, and carried to America in the money pouches of Norsemen. In England, Scotland, and Ireland, many Norsemen settled down, married Saxon or Celtic maidens, and gave rise to many a British family that still carries a Norse name. Is there any reason why visiting Norsemen in Eastern America might not feel tempted to do the same? Probably not. The blue-eyed Indians of the Northeast encountered by several early explorers, the fair-haired corpses found by the Pilgrims when they opened mounds near Plymouth, and the light-skinned people of Rhode Island who fascinated the visiting Italian crews thirty years after Columbus, may all have been descended in part from Norsemen, as other writers have already suggested.

Although no mention of the fact can be recognized in sagas that have been preserved, it would appear that these early Norsemen also sailed south to the Gulf of Mexico and ascended the Mississippi. For when Oklahoma was settled by displaced Cherokees and other eastern tribes in the early 1800's, inexplicable rock inscriptions were discovered. Knowledge of these was passed on to the European colonists who were later admitted into the then Indian Territory, and they in turn showed the inscriptions to their children and grandchildren. One of these was Gloria Farley. In later life, recalling what she had seen as a child, but finding that no one any longer remembered where the inscriptions are to be found, she set about rediscovering them. The strange letters proved to be runes.

The best known of these finely cut texts, written in the Old Runes of the Viking Age, and therefore probably not later than about 1050 A.D., are located near Heavener and Poteau, and another has been found at Shawnee, Oklahoma. They are shown on page 348. A fourth inscription of matching aspect but using letters like those of the Sabean alphabet of Arabia has not yet yielded any plausible decipherment. These inscriptions have been the subject of much debate and uncertainty, but not as to their antiquity; it is the decipherment that has proved difficult. Earlier suggestions that they represent concealed dates appear improbable to me and to Scandinavian authorities. Madok is a common Celtic name found in Ireland, Scotland, and Wales, and one likely to be acquired by Norsemen of partial Celtic ancestry. The Oklahoma Madok is unlikely to be related to the Welsh prince of that name who is reputed to have come to America some centuries later, for the runes are of too old a style. A Welsh gravestone in vowelless Ogam, bearing the same name, is also shown on page 348. For information on this latter I am indebted to my colleague James Whittall.

After the eleventh century, the shapes of the runic letters used in Scandinavia underwent much change, and the number of letters in the alphabet was reduced. Some differences also arose between the particular alphabets used in different countries of Scandinavia. Hence it is possible to assign approximate dates to runic inscriptions merely by examining the type of letters employed. In this

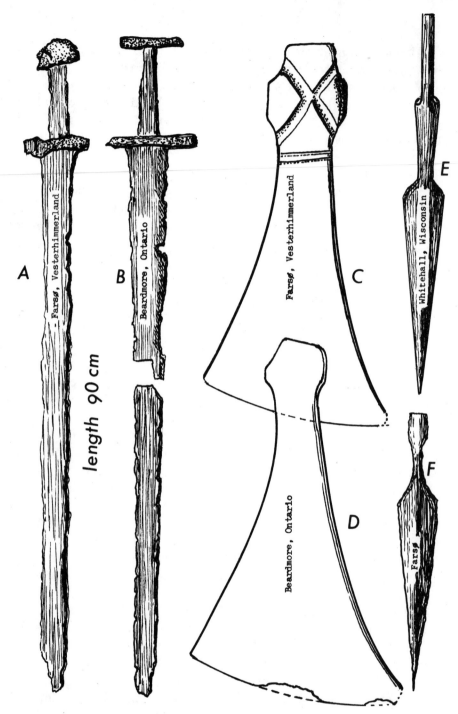

Sword, battle-axe and spearhead from Beardmore, Ontario, A, D, and from Whitehall, Wisconsin, E, compared with corresponding Norse artifacts from the Faeroes, A, F, C.

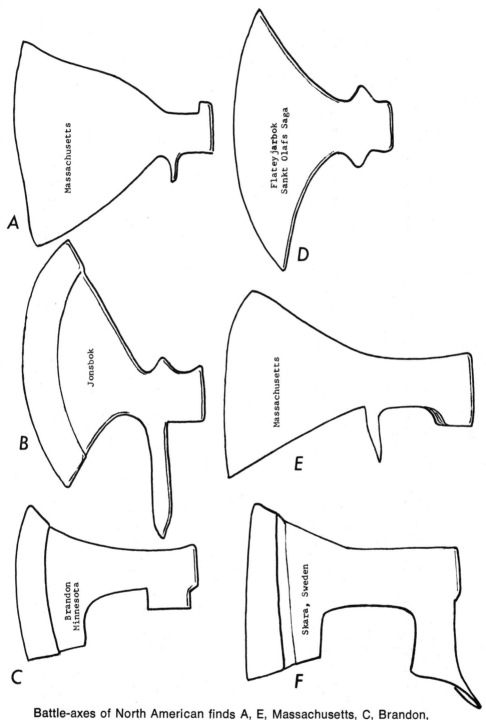

Battle-axes of North American finds A, E, Massachusetts, C, Brandon, Minnesota, compared with corresponding forms from Skara, Sweden, F, and illustrations in the Copenhagen copies of the sagas *Jonsbok*, B, and *Flateyjarbok, Sankt Olaf's Saga*, D.

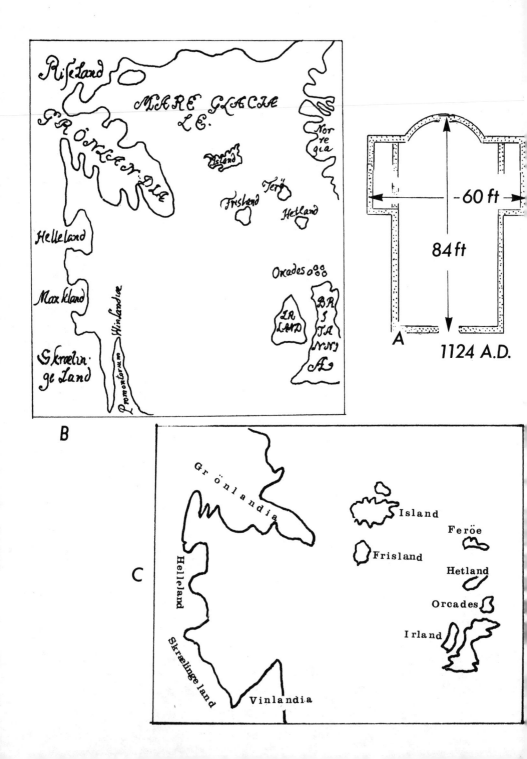

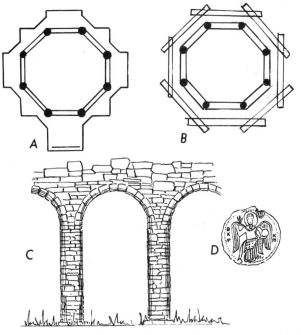

From the 1100's onward, Norse churches were provided with Romanesque arches and were built under the influence of early Byzantine architecture that became familiar to many Norsemen when they served in the palace guard at Constantinople. Early Byzantine chapel (A) and its later derivatives in northern Europe. A, church at Mastara, Armenia, 650 A.D. (After De Vogüé). Wood bell-tower of Tsyvozero, 1658, the outer shell of lap-jointed pine trunks. C, arches in Romanesque style in the ruins of the Domkirke at Hamar, Norway (1152 A.D.). D, Byzantine seal of Michael III issued to Norsemen of the palace guard in Constantinople, found in Denmark.

Opposite page: In 1124 A.D. Pope Callixtus II authorized the permanent bishop's seat at Gardar, for the Greenland settlements. The ruins of the cathedral, A, excavated by Dr. Poul Nörlund, disclose a fine cruciform stone building to serve the sixteen stone churches of the Greenland parishes. The extensive bishop's residence, larger than the cathedral, and including a barn to hold over a hundred cows of the bishop's herd, together with the lumber needs of the resident population, undoubtedly required continuous voyages to Vinland for supplies. Yet, despite this, the two oldest maps of Greenland and Vinland held by the bishop of Skaholt, in Iceland, dating from 1570 and shown in B and C, reveal an imperfect knowledge of the east American coast no better than can be inferred from the record of Leif Eriksson's original voyage of 1000 A.D. It is apparent that the bishops of Greenland and Vinland did not disclose the extent of their see to the Icelandic bishops. Rhode Island, where a stone episcopal church was built in the 1300's, does not appear at all in the Icelanders' maps, which terminate at the northern promontory of Newfoundland. The strait leading to Hudson Bay is similarly omitted. The two maps are later copies now held in the Royal Library in Copenhagen. The nonexistent island of Friesland must derive from some erroneous sighting reported around 1000 A.D. The determination of latitude was well understood by Norse mariners; therefore the portions of the American coast shown in the same latitude as Britain can be recognized as Labrador.

America's oldest Christian building, the fourteenth century Norse church tower at Newport, Rhode Island, photographed in summer 1942 by Malcolm Pearson, on the occasion when the Norse runes were discovered inscribed on the tower.

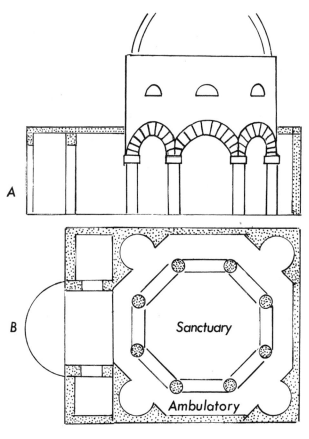

Early Byzantine church of Saint George at Ezra, Syria. The free-standing octagonal-based tower, with eight columns supporting Roman arches, encloses the sanctuary. Date of construction 515 A.D. When intact, the Newport tower was presumably free-standing, within a timber outer shell. Byzantine influence was strong in Scandinavia, and early visitors reported church buildings with outer walls of timber. A, elevation. B, plan. (*After De Vogüe.*)

A

B

Sanctuary

Ambulatory

The Norsemen who took service under the Byzantine Greeks after 839 A.D. were known as the *Vaeringer,* and comprised among others the palace guard in Constantinople. This lead seal dates from the reign of Michael the Drunkard, Emperor from 842 to 867 A.D., and was carried by an interpreter called Lancelot, probably an Englishman. It reads: "Admission-pass of Lancelot to the Palace for resolving translation problems for the Hired Palace-Guard. Michael." (Data from Johan Ottosen, Copenhagen, transl. Fell.) The combination of Latin and Greek letters may be a protection against forgery, as purely arbitrary substitutions of one letter for another occur.

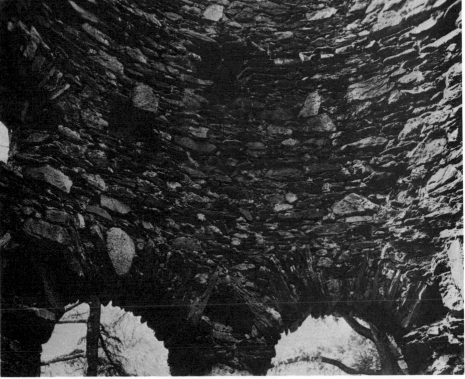

The Newport Tower in the cool season, when the trees around it are leafless. *Photo Earl Syverson.*

Opposite page: Two views of details of the construction of the Norse Christian church tower at Newport, Rhode Island. *Photos Malcolm Pearson.*

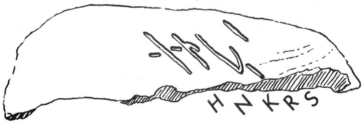

Norse runes reading H-N-K-R-S, and signifying the church "of the Bishop's stool," i.e., cathedral church, found in 1946 by Magnus Bjorndal and Peer Lovfald, and photographed on that historic day by Malcolm Pearson.

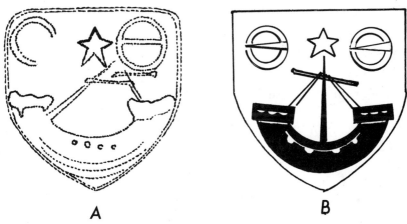

A   **B**

Relic of the last of the Celtic-Norse voyages to America dating from 1396. The coat of arms A, engraved as part of the accoutrements of a faintly delineated figure of a fourteenth-century knight, was discovered by the late Frank Glynn at Westford, Massachusetts, in 1956. In 1961 Charles M. Boland and Frederick J. Pohl independently proposed a connection with the recorded fourteenth-century voyage of Sinclair Earl of Orkney. In 1967 Sir Iain Moncrieffe, a Scottish authority on clan heraldry, identified the arms as those of a sept of the Sinclairs, the Gunns of Caithness, originally Norse, in which form the name is Gunnr. It is known that the Earl of Sinclair was closely linked with Crowner Gunn, whose famous plaid brooch is featured on the arms, B. (*From photograph by James Whittall.*) For the record of this last crossing of the Atlantic before Columbus, in 1398, see Frederick J. Pohl, *Prince Henry Sinclair* (London: Davis-Poynter, 1974).

way, Scandinavian scholars have recognized a later generation of rune scribes in Greenland and in nearby areas of northern North America, men who were writing short inscriptions in the 1300's. But the inscriptions are very few, and they relate to trivial incidents, briefly reported. They tell us little indeed about historical events in either Greenland or North America.

Part of the reason for this paucity is to be found, I believe, not in a lack of literacy on the part of the Greenland Norse, nor among their Vinland relatives in North America. Rather it is to be related to the course of events in their nearest Scandinavian neighbor,

Iceland. For here runes went out of fashion, and parchment replaced stone as a writing surface.

The Icelanders, after a century or two of unparalleled blood
feuds and internecine rivalry to beat all other possible contestants
for laurels in this department of human vanity, had undergone a
mysterious transformation. They proceeded, by some genetic mu-
tation or gift of providence, to breed a race of literary giants who
bequeathed to the entire Nordic world the splendid series of sagas
that relate the history of their times, of their predecessors, and, indeed, of the entire world since its creation by the gods. This pagan
mythology was set down on parchment in the beautiful hand of the
medieval Celtic scribes, adapted to the needs of the Norse language. Together with the real history and the novels that illuminate
such history, they form the corpus of medieval Norse literature. In
keeping with this sudden civilization of the most isolated island of
Europe, the old Norse runes passed almost out of use, to be replaced by the decorative letters already mentioned. So it happens
that it is in the province of Uppland, Sweden, that we must seek
the best ruinic inscriptions, for some 3,000 of them occur there.

For the same reason, presumably, there are not many Norse
inscriptions using the later styles of runes in Greenland or on
neighboring American territory. Examples that have been accepted
as genuine are illustrated on pages 348 and 349. In partial compensation, an ever-increasing tally of Norse artifacts, particularly
iron weapons such as battle-axes and swords, have been coming to
light on American territory, in Canada, and New England. Examples accepted as genuine by Scandinavian authorities are shown on
pages 358 and 359. One other well-known inscription, called the
Kensington stone, purporting to date from the 1300's, is written
in a dialect so close to nineteenth-century Swedish-American as to
be regarded as a forgery by present-day Scandinavian scholars, following the analysis of its language and signs carried out by Dr.
Sven Jansson (1950). Certainly its language has a very modern
character, not at all like that of the other runestones. It is as if
an inscription referring to an event in the time of Chaucer were
written in the kind of English that George Washington used.
For another view, however, the writings of Hjalmar R. Holand
may be consulted. In certain districts of England, a dialect of

English very similar to modern English arose during the Middle Ages, and indeed became the parent of modern English. Thus it is conceivable that the Kensington stone may one day be vindicated (it reports a bloody encounter between Norse explorers and Indians); but at present a majority of specialists reject its authenticity.

On account of the flowering of literacy in Iceland and the adoption of parchment and Celtic script for writing, it seems likely that the Greenland Norse would follow suit. Similarly, one presumes, the civilized behavior of educated people would replace the violence and savagery of earlier times. On the witness of reliable ecclesiastic visitors, we know that the Greenland settlements of the fourteenth century were peaceful pastoral farms and villages, rearing cattle, sheep, and poultry, and under the spiritual care of priests and a bishop. But trees large enough to yield timber for their houses and barns were lacking. The nearest sources were the forests of Labrador. Here, undoubtedly, they sailed, and here they would also build new ships to replace those that became unserviceable. Here also they would encounter Amerindians and, in the light of their reformed manners, might be expected now to enter into friendly and mutually beneficial relations. Encouraged both by these circumstances, and also by the recollection of what earlier Greenland Norsemen had apparently found when they sailed up the Mississippi, we might infer that this new generation of Greenland Norsemen would sail similar routes.

Whether or not the foregoing inferences are correct, it is a fact that inscriptions that can only be related to those found in surviving copies of the sagas can now be recognized in Colorado. I give a selection of them on pages 377 to 380. Many were originally discovered by Professor E. B. Renaud in the 1930s, although he did not recognize their Scandinavian affinities. It is my impression that isolated pages of particular saga manuscripts are the models from which the Colorado petroglyphs are carved. I infer that the Greenland Norse possessed parchment copies of some of the same sagas as have been preserved intact in Iceland, and which now lie in the Royal Library and other repositories in Copenhagen.

It is also obvious that a spirit of ridicule has entered into the work of the artists who made the petroglyph copies. It is difficult to attribute such travesties of Christian art to mere naïveté on the part of Amerindian copyists. My own belief is that people of mixed Amerindian-Norse descent made the petroglyphs in an age when Christianity had been rejected. They resemble nothing so much as the mocking anti-Christian graffiti that are to be seen scrawled on the walls of Pompeii; depicting, for example, the worship of a crucified ass, and similar themes.

These inscriptions, whose interpretation as anti-Christian or antireligious mockery seems unavoidable, may well be related to medieval ecclesiastic documents that Scandinavian scholars have brought to light. I discuss these in the next chapter.

Pagans Triumphant?

In 1845 the Albany Academy was presented with a boulder, engraved with Latin letters, discovered by settlers in the Onondaga area near Lake Ontario. The inscription was illustrated by School-craft in his *History of the Indian Tribes* submitted to Congress. The lettering (page 375) was interpreted by contemporary archeologists as reading "Leo VI 1520," and since then no further attention has been paid to this apparently meaningless text, supposed to be a gravestone of an unknown explorer named "Leo Vi" who entered the St. Lawrence River some fourteen years before Jacques Cartier. Other markings on the stone were incomprehensible.

In reality the stone is readily decipherable, if the Latin text is read horizontally as is normal, instead of vertically as the finders did. The text as written in abbreviated form is *Leo Dec(imus) VI 1520*. Pope Leo X was reigning in June 1520, and it is his personal coat of arms that is depicted to the right of the Latin text. His monogram L-X is interwoven with an heraldic yoke (*iugum*) and topped by an heraldic hyacinth (signifying the Latin word *suave*), and thus giving his personal motto: *Suave iugum* ("Sweet is my yoke"). The object carved to the lower right appears to be the triple tiara of the popes, giving the title *Pontifex*.

The stone evidently records a voyage made under the direction of Pope Leo X, but not hitherto made public. The era is post-Columbian, and beyond the range of time covered by this book, but it has a direct relevance to a matter that does fall within the context of Norse settlements. For, as Danish and Norwegian historical documents have disclosed, long before Columbus, the medieval Church had become deeply concerned at reports of paganism on the part of the Norse Christians of Greenland and

371

Vinland. It was argued that voyages should be undertaken to establish the truth of the disturbing news. The Onondaga stone may be related to these matters, and at least it is evidence that a voyage was inspired by papal direction, and not advertised to the world at large.

Some time prior to 1341 A.D., the bishops of Greenland and Vinland at their seat at Gardar seem to have lost touch with the congregations of the west coast. It is not known why, but a change in population distribution would seem to be a likely cause. In that year a Norwegian priest named Ivar Bardson was commissioned by the bishop of Bergen to sail to Greenland to investigate the situation. His report, since published by Danish historians, disclosed that the former cathedral church of the west settlement was still standing, but abandoned. He could find no trace of any living people, either Christians or Eskimo; yet there was no sign of any bloodshed. The entire settlement appeared to have been abandoned by the inhabitants who, however, had left part of their farm stock behind, for cattle, sheep, and chickens were found running wild. Bardson and his companions captured some of the cattle and sheep and took them back to the east settlement. Bardson remained in Greenland as a steward to Bishop Arne and subsequently related his experiences to later investigators.

Historians have speculated on what became of the west Greenlanders: whether they took ship to Iceland and perished en route, or whether they removed to Vinland and there integrated with the Indians. Opinion has generally favored the latter view, though proof has been lacking.

A document dated 1342, the year after Ivar Bardson's visit, was still in existence in the seventeenth century, at which time a Bishop Gisle Oddson made a Latin summary of it which still exists. It records that in 1341 the inhabitants of Greenland voluntarily gave up the true faith and Christian religion, and after renouncing all good manners and true virtues, turned to the people of Vinland.

In 1347 the remaining east settlement was in trouble, probably from attacks by Eskimos. That year a ship manned by seventeen men arrived in Iceland, claiming to have sailed from Markland (Labrador). They reached Bergen, the Norwegian capital, the following year and are presumed to have appealed to the king for help. The king, Magnus Eriksson, had been commissioned by Pope Clement VI to make a military expedition against Russia with a view to converting the Orthodox Church to Rome. Plague in Europe and Russia, however, made this impracticable, and Magnus now redirected the pope's money to financing an expedition under Paul Knutsson to visit Greenland and to restore the Christian faith there. Norwegian scholars believe that the expedition sailed in 1355, and remained away from Norway for eight years. The records of the expedition have not yet been found. Norwegian scholars believe that Knutsson, after finding Greenland partially deserted, went in search of the Norsemen in American waters.

Until now the only other information we have had on the subject derives from the voyage of the Italian explorer Giovanni de Verrazano in 1524. He sailed northward from Florida to Labrador, and one of his notable discoveries was Long Island Sound and the Hudson River (R. del Soie). A bridge in New York now commemorates his feat. Verrazano's course took him along the Narragansett coast where he was astonished to glimpse a tall stone-built "Norman villa." He went ashore to investigate and found the region inhabited by friendly Indians who appeared to be much the most civilized people he had ever encountered in America, and some of whom had fair skins. They could remember nothing of how the Norman villa had been built.

On his return to Italy, his brother Girolamo prepared several maps and one globe illustrating the discoveries Giovanni had made. It is generally stated that Giovanni was in the service of Francis I of France. However, he would seem to have served several sovereigns, for what appears to be the original of his map of the American coast is in the Vatican library. Another was seen by the English historian Richard Hakluyt in the possession of Master Locke, Keeper of Maps to King Henry VIII in London, "An olde excellent mappe wh. Master John Verrazanus, who had been thrise on that coast, gave to King Henry." One published version of Verrazano's discoveries appeared in 1542 and is lettered in a mixture of Latin, English, Italian, and Spanish. Part of it, illustrating the country he named Verrazana, or New France, and including the "Norman villa" is shown on page 376. The Norman villa is undoubtedly the Round Tower of Newport, Rhode Island, also referred to in an English document proposing the settlement of Rhode Island and giving the presence of the tower as an added reason for why such a settlement should be made. The local Rhode Island name for the structure is often given as "Governor Arnold's Mill," for the first governor made use of the tower when he needed a flour mill.

Authoritative scholars in the area of ecclesiastical architecture and Scandinavian history are all agreed that the tower conforms to the specifications of similar structures built in Scandinavia in the 1300's. Indeed, similar buildings for church use date back to Byzantine times, and are still to be seen in versions constructed from logs in northern Europe and Russia. All that now remains is the central tower standing on eight pillars which support eight arches, and which initially housed the central sanctuary. A timber one-story surrounding edifice, roofing the ambulatory, has decayed long since; but the recesses that supported the roof beams can still be seen. The upper part of the tower served also as a lighthouse for ships seeking the harbor.

The Newport Tower is thus America's most ancient church, a fourteenth-century edifice whose builders must have been Norsemen. But were they American Norsemen who had not yet given up the Christian faith, an earlier offshoot of the west Greenland settlement? Or were they men from the east Greenland settlement who never gave up the faith? Or were they yet other Norsemen— such, for example, as the men on board Paul Knutsson's ship, who were unaccountably absent from Norway for eight years?

Some hint as to how to answer the question was provided in 1946 by Magnus Bjorndal and Peer Lovfald when they discovered five runes cut into one of the stones of the tower. Malcolm Pearson who, it will be remembered from *America B.C.*, is largely responsible for leading archeologists to the mysterious stone-built sites of the Northeast and who became an expert photographer of obscure inscriptions, was present on that notable occasion, and the photograph he took is shown on page 366. It shows runes of the late type, in agreement with the late date of the building itself, and they read HNKRS. Some have supposed this to be the misspelled runic abbreviation of the Latin name *Henricus*, and have attributed it therefore to Bishop Henricus of Greenland and Vin-

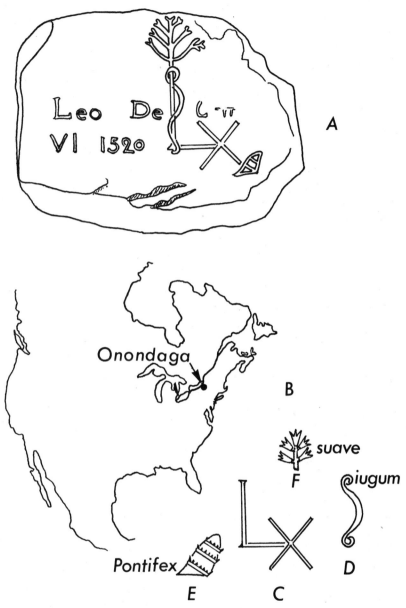

The Onondaga inscription recording a previously unknown voyage by an exploring ship that entered the St. Lawrence in June 1520 and left behind the inscribed rock giving the name, titles, monogram, and motto of Pope Leo X (see page 371).

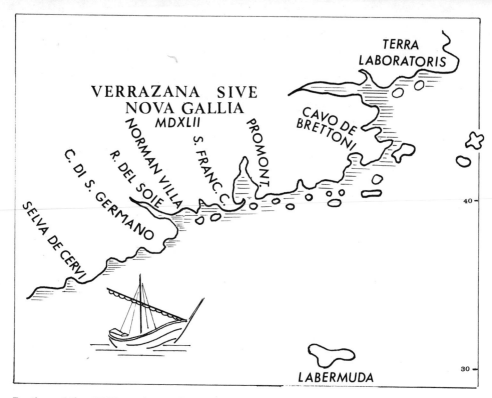

Portion of the 1542 reprint of Giovanni Verrazano's map of "Verrazana or New France" showing Virginia (Selva de Cervi, Deer Forest). Long Island Sound (R. del Soie), with the Newport Tower (Norman villa) shown. The map was drawn in 1524, and its original version appears to be that in the Vatican Library. His sighting and onshore investigation puts Verrazano's record of the Newport Tower one century ahead of Governor Benedict Arnold, who has traditionally been credited with building this Norse church.

Opposite page: The alarming reports reaching Norway, Denmark, and the Vatican in 1342 of serious reversions to paganism occurring among the Vinland Norse seem to be confirmed by a series of petroglyphs from sites in Colorado first recorded by Professor E. B. Renaud. On comparing them with illustrations in the extant copies of the Iceland sagas, it seems that the Colorado petroglyphs must have been copied from a second set of the sagas, presumably those held by the Greenland Norse, and later brought to Vinland. Icelandic manuscripts of the 1300's contain the prototypes A, C of the Colorado petroglyphs B, D recorded by Professor E. B. Renaud in 1938 from his sites N.M. 224, 235. A, medieval flute-player in marginal decoration of the *Flateyjarbok,* now in the Kongelige Bibliotek, Copenhagen. B, its first recognizable Colorado imitation, the theme subsequently repeated widely over New Mexico with increasing emphasis on the twisted torso of the original, to give the well-known "Humpback flute-player" motif. C, the bishop of Iceland as depicted in the *Jonsbok,* Arnamagnean Samling, Copenhagen. It is inferred that copies of the Icelandic manuscripts were taken to the Greenland settlement, and later fell into the hands of the Colorado graffitist, whose mocking inscriptions invited comparison with the anti-Christian graffiti found engraved on walls in Pompeii. An alternative explanation is that fragments of the manuscripts may have served as models to an illiterate engraver who merely misunderstood the subject matter.

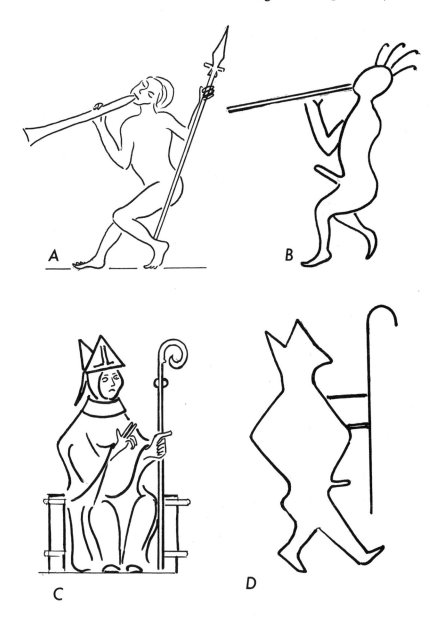

A

B

C

D

Knowledge of the elephant came to America in various ways, on coins of Rome (see page 214), as statuettes imported from China (see page 287), and also in this extraordinary manner by way of Icelandic manuscripts. An ancient Greek work, *Physiologus,* was translated into Arabic, and as it contained pictures of animals, it served as a natural history in the Dark Ages. The elephant, of which the Arabic name is *Fil,* is recorded in an Icelandic manuscript of the 1200's by the peculiar drawing A, where it is "called in our language *fill,* but *elephans* in Latin." This shows that the Icelandic scribe copied directly from Arabic, not amending the word "our" in the translation. There is no Norse word *fill* meaning elephant. The Icelandic *fill* probably was the model for a Greenland copy, which in turn became the model for the Colorado copies, two examples at B, C being from Renaud sites, and others have been discovered by Gloria Farley on the Cimarron cliffs, separating Colorado from Oklahoma. For years the puzzling petroglyph was called by Gloria "The four-legged bird" until Fell's identification in 1978 as the Icelandic *fill.* D exemplifies the Icelanders' idea of kings, as depicted in the *Jonsbok* of the 1300's. Figures E, F, G are from Renaud's Colorado sites NM-336 and NM-337, and seem to be copies either inspired by the *Jonsbok* or some similar work, presumably in the hands of the Greenland Norsemen. G, however, could well be a copy of a saint as depicted on the obverse of many Byzantine coins which, as we know from other evidence, were the principal Colorado currency in the medieval period.

More subject matter from the Icelandic *Jonsbok*, as rendered in the Colorado inscriptions, and a Colorado version of the Creation, as depicted in Icelandic drawings. A, from a later copy made in the 1400's, now in the Arnamagnean Samling, Copenhagen. C, its Colorado copy, at Renaud's site NM-336, in turn a model for other versions. B, Icelandic lady in festal attire, from the copy of the *Jonsbok* in Arnamagnean Samling, Copenhagen. D, its Colorado mimic at Renaud's site NM-235. In C the Colorado copyist has interpreted the picture as a snake charmer, suggesting that the model has already suffered damage, losing part of its ornamental border, before it was seen by the American engraver.

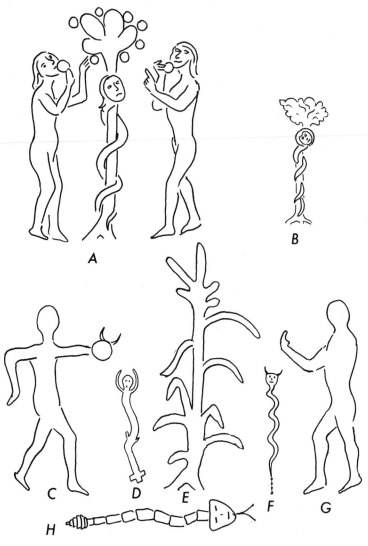

Comic-strip versions of the Bible, for the edification of illiterate Christians, circulated in Iceland under the general name of *Stjorn*. The Garden of Eden scene at A, depicting our first parents' fall from grace, seems to be the model for numerous Colorado petroglyphs, B, C, D, E, F, G at Renaud's sites where nude men and women brandish circular objects resembling apples, while coiled rattlesnakes have spherical heads and faces like the Serpent of Eden. In general one gains the impression of a disrupted Temptation scene from which the participants, bearing apples, scatter in all directions.

The grinning Norse devil, with spikes in place of hair, that decorates the *Snorra-Edda*, appears to be the model for countless similar petroglyphs that range the whole area where other Norse motifs are evident, from Colorado north to British Columbia. Forms such as E and F in turn give rise to numerous variants along the northwest coast as far as Alaska. D, G, H, I are whimsical Colorado versions, some of which merge with what appear to be pictures of medieval jesters.

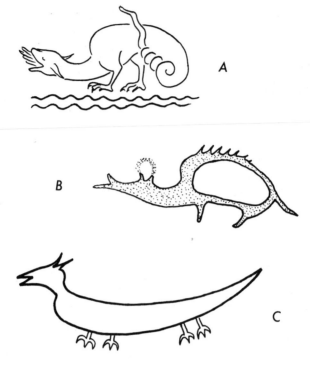

A, the Nile crocodile, as it was depicted in the Icelandic version of the Arabic version of the Greek *Physiologus,* dating from the first century A.D., reached North America in its Icelandic form, probably by way of the Greenland Norse settlements. It appears widely in forms similar to B, found all along the areas penetrated by Norsemen entering the Gulf of St. Lawrence, and was repeated by Algonquian carvers and rock painters over the Great Lakes region. The southern form, C, as amended by a Colorado revisionist, probably takes acount of critical comments made by art patrons who had encountered the alligator, which in former times extended much farther north than its present range.

land, better known in Scandinavia by his Norse name, Erik Gnupsson. But this bishop was appointed in the year 1112 by Pope Paschal II. *Episcopus Groenlandiae et Vinlandiae in partibus infidelium*—bishop of Greenland and Vinland in the pagans' territories—were his titles. The location agrees, the date does not; for it is unlikely that a stone church with romanesque arches would be constructed two centuries before they became fashionable in the Scandinavian homelands. In any case, the letter order is wrong.

I believe that here, as in the case of the older runes in Oklahoma, we are intended to read the runes just as they appear. *Hnakr* is an old Norse word meaning *stool*. In Scandinavia to this day, the word stool—spelled *stol*—is used for a bishop's seat, applying to the church or cathedral church where the bishop's *stol* is located. It matches exactly the Latin *cathedra*, used for a bishop's stool (or nowadays a throne). The adjective *cathedralis* "pertaining to a stool" is applied to a bishop's church, which in English we call a cathedral. Similarly, in Old Norse, the possessive case of *hnakr* is *hnakrs*, and means "of the stool"; applied to a church, it simply means "cathedral church."

If this reading be accepted, as I believe it should, then the Norfolk Tower is the last remaining portion of what was the cathedral church of Vinland in the early fourteenth century, when the Catholic faith was still universal, and when the bishops in Greenland still exercised authority over the faithful in America. It antedates the Reformation, of course; a fact that probably encouraged the Puritan fathers of New England to overlook the fact that it existed before the *Mayflower* landed. In our age of tolerance and respect for ancient relics, all Americans of whatever persuasion can only rejoice that a beautiful and historic Christian church has survived through seven centuries to give us pleasure today.

We remain in ignorance, however, as to the names of the builders, though we know they cannot have lived earlier than the 1300's.

Despite the presence of the church, Christianity virtually disappeared from New England and Nova Scotia. Two hundred years after its construction, the early Jesuit missionaries found that the Micmac Indians venerated the cross and believed in a heavenly father-spirit. Such beliefs may descend from a Christian past, though not necessarily, for they are shared by other faiths of older vintage. John Gallagher and Frederick J. Pohl are presently investigating a site in Connecticut that appears to have been an early Christian church. The eastern Cherokees claim a knowledge of biblical matters antedating the Christian missionaries of colonial times; that, however, is a matter requiring further investigation.

I turn now to the southwest desert states, and especially to Colorado, where there are petroglyphs indicating a Norse presence, as mentioned in the previous chapter. These seem to imply the introduction of Christian and also Norse pagan concepts, apparently through the medium of copies of the Icelandic sagas. The copies seem to have had the same illustrations as the surviving ones we know from Iceland itself, now preserved in Copenhagen. Since we know that at least two of the Greenland Norsemen became poets, it is likely that the Greenlanders were a literate people in their latter days, using parchment manuscripts that they would themselves manufacture from lambskin, and written by their own scribes. Such scribes could well have seen to it that the Greenland colonies were provided with copies of the literary works of the Icelandic poets and annalists.

Somehow these works were brought to Colorado—perhaps by way of the route to Oklahoma. Somehow they became the property of people who no longer revered the Christian faith. They carved mocking travesties of the original illustrations on the pages of the sagas. Was this, then, the work of those same west Greenlanders of whom complaints had been sent to the bishops and to Rome—those who renounced "good manners and true virtues, and turned to the people of Vinland?" Perhaps. I can think of no other explanation.

Paganism is the Church's jargon for belief in a religion other than its own approved variety. A great many pagans, such as Virgil, Julius Caesar, the emperor Trajan, and a host of other famous men, would probably not feel particularly out of place in a modern society such as ours; their moral values were the universal values that most of us today accept, and they were a good deal more tolerant of other faiths than Christians have been prone to be. It is not for us to pass judgment if paganism was found to be more acceptable to the erstwhile Christians who found refuge in America.

Barbarians at the Gates

Having regard to the savagery of the Norsemen—those who raided Britain and Ireland left an indelible memory of ferocity—at the time when the first Norse settlements began in Vinland, it is a moot point whether we should list these as among the vanguard of barbarians that were soon to bring devastation to the various civilized communities of North America.

Harold Gladwin's scholarly but eminently readable *History of the Ancient Southwest* gives the end of the tenth century as the date of the first serious incursions of the Athapascan tribesmen into the Pueblo areas. His dating is authoritative—the basis of all detailed sequences for the desert states—and rests on tree-ring analyses in which he achieved unrivaled accuracies, exceeding the best that carbon dating has so far managed.

About the same time, the settled tribes of the Mississippi probably began to feel the sting of Iroquois attacks—not from the north, as was later the case, but from the south; for there are reasons for suspecting that these fierce warriors came to North America via the Gulf of Mexico, presumably from South America.

These tribal movements initiated a new period for North America, one of upheaval and, in many cases, disaster. The subject is complex, and its implications for the civilized tribes of the Southeast cannot be discussed here, since the southeastern tribes have not formed part of the history inferred in this volume. I therefore leave the subject for a later book, and here do no more than say that as the year 1000 A.D. approached, there were gathering clouds on the horizon. The civilization whose roots we have surveyed continued on in many places for another century or two, but a bleak prospect lay in view: one in which much of the continent was to be plunged into barbarism or semibarbarism in much the same way as Europe had been in the fifth century after Christ. For now let us take leave of the North American scene, still in its prosperous days: a peaceful continent with many different communities—some truly indigenous, others dominated by colonists from abroad, most, however, being of mixed derivation—a peaceful continent, where schools of learning flourished and where the young men went off on adventurous voyages overseas.

Sufficient unto the day is the evil thereof, and that day is not within the compass of the present book. There are other ancient North American civilizations yet to be considered before we examine the tragedy of the widespread collapse of civilization that preceded the arrival of Columbus and the conquistadores. For the time being, then, we may let the Western geometers experiment with the division of the circle and leave the astronomers to their zodiacs and the motions of the sun and moon. There is much more to be said about that, too—but alas, no room in these pages.

And where should I end this book, itself only one more chapter in a much longer record of travel and exploration? I already knew where it would have to end one December evening before I had set pen to paper. As the sun sank behind the mountains of Cyrene, historic mother-city of queens of Egypt and of Libyan navigators and astronomers, I realized that here, where it all began, must also be my place of departure.

EPILOGUE

Sunset at Cyrene

Cyrene, in her aristocratic majesty in the fifth century B.C., can exist for us now only in our imagination; so forlorn are the ruins today, and yet so beautiful. To see the splendor of ancient Libya one must visit the Roman cities of Leptis Magna or Sabratha, beloved of the North African emperors of Rome who spared no expense in honoring Tripolitania.

Cyrene is of an older era in man's reckoning, and is built to the sterner and more classical Doric mode. Her first king and founder was a Greek colonist named Aristotle, but the Libyans called him Battus. Herodotus tells us that Battus was actually the Libyan word for *king,* and now an American tablet has proved him correct, for a Libyan queen is cited by the title *Batut,* and that would be the Libyan feminine form of the same word. Legend says that hospitable Libyans led Battus to the site he chose for his city, for there was a wondrous fountain there to provide copious water at all seasons: a rich dowry for any desert city. The fountain flows now as it has done all through recorded history; an artesian gush that pours from a cave on the Acropolis, and sends a stream down the hillside to feed many man-made pools and fountains on the way. The ancients called it the Fountain of Apollo. And the god of the muses rewarded Cyrene by granting the divine gift of inspiration to one of her sons, Callimachos, the greatest of the Libyan poets and predecessor of Eratosthenes as librarian of Alexandria. For Cyrene, in the days of the greatness of the early Ptolemies, sent all her gifted sons to Egypt.

Cyrene today stands aloof, silent, neglected it seems (though only because her streets and terraces are without people—the ruins are cared for by respectful guardians).

387

All around are the long afternoon shadows of midwinter, when North Africa assumes the coolness of the late fall in New England. The ancient city will come to life again next summer, when the archeologists return, and colleagues from Oberlin and the University of Pennsylvania resume their labors in the Temple of Demeter and Persephone, beyond the Acropolis. I am reminded of the Pima in far-off Arizona, whose religious chants still speak of the Corn-Goddess and her daughter, ravished by the God of Darkness. Cyrene is an aristocrat among cities, a fit birthplace for queens— and indeed several queens of Egypt were born princesses of Cyrene, as Berenike and Arsinoe, wed to the first Ptolemies.

For the pilgrim from America, Cyrene is sacred ground in every sense. Here lived the very people who sent their sons to discover, colonize, and civilize our lands. Here Eratosthenes was born. We can walk the very streets he trod, visit the temples of Apollo and Artemis, as he did, and drink at the selfsame sacred fountain. It is a noble city, built upon two hills on the seaward slope on the Green Mountains, surrounded by hillside pasture and rocky crags, all of which add a feeling of mystery and of solitude and of magic—for who would expect to find temple columns and fountains in so rugged a setting? And for those of a religious turn of mind Cyrene is remembered as the home city of Simon, who carried the Cross on the road to Calvary. Local tradition also says that Saint Mark wrote a part of his gospel here, before his journey to Cairo and martyrdom.

There is an overwhelming air of sadness in Cyrene, or so it seems to me, as the sun sinks and the evening shadows deepen in the empty temple courts. As the light fails, Peter puts away his cameras. Our colleagues from Tripoli and Benghazi walk back toward the car. I am grateful to be left alone a little while to gaze on this astonishing vista, so steeped in history; these cool, green uplands so unlike the rest of Libya, though the desert sands are not far away.

How many sons of Cyrene sailed away, never to return? Did friends ever bring back news of them in the New World? Did parents or children never know if loved ones were lost at sea? Certainly there were many tragedies, for Callimachos himself was often called upon to compose epitaphs for such occasions. Most of his poems have been lost, like so much else that was written in Cyrene, yet in the surviving fragments we find him mourning friends or acquaintances who were drowned at sea or disappeared without trace. And that other facet of tragedy at sea was not unknown here: the lifeless bodies of men from other cities, cast ashore on the

CYRENE:
Fluted columns of the Propylea, the entrance to the Acropolis of Cyrene, built in the fourth century B.C. This was the most sacred part of the city, located at the highest levels, though overhung by the Green Mountains, the easternmost extension of the Atlas.

CYRENE:
Another view of the Propylea. Dr. Mohamed Jarary, Director General
of the Libyan Study Center, University of Tripoli in the foreground, and
beyond the columns the northern slopes of the Green Mountains.
Photo Peter J. Garfall.

CYRENE:
Forlorn solitary
column standing
among the ruins of the
Temple of Zeus at
Cyrene, as the last
glow of the sunset
illuminates the site.
The oldest sacred
buildings date from
the fifth century B.C.,
the temples of Apollo
and Artemis, and the
nearby temple
dedicated to the
Heavenly Twins
(Dioscuri).

CYRENE:
The sacred waters of
the Fountain of
Apollo flow from a
cave in the cliff-face
behind the Acropolis,
first into a natural
pool, then by natural
runnels down the
hillside, through the
temple area of the
Acropolis to reach
this man-made pool;
from here further
runnels lead the water
into man-made
fountains at succes-
sive lower levels.
Voyagers to the New
World must frequently
have passed this way
after paying their
last respects to the
gods of the city.

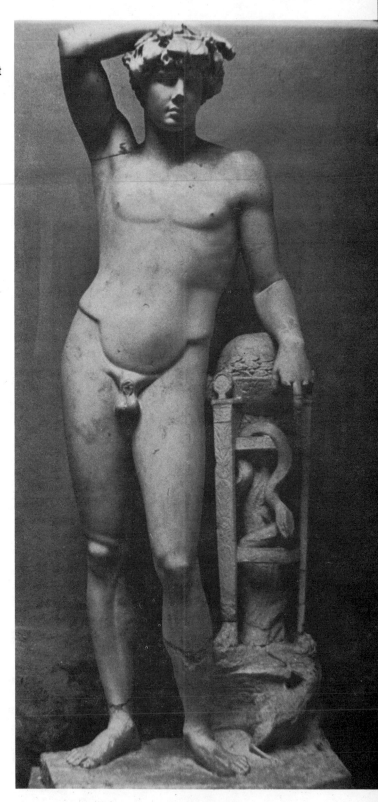

A young Libyan Greek of Classical times seems to symbolize the spirit of adventure in exploration—an aspiring youth with a globe, perhaps representing the globe of the earth as explained by Eratosthenes. *Photo Peter J. Garfall, National Archeological Museum, Tripoli.*

The tombstone of one who stayed behind. The Greek inscription on this monument at Cyrene tells us that it marks the resting place of one Felix Betranos who died at the age of 58 years. *Photo Peter J. Garfall.*

ASKHOLOS MNEIA, *Askholos, In Memoriam,* an American tribute left
by shipboard companions to one of their number who never returned to
his loved ones. This inscription, in artless Greek, was found by
Professor Da Silva Ramos, cut in rock at Serra de Parentin, Brazil.
Was this, perhaps, one of the lost sons of Cyrene for whom Callimachos
wept? Epigraphic Museum replica. *Photo Dr. Julian Fell.*

Cyrenian coast. For one such, Callimachos wrote an epitaph at the
request of his friend Leontichus, who met the funeral charges. For
Lycus, who never returned from a voyage, the poet wrote another
poem that was engraved on his empty tomb. Yet another friend
Sopolis met the same fate, and for him, too, Callimachos wrote
sad lines.

There have been other poets hereabouts, not all of Greek parent-
age. Callimachos sang the praises of the famed fountain of Apollo,
not omitting to mention that he himself was descended from Battus, the princely founder of the city-state. And I remembered this
line from the hand of an unknown Berber:

$$| \because \odot \vdots 3 \Upsilon \quad \Upsilon \cdot \rfloor \cdot | \quad \cdot | + \cdot || \cdot \quad \cdot 3$$

"I too have drunk of the waters of that Fountain."

The centuries rolled by, and men came to Cyrene bringing word of new stirrings of religious thought. Even before the Ptolemies, the Persians had invaded Egypt under Darius, and their soldiers inspired many in North Africa by their belief in the brotherhood of man, under the light of the one god Ahuramazda, Lord of the Sun, and his adjunct Mithras. Later still came Mark and his Christian brothers, and many were converted to his Faith which spoke also of the brotherhood of men as sons of God. But many were martyred for this belief.

Three centuries later, Constantine declared the entire Roman world to be Christian, and churches were built in Cyrene, which now became the seat of a bishop. The Vandals, claiming to be Christians, though dissident from Rome, brought havoc to North Africa; but a Berber army in Tripolitania barred the way to Cyrene, and turned back the barbarian tide. Rome now fell under the invading hordes, and Byzantium took her place as the seat of administration for North Africans. But the times were corrupt, and when a new star shone in the east, it heralded the westward tide of Islam. The harbinger of the new faith in the One God was a personal companion of Mohamed named Ruwaifa, the apostle of the Libyan Moslems. He is buried among the hills to the west of Cyrene, a holy place of pilgrimage.

And through all those centuries of change, on into the Moslem era, men still felt the ancient urge to cross the oceans, to seek a paradise on earth. So it was that God-fearing wanderers came far across the seas to find a refuge in America, and dwelling places among the great mountains. And from the record that survives of their faith and deeds we may be sure that they sang this song of Thanksgiving in their New World:

In the name of God, the Beneficent, the Merciful,
Who created the heavens and the earth, wherein is beauty for you,
And God's was the direction of the way
To the land you could reach only by great effort.

He caused the night and the day, and the sun and the moon,
To serve your needs,
And the stars were made to serve you by his command.

And he caused the sea to be at your service,
That you ate fresh food from thence,
And behold, your ships plowed it, and for landmarks
The stars by which to find the way.

And God has given you a place to dwell,
And hides of cattle to make your tents,
Easy to carry on the day of migration,
And on the day of pitching camp.

Wool and furs for clothing to comfort you,
And God has given you shelter from the sun,
And a place of refuge among the mountains.
God is with them who do their duty,
And with those who are the doers of good

—from Surah XVI of the *Koran*

My Arab friends tell me that these beautiful words were first set down in writing from the dictation of Mohamed, soon after 622 A.D. Were they, perhaps, addressed in part to those who had crossed the ocean to pitch their tents beyond the great Sierra?

I should like to think so. And I look to the day when Arab colleagues will climb the Sierra to visit the hanging valleys where the name of the Prophet lies cut in American bedrock by sailors who found peace there so long ago.

If most of the wanderers in those later centuries were Moslems, many were certainly Christians, and others Hebrews, as we know from the inscriptions at the Oasis of Figuig, and as the American inscriptions also tell us. From the ancient Arab historians we learn also that Hebrews and Christians lived among the Moslems of North Africa, as many still do to this day: for Islam had become a tolerant faith, and the Koran speaks of Abraham and of Jesus as great prophets of God. Of these various faiths, men of Cyrene came to the New World.

It has grown dark. Already the imam of the nearby village of Shahat has summoned the faithful to prayer. His voice brings me back to the present. Dr. Mohamed and my other friends have grown impatient and call out to me from the hillside road above the Acropolis, so I make my way back to the gates of the deserted city. To my surprise, a robed figure in the dusk waves me on with a friendly gesture, and I hear the lock turn behind me. But when I asked afterwards who he might be, they told me he was a local Bedouin, and that he wore no robe, but an old army greatcoat! Why argue? What I saw, I saw, and I remember it that way. Besides, another Berber poet has explained it, perhaps:

You were dazzled by the rays of the setting sun,
So gaze no more on the light that blinds.

Al-Jabar the Mighty Hunter, whom we call Orion, was already rising over Egypt as we slipped quietly away into the night. And so I returned to the winter snows of New England, to our pillared house by the lake, to write this book.

APPENDIX

The Language of Plutarch's Greeks

Vocabularies are not the stuff from which interesting chapters can be made. They are, however, very necessary in any study of the origins of the Amerindian languages. Many readers of *America B.C.* wrote to me asking for more details on this matter, and the short answer is "Consult the *Occasional Publications* of the Epigraphic Society (obtainable by inquiry directed to the Society at 6 Woodland Street, Arlington, MA. 02174). In respect of the Greek roots in the northeast dialects of Algonquian, corresponding to the dialect that Plutarch said was compounded from Greek and native speech, the following tables support Plutarch's claim. It should be noted that by *Ptolemaic* is meant that dialect, mainly Greek, that was spoken in Egypt and parts of Libya for several centuries before and after the time of Christ. It is a mixed language, mainly of Greek derivation, but amplified by Egyptian words like those that also occur in the later Coptic language. In addition, the vocabularies show a regular proportion of Arabic roots. These point to a Libyan—rather than Egyptian—origin, for Arabic speakers were already present in Libya long before the Moslem invasion of Egypt and North Africa in the seventh century A.D. As mentioned in Chapter 5, Dr. Silas Rand, the great lexicographer of the Micmac speech, had already detected and drawn attention to the Greek elements in that Algonquian tongue. As these representative vocabularies show, recent statements that no Old World vocabulary occurs in an Amerindian tongue, and similar claims, are without foundation.

Although the inscriptions show that the Greek alphabet was once in use in North America, no modern Amerindian language inherits a writing system derived from the Greek. In contrast, however, a very large number of Greek roots occur as part of the vocabulary of the Algonquian Indians. These words, if written in Greek script instead of Latin (as is customary), are immediately comprehensible to Greeks. It is impossible here to give more than a brief list of representative examples of such words, taken from the northeast dialects of Algonquian, using the dictionaries of Rand.

English	Greek	Algonquian*	English	Greek	Algonquian
a far shore	ap'aktes	ab'akt	set aside	apoduo	abada
redeemed	apetelessa	abatelase	ache	ponos	pina
unjust	adikos	adagi	to make	ago	aga
travel	aleo	alea	all	pan	pan-
work	aroka	ergon	alone	enikos	enekut
distraught	anodomenos	anodomina	against	anti	anti
on, at	epi-	api-	arrive	pao	paio
ashes	pinos	pingui	hide, skin	askos	askon
go	bao	ba	big	mega-	mag-
uncovered	menutes	menadu	young	ne-	na-
bright	meniskos	meniskuk	come	pao	paio
capsized	katakulthe	ketkookwa	talk	mileso	milese
cowardly	menetos	menadi	dove	pelos	pules
dive	katabasis	katabase	water	nipsis	nebi
opinion	thuma	dum	earth	ge	ki
have	ekho	eek	egg	o'on	wowan
lie down	keisthai	ekase	fever	kausos	kez-
fish-	peska-	pasko-	rod	rabdon	obdon
feet, legs	poda	poda	freezing	pegnumai	pekuami
table	tetrapoda	tawipoda	solid	pagios	pogui
inform, say	ideazo	idozik	hot	kausis	kesuae
hand-held	khermas	kelnoos	ice	pagos	pege
cut notches	katatemno	ketkoktam	reside	katoikea	ketkoone
overwork	katakourazo	ketakase	stone	kounos	kundao
talk	laleo	lalomo	see	noemi	nami
intercourse	mixis	miskase	and not	oude	oda

*Abenaki/Micmac

Sample vocabulary of the maritime Algonquians of New England and Nova Scotia, showing that an effective vocabulary of nautical terms of Egypto-Libyan origin already existed in North America prior to the coming of modern European settlers. Note that English or French words were not borrowed to convey the sense of equipment such as the magnetic compass, of which ancient dials have been found in Spain and North America.

Mariners and Navigation

English	Abenaki/Micmac	Ptolemaic	Arabic
travel, to sail	alea	aleo, aleomai	
sailor	alategw	aletes	
coastal seas	sobagwa		sobagwa
magnetic compass	el-ugwech		al-hukk
plumb, level	el-amkadu		al-imam
mast, rigging	el-dukadegw		al-daqal
sail, spread sail	siba-		sabih
cable, anchor-rope	rabanbi	ribi	
cordage	pelum		barin
dive, plunge	katabase	katabasis	
journey afar	aksit		aqsa
the world, the earth	ki	ge	
waves	tegoak	teggo	
to fish by hook	oma	oeime (fishhook)	
blow, spout	putu	putizo	
whale	putup	putizo (to spout)	
fishing net	abe	abo	
make a net	abe-ago	abo-ago	
ship's clerk	komi	keme	
haul up a trawl	natk-abea	hntok-abo	
shore	senojiwi	shna	
fish-(compounds)	pask-	peska-	
wind, weather	awan		ahwa
east	waban	weben	
calking pitch, resin	lamegusum	lamchat	
circle, meridian	owo	owow	
capsize	ketkukwa	katakulthe	

Astronomy and Meteorology

English	Abenaki/Micmac	Ptolemaic	Arabic
the day following, day after tomorrow	achakuiwik	echakik	
dew	nebiskat		naba saqt
halo	owealusk	owow lukes	
ice	pege	pages	
light	-lusk	lukes	
sunrise	sposw		asbah
immediate	nitta		nitaij
summer, heat	niben	nbibi	
by night (adv)	niboiwi		nabiha

English	Abenaki/Micmac	Ptolemaic	Arabic
err, erroneous	ebulea	obeleia	
star	alakws		allaq (twinkling)
bear, Ursa Major	mooin, muin	mouie	
constellation	kulokawechk		el-kaukab
to measure	tebe	teebe	
cold weather	tek, teg	teko (ice-melt)	
ten	mtara	mete	
icicles	pkumiak	pegnumai (freeze)	
falling rain	-nun	noni	
falling rain	soglon		seqlaba
sprinkle of rain	ran	ranis	
rainbow	managwon		mantaqa (girdle) used for zodiac
tomorrow	saba		sabah

When the French and English colonists introduced legal procedures into New England and Nova Scotia, a pre-existing legal terminology of Libyan origin (partly Ptolemaic) continued in use among the maritime Algonquians, who found no necessity to borrow English or French terms. The sample vocabulary in the table below points to the earlier existence of orderly administration of law and government in America before the advent of modern European colonization.

Justice and Administration

English	Abenaki/Micmac	Ptolemaic	Arabic
forced labor	kba	kba	
arrest	channo	cheno	
cross-examine	ketukash	katekhizo	
confidential	keme	kmeme	
guard in jail	hodwi	htor	
slayer	keneb (warrior)	kenes	
the rod	obdon	rabdon	
one in command	tagos	tagos	
offense, error	obulea	obelos	
versus	anti-	anti-	
respond	apa-jekeluse	apo-krinesthai	
rebellious	el-istum	el'atsotm	
valid, firm	pogui	pagios	
unlawful	adagi	adikos	
equity, equality	tatebi	tebe	

English	Abenaki/Micmac	Ptolemaic	Arabic
state, proclaim	ojao	oeish	
give evidence	ido-zik	ideazo	
false statement	kabawa		kabwa (false step)
punishment	kalama-		kalal
insolent, malicious	majigo		majin
authority, king	malki-		malk
king	el-Agawit		el-Agelid (Libyan)
master	al-susit		al-usteth
slave	kesteju	oiketes	
trespass	pad-adega	adikos (unlawful) + badda (occupation)	
lie, be a liar	kelus-kabawa	kelozo (speak) + kabwa (false steps)	
proposal of marriage	kelu-lawa	kelozo (speak) + lau'a (of love)	
equitable	sasagi	soshe	
remorse, feel bad	madamalso	metamelese	
speak	milese	milesa	
Drop dead! (expl.)	Jok!	Chok!	

Medical and Anatomical

English	Abenaki/Micmac	Ptolemaic	Arabic
physician	mpe-soona	mpe-saein	
pain, suffer pain	pina	poine	
affliction	kalama-		kalal
ague, chill after a high fever	zabeze	sebesis	
malaria (fever and chill alternating)	kez-zabeze-	kaus- (fever) + sebesis	
beard	poogwe	pogon	
fracture	wagi	wakip	
breast (female) to give suck	memu-lik	maman-likanos	
castrate	men-suk	menos (libido) + sok (drain away)	
coitus	lamo-		l'am
delirium	legwasowogan	logismos, paralogismos	
hoarse	chacha	chache	
ill	madamalso		madad + mall
intestines, viscera	mlagzial	malakia	

English	Abenaki/Micmac	Ptolemaic	Arabic
intercourse	mikase	mixis	
vein, sinew	kojo	khorde	
intoxicated	saupa	sau	
duct	hanngan	hone	
ejaculation	utikua	uotn	
finger	meto-luigun	meta-likhnos	
louse	kemo	komf	
orgasm	lawa		lau'a
eviscerate	keleolaje	koiliazo	
be exhausted	ketunumi	katanomai	
adolescent	kiabes		kabr
nose	kiatam	kiatm	kiatm
penis	udauehanngan	aidoia + hone	
testicle	wreswa	worshf	
penis	wiraghe	oura	
scrotum	ulsook	al (testicle) + sok (bag)	
uterus	mas	metra	

English	Abenaki/Micmac	Ptolemaic	Arabic
adolescent girl	kwet		qatquta
libido	kaza-l'mo		qassa (yearn for) + la'm (coitus)
laceration	lagun	ragas	
sleep	ekase	keisthai	
become swollen	maguizo	megesthono	
hand	melji	marchoche (mitten)	
disclose, denude	menadu	menutes	
animate	muk	moukh (sensitive)	
shoulders	mutug	mote	
child	na◄	neos, nea	
youth	na-kabet		na+kabr
sneeze, cough	nakwhomo		nakam
see	nami	noemi	
tremor	nanam	noein	
breathe	nasawan	nousth	
pregnant	tetkwit	titektein	
tongue	wilalo	lalo (speak)	
urinate	seghi	sek-	
insane, distraught	wanodomina	anodomenos	
feverish, hot	kesuae	kausis	
stammer, hiccup	psolo	psellos	

Household and Clothing

English	Abenaki/Micmac	Ptolemaic	Arabic
belt	taktek (Pima tkak)		tikak
bracelet	mpedi-nobi	pedi-nob	
cloth	munedo (Ojibway)	mounk	
waist-cloth	nesunk		nazala-aniq
basin	kwat	kot	
plaited basket	aba-znoda	abo-snod	
dish	wlogan	lekane	
iron, iron tool	kusawok	kies-woch	
drink, water	nipi, naba	nipsis	naba (spring)
dwell, reside	ketkoone	katoikeo	
egg	owan, oow	oon	
kiss, greet	wajad	washt	
grind	-seguis	sike	
stone	kundao	kounos	
to hold, handle	lum		lams
fruit bush	mozi	mose	
table	tawipodi	terapodi	
to thread	napa		nafad
wash	paka	pagaomai	
mirror	ank-amsuda	ankh, onq	
small dish	wloganis	lekanis	

Opposite page: Excavations at Pujol, Castellon de la Plana, near the coast of Valencia in southeastern Spain brought to light a lead lamina some 15 inches in length and 3 inches wide, believed to date from about the third century B.C. It carries four lines of script in Iberic letters, which however, yielded no possible decipherment in any known form of Iberic language. Placed on exhibit in the National Archeological Museum, Madrid, the inscription was copied by James Whittall and brought back to Harvard for analysis. The language was eventually found to be a dialect of Greek, presumably of the Greek colonies in Catalonia. The decipherment was published by Fell (1976), and shows that the document is a short report on a voyage from Libya into Egypt. The decipherment was promptly confirmed by Professor Linus Brunner of Switzerland, who has suggested some possible alternative readings for certain phrases, and who has published a reconstitution of the text in classical Attic Greek.

(1)

Λ Ι	Φ Τ Λ Υ Μ Σ	Λ Ι Β Υ Ε	Υ Ξ Β
Leaving	Ptolemaios,	from Libya	(we) departed.

Ξ Υ Ν Κ Ρ ΤΙ	Ν ΟΥ	Φ Ι Σ		θ Ε Β Ε
In collision (was)	the ship	after	(we left)	Thebes.

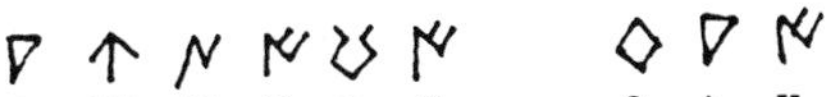

Λ ΟΥ Ν Υ Ρ Υ	Ο Λ Υ.	
Was broken	everything.	

(2)

Λ Σ θ	Ρ Υ Ψ	Λ Υ Ν :	Ε Λ Φ Υ ΟΥ	Κ Λ Ε Υ Ζ θ	
Thieves cast aboard		a net	(and) unloaded	and	removed a locked

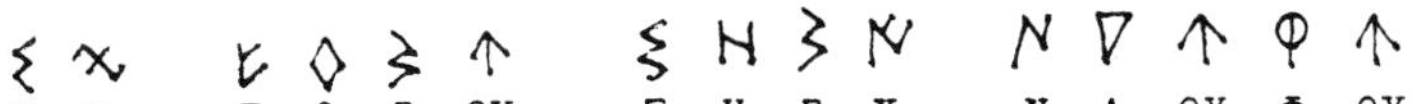

Σ Μ	Ε Ο Σ ΟΥ	Ξ Η Σ Υ	Ν Λ ΟΥ Φ ΟΥ :
cabin trunk of Jose's.	The lawless ruffians were barefooted.		

(3)

Κ Φ Ρ Ο Ν Ζ Ε ΟΥ	Χ Σ Η Ι Γ	Ι Ν Ο	Ζ Μ :
"Kephronesiou" (so-called),	banded together	in order to	rob;

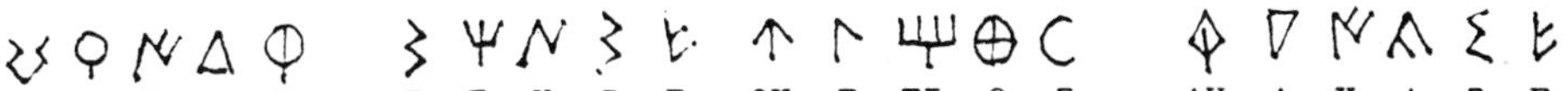

Ρ Β Υ Λ Φ	Σ Τ Ν Σ Ε:	ΟΥ Γ ΤΙ θ Σ	ΔΗ Λ Υ Λ Σ Ε:	
A magistrate	I sought,	(?) an Egyptian,	desiring him	

(4)

Λ Ο Σ ΙΤ Σ	Λ Ε Φ Σ.	Ι Λ Ο Λ ΟΥ	Φ Λ Υ Κ Σ
to have them seized.	The arrest was	authorized,	and into prison

Ι Ν θ Σ Ι Ν	Υ Λ Λ Φ Σ Ε.
they were placed	forthwith.

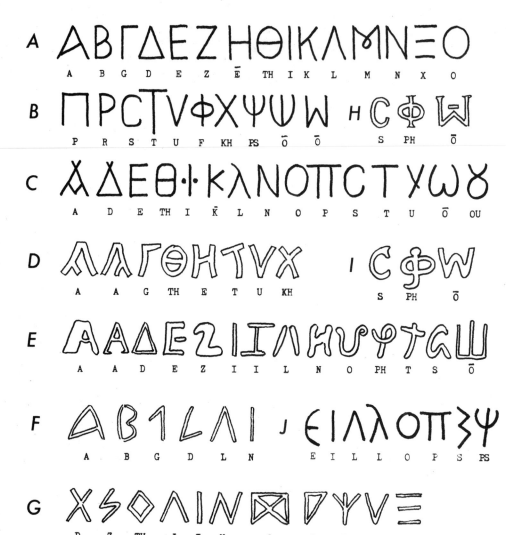

Greek and Iberic Alphabets. A, B, Constantine (Algeria) ca. 400 A.D.
C, Cripple Creek, Colorado, showing Coptic influence ca. 500 A.D.
D, Tripoli (Libya) ca. 200 A.D. E, Inyo County, California ca. 500 A.D.
F, Tartessian Iberic, Medicine Rock, Pershing County, Nevada, ca.
200 B.C.–100 A.D. G, Iberic, Grand Traverse Bay, Michigan, ca. 200 B.C.–
100 A.D. Note: Older styles persist into later epochs in America, making
dating uncertain unless other evidence is available. H, El-Beide (Libya)
ca. 250 A.D. I, Grimes site, Churchill County, Nevada (compare with H).
J, Lagomarsino, Nevada.

BIBLIOGRAPHY

PERIODICALS

Archaeoastronomy, Center for, University of Maryland, *Bulletin* (1978-cont., since vol. 2 (1979) renamed *Archaeoastronomy*). Reports research on ancient astronomical sites and buildings, espec. of America.

Early Sites Research Society, RFD-2, Danielson, CT. Issues *Bulletins,* a *Newsletter* and *Work Reports.*

Epigraphic Society, International, with European, African and American offices. Issues *Occasional Publications* (1974-cont., vol. 7–1979) and special publications, on decipherment of ancient inscriptions. Numerous papers on ancient sites in Mediterranean, North Africa, North America and Pacific Islands.

Antiquities, Department of, Tripoli, Libya. Issues *Libiya al-Qadima* (Arabic and other languages) on ancient Libyan sites, and special publications.

OTHER PUBLICATIONS

Works dealing with ancient megalithic ruins of America and ancient inscriptions:

Fell, Barry: *America B.C.* (Times Books, New York, 1976; softcover ed. Pocket Books, Simon and Schuster, New York, 1978; also British ed., Wildwood House, London, and other foreign editions).

Fell, Barry: *Inscriptiones Gadelicae Americanae* (National Decipherment Center, 1978).

Trento, Salvatore Michael: *The Search for Lost America* (Contemporary Books, Chicago, 1978).

Whittall, James: *Sean Seomrai Cloiche de an Nua-Sasana* (Early Sites Research Society, 1977).

Research reports on Amerindian and North African linguistics:

Fell, Barry, various papers in *Occasional Publications* of the Epigraphic Society, in particular: *Arabic Dialect in Ancient Moroccan Inscriptions,* vol. 3; *The Roots of Libyan,* vol. 3; *The Pima Myth of Persephone,* vol. 3; *Takhelne, a Living Celtiberian Language,* vol. 4; *Libyan Expedition papers,* vol. 6; *Medical Terminology of the Micmac and Abenaki Lan-*

407

guages, vol. 7; *Radicals in Takhelne, a North American Celtic Language,* vol. 7; *The Micmac Manuscripts,* vol. 7.

Research reports on artifacts in North American sites:

Johnson, Gertrude: *Comparison between ancient western North African and New England Sherds and Artifacts,* Work Report on the Early Sites Research Society, (in) *Occasional Publications* of the Epigraphic Society, vol. 7.

Totten, Norman: *Carthaginian coins found in Arkansas and Alabama, Occasional Publications* of the Epigraphic Society, vol. 4.

Whittall, James and Fell, Barry: *Amphorettas from Maine, ibid.,* vol. 4.

Whittall, James: *Naufragrium Romanum, AVC M, Ipswich, Bulletin,* vol. 7, no. 2, Early Sites Research Society (1979).

North African archeology:

Anag, Giuma M.: *Horizons on Libyan Culture,* Department of Antiquities, Libya, 1977.

Bakir, Taha: *Leptis Magna,* Department of Antiquities, Libya (N.D.).

Goodchild, Richard: *Cyrene and Apollonia,* Department of Antiquities, Libya, 1970.

Haynes, D. E. L.: *Antiquities of Tripolitania,* Department of Antiquities, Libya, 1965.

Kane, Susan: *The Sanctuary of Demeter and Persephone in Cyrene, Archaeology,* March 1979.

White, Donald: *Reports on University of Pennsylvania excavations at the Temple of Demeter and Persephone in Cyrene,* (in) *Libiya al-Qadima* (*Libya Antiqua*), vol. 8 (1971), vol. 9 (1977); and in *American Journal of Archaeology,* vol. 79 (1975), vol. 80 (1976); also in *Expedition,* vol. 17 (1975), vol. 18 (1976).

American petroglyphs:

Corner, John: *Pictographs in the Interior of British Columbia* (Corner, R. R. 6, Vernon, B.C., Canada, 1968).

Duff, Wilson: *Images Stone B.C.* (Hancock House, Saanichton, B.C., Canada, 1975).

Farley, Gloria: various reports of field research and discovery, especially papers in *Occasional Publications* of the Epigraphic Society.

Grant, Campbell, Baird, James W., and Pringle, J. Kenneth: *Rock Drawings of the Coso Range* (Maturango Museum Publications, no. 4, 1968).

Heizer, Robert F., and Baumhoff, Martin A.: *Prehistoric Rock Art of Nevada and Eastern California* (Univ. of California Press, 1962).

Hill, Beth and Ray: *Indian Petroglyphs of the Pacific Northwest* (Hancock House, Saanichton, B.C., Canada, 1974).

Meade, Edward: *Indian Rock Carvings of the Pacific Northwest* (Grays Publishing Ltd., Sidney, B.C., Canada, 1971).

Radio carbon dating:

Whittall, James: *Archaeological Survey, Drystone Chamber WD-16, Windham County,* Vermont, *Bulletin,* Early Sites Research Society, vol. 7, no. 1.

INDEX

A

Abaci (calculators), American 321, 328-9
  decimal, in Indiana 328
  Libyan 325
Adams, John Quincy, records ancient coins from Massachusetts 26
Aeneid of Virgil, quoted in Maine inscription 131
Aerial photography 36-7
Aesop's *Fables*, in Pima chants, 312-3
Aethelred's coins imitated by Iroquois bead-makers 346
  and by Algonquians 346
Agapitus II, Pope 342
Ahuramazda, God, in Texan inscription from Big Bend 165
Alabama, Punic coinage in 59
  Roman pottery in 117 *ff*, 125 *ff*
  Madoc of Wales lands 348
Alexander, Aileen 58, 115
Algonquian (Eastern), Ptolemaic and Arabic roots
  navigation terms 400
  astronomical terms 400-401
  legal and juridical terms 401
  medical and anatomical 402-3
Alpha and Omega, at Christian sites 183
Alphabets in ancient America
  Arabic 229, 241, 332, 335-7
  Berber 227, 228
  Carthaginian 58, 65, 174
  Celtic 38, 304-10
  Cree 222, 229

Cypriot 68, 69
Greek 95-7, 175, 177, 178, 183, 394
Hebrew 167, 168
Hiragana 324
Iberian 129, 130, 166, 229
Kufi 229, 232, 241, 335-7
Latin 130, 131, 245
Libyan 228, 241, 301-3
Minoan 68, 69
Naskhi 335-7
Norse 377-82
Punic 58, 65, 174
Tifinag 227, 241
Alphege, Archbishop, murder 343
Alrutz, Robert 122, 123, 156
America, ancient names of
  Mer (Libyo-Egyptian) 291
  Epeiros Occidentalis (Graeco-Roman) 88
  Asqa-Samal (Punic, Libyan) 171
  Vinland (Norse) 341 *ff*
  Vinlandia (Church Latin) 374
  Meirica (Celtic), from Mer 291
America, routes to, Plutarch on 64 *ff*
  Pacific routes 266
America's oldest church 366, 374
American arithmetic 317, 374
Amerindian tribes xi
Andress, Gene 117-9, 124-5
Anti-Christian petroglyphs 377-82
Antiochus IV, coin find in Illinois 153
  Hebrew persecutions and Tenn-Ky refugees 147-8

413

Some Representative Dates and Events in Ancient and Medieval American History.*

Time Scale	America	Europe and Mediterranean
325 B.C.–250 B.C.	Carthaginian trade. Imports; Phoenician manufacturers.	Carthage and Rome dominate western Mediterranean, come into confrontation.
	Exports; lumber, gold and furs.	Libyans cross Pacific to reach west America.
264 B.C.–241 B.C.	Carthaginian trade ceases.	First Punic War. Fleets of Carthage destroyed.
	Libyan Greeks integrate.	
250 B.C.–100 B.C.	Trade with Europe disrupted.	218 B.C.–201 B.C. Second Punic War. Hannibal.
	Token coins issued to relieve currency shortage.	149 B.C.–146 B.C. Third Punic War. Carthage destroyed.
	North America mapped.	
100 B.C.–400 A.D.	Roman traders, mainly Iberian, active in America.	31 B.C. Battle of Actium. Rome dominates world.
	Roman currency adopted.	27 B.C.–476 A.D. Roman Empire.
69 A.D.	Jews settle Kentucky and Tennessee.	Destruction of Jerusalem.
132 A.D.	Second wave of Hebrew refugees.	Second Revolt of Jews.
425 A.D.	Stone chamber in Vermont carbon dated to this time.	Some stone chambers in Europe known still to be in use at this time.